GERMAN PSYCHOLOGICAL WARFARE

GERMAN PSYCHOLOGICAL WARFARE

Edited by Ladislas Farago

For the Committee for National Morale

Lewis Frederick Gittler *Assistant Editor*
with the co-operation of
Prof. Gordon W. Allport *Harvard University*
and
Prof. Edwin G. Boring *Harvard University*

Interpretative Summary by Prof. Kimball Young
Queens College

COACHWHIP PUBLICATIONS
Greenville, Ohio

German Psychological Warfare / Ladislas Farago, editor
© 2018 Coachwhip Publications

Reprint of second edition (first definitive edition), 1941 / 1942
No claims made on public domain material.
Cover image: Barbed wire © PanaceaArt

CoachwhipBooks.com

ISBN 1-61646-462-3
ISBN-13 978-1-61646-462-2

CONTENTS

ACKNOWLEDGMENTS

For invaluable aid, advice and encouragement, the Committee for National Morale and the Editors acknowledge their debt of gratitude to:

Dr. H. L. Ansbacher of Brown University
Dr. John G. Beebe—Center of Harvard University
Colonel Percy G. Black, U. S. A.
Major William Moseley Brown, Specialist Res., U. S. A.
Lieutenant William Exton, U.S.N.R.
Lieut. Col. J. I. Greene, Editor, *The Infantry Journal*
Dr. Herbert Rosinski of the Fletcher School of Diplomacy
Dr. Floyd L. Ruch of the University of Southern California
Dr. Stanley S. Stevens of Harvard University
Edmond Taylor of the Office of War Information
Professor Robert M. Yerkes of Yale University

Special thanks are due to Admiral Chester William Nimitz, now commander-in-chief of the U. S. Pacific Fleet, for his generous understanding and help that made a first revision of this Survey possible.

HOW TO READ THIS BOOK

It is suggested that the Survey be read in its continuity, disregarding at first the key numbers referring to the abstracts in the Bibliography.

To obtain a more complete picture of the subject, however, the Bibliography should be read as well, since the abstracts contain additional information and biographical notes on the authors wherever they were available.

COMMITTEE FOR NATIONAL MORALE*

Major George Fielding Eliot, *President*

Arthur Upham Pope, *Chairman*

Dr. Alfred E. Cohn, *Chairman of the Executive Committee*

Hon. Robert P. Bass   Hon. Gifford Pinchot
Mrs. J. Borden Harriman   Herbert Bayard Swope
Dr. Frank Kingdon
Vice-Presidents

Gregory Bateson, *Secretary*

Board of Trustees
Dr. Phyllis Ackerman
Frank Altschul
Dr. James Rowland Angell
Edward C. Carter
Clark Eichelberger
Ladislas Farago
Austin M. Fisher

* For a description of the Committee's aims and functions, and a complete list of its membership panel, see end section.

11

GERMAN PSYCHOLOGICAL WARFARE*

The title of this book is used in the broadest possible sense of a phrase which is becoming increasingly "popular." It is, indeed, a composite title, just as the book itself is the composite picture of one of the truly important features of the present war: the Germans' skillful use of psychology in revitalizing military strategy and tactics to fit the changed requirements of total war.

* This is the first regular edition of a survey prepared and privately published by the Committee for National Morale. The present edition has been revised, enlarged, and brought up-to-date. The chapters on morale and the offensive in psychological warfare, including propaganda, have been considerably expanded. The Committee and the Editor want to acknowledge a debt of gratitude to the Publishers whose interest and generous cooperation made this definitive regular edition possible. Since the first line of defense against the Nazis' aggressive program is knowledge, the Committee for National Morale has always felt that a clear and concise statement of the whole German theory of psychological warfare was urgently needed. This authentic survey was drawn up to meet the demand, but its circulation, limited as it was to a comparatively small number of "insiders" and technicians, prevented the wider dissemination of the message it implicitly bears. With the aid of the Publishers, the Committee is now enabled to secure a wider audience for what it thinks is an important contribution toward the better understanding of this war.

When it first burst upon the world, the tremendous striking power of this revamped German strategy derived its primordial fury from overwhelming psychological motivations: the Germans' stunned disappointment over the defeat of 1918, their blind faith in Germany's "historic world mission," and a steadfast conviction in German superiority and ultimate victory.

For the exploitation of these largely synthetic motivations, the Nazis mobilized German psychology and made it into an integral part of their political machine.

The High Command of Germany's armed forces has gone even beyond that.

Today, it uses *defensive psychology* to select the best man for the right place, to bolster the morale of the whole German "nation in arms," to habituate its soldiers to the hazards, dangers and strains of technical warfare, to cushion the shocks of combat and increase the efficiency of military life, to regulate relations between officers and men, and to solve all the complex problems of human behavior raised by war.

Offensive psychology is used to break down the morale of Germany's enemies both on the military and the home fronts, to conquer public opinion in neutral lands, to pave the invader's way into unprepared countries by disintegrating the political, social, and intellectual structure of nations singled out for future attacks.

Aside from the rare editorial interpolations and interpretative remarks which were kept to a minimum, the Survey is exclusively based on the writings of German military theorists, psychologists, and Nazi "philosophers." Their books and articles have been carefully orchestrated, but no attempt was made to evaluate their theories. By its very nature, such a survey cannot anticipate a finished portrait of German war psychology in action. We shall have to wait to see how valid many of these theories proved in the acid test of their actual application.

There is a Nazi policy *in books* and a Nazi practice *in action*. It must not be assumed that the two always agree. Many of the sources reported in this volume present *programs, aspirations, or blueprints,* by no means all of which are realized in actual practice. For example, it is doubtful whether the elaborate program of testing for the selection of officers, even with the aid of a large psychological staff, has actually been carried out for any large proportion of the (approximately) 400,000 officers in the German Army. Although many of the sources cited contain authenticated reports of actual procedures and actual accomplishments, the reader should be on his guard against assuming that all the plans and policies the Nazis express in their florid military and psychological writing are invariably translated into efficient action.

At the same time the Nazi program outlined in these pages represents a consistent unity whose impact as a whole is one of power and one of menace. The reader must beware lest his critical attitude toward extravagant claims blind him to the overall effectiveness of Nazi mobilization. Even though in respect to specific items he may suspect a divergence between Nazi "law in books" and the Nazi "law in action," still his residual impression of a vigorously unified and dangerous machine is unquestionably valid.

While, thus, it is appropriate to caution against accepting every single German theory at face value, many of the German suggestions are adaptable to specific American requirements of national defense.

Americans should have no qualms about adopting some of the best features of German military psychology. The Nazis have, on their part, expropriated the findings of many American scholars whose contributions to military psychology (particularly those of the Division of Psychology, U. S. Army 1917-18) were of the greatest interest and value when psychology was introduced as an integral part of the German war machine.

American psychologists like Yerkes, McDougall, Thorndike, Terman, Allport, Yoakum, Strong, O'Connor, Ligon, Dodge and others have had an unmistakable influence on German military psychology, although their theories and practical suggestions were more or less distorted after going through the Nazi mill.

American political scientists like Harold D. Lasswell and Leonard Doob have attracted Nazi attention and imagination. Lasswell's *Propaganda Technique in the World War* and Doob's *Propaganda, Its Psychology and Technique* were carefully read and digested in Germany.

Nor were the Germans the first to discover "psychological campaigns." General Sherman Miles, former chief of our own Military Intelligence, surveyed the nature of modern war almost fifteen years ago in an article published in the *North-American Review*. It is known that his article received the most careful attention of German military circles (347). Long before Hitler wrote his *Kampf,* Banse and Ludendorff their blueprints of Total War, or Blau his secret propaganda textbook, an American, Colonel (now General) Walter Campbell Sweeney, described the changed character of modern wars in a prophetic little book entitled *Military Intelligence—A New Weapon of War* (New York: Stokes, 1924).

Written almost eighteen years ago and now all but forgotten, it was, in fact, the first warning and outline of "psychological warfare." Colonel Sweeney wrote:

> While espionage is still one of the recognized agencies in the collection of military information, its field of action has been so extended . . . as to make its military phase an unimportant one. . . . It may be called War Propaganda . . . and it is not a military weapon but a national one. It is not operated by military personnel but by civilians. Even in war the attack chiefly is directed against the civilian population in the homeland and only partially against the military forces. Its main object in war is to weaken the enemy by destroying the faith of his people in their government. Its main object in peace is to select and prepare agencies which will be of value to it for the purposes when the time for the use of military force arrives.

The Fifth Column was clearly foreseen by Colonel Sweeney:

> A possible method of acquiring information of value under such conditions but one whose use would not even be considered by the United States lies in establishing within the enemy country a system whereby local resident inhabitants act as spies and agents and make their reports to representatives who pass through at regular intervals. Such a system to be effective must be one that has been built up years before the commencement of the war.

And the warning:

> It appears to be evident that a new agency with a new method of attack has come into existence. It was born out of the modern industrial necessities of the armies and the need for having full support of the public in prosecuting a war.
>
> New methods of attack require new methods of defense. The new weapon, war propaganda, as described, has developed the new method of attack and has brought us to the point where we must create a new agency and method of defense.

The present war is, in large measure, ideological. Ideas are being used for political and military purposes with greater skill and ruthlessness than ever before. Germany has mobilized and employed the resources of scientific and popular psychology with an unprecedented audacity and thoroughness which, in their view, mark the latest advance in the art of war. Equipped with vast sums of money and full political power skillfully co-ordinated with military action, this new type of warfare is a serious menace against which sporadic efforts, improvisations or the conventional applications of force are quite insufficient.

In this respect, this book may be regarded as a guide to the complex structure of total war.

NEW YORK, SEPTEMBER 1, 1942.

ARTHUR UPHAM POPE
Chairman of the
Committee for National Morale

WHAT IS TO BE LEARNED FROM THIS SURVEY? AN INTERPRETATION

This study dismisses any doubt that Germany is waging an all-out total war for world domination. It reveals in a simple and painstaking manner how Nazi aggressive ideology has been converted with the help of psychology into a dynamic military system of life.

This Nazi aggressiveness, this dynamism, this complete upsurge of actionism runs throughout the entire picture. German military psychologists seem to scoff at the "fortress" mentality. They seem to point a finger of contempt at Americans who set as much store in "protective oceans" as the ill-fated Frenchmen did in their now-defunct Maginot Line.

The Germanic theories of warfare—as they unfold in this study—are something awesome, strange, almost otherworldly. They are confusing; they do not fit easily into any of our preconceived ideas; they leave us without means of defining our future role. Yet this, to us, artificial and "unreal" character of German ideology is not only accepted by the army but by large sections of the population ruled by Hitler. To quote W. I. Thomas, "If men define situations as real, they are real in their consequences." What may seem strange, barbaric, and bizarre to us is the very core of the "New Order" which the Nazis are trying to build. In other words, the impact of such cultural values on the German man, woman, or child today or in the future—if Hitler wins—will determine the kind of individuals with whom we must deal in the coming years.

It behooves us to understand the revolutionary nature of these changes, if we would not be misled.

But in spite of our anxiety and dismay over the Nazi successes, we do have one great advantage. We can never say we misunderstood the Germans. We can never say that we were not warned and informed of Nazi aims and aggressive techniques, as were the French and British who were deluded, first, by an appeasement policy without resort to arms, and, second, by the belief that modern wars can be successfully fought merely by providing adequate defense.

Yet the average American still thinks in terms of "defense." Either he is indifferent to the implications of Nazi offensive strategy, follows a pseudo-socialist line of self-sufficiency, or believes with an utterly unrealistic naiveté that we are still living in a world of nineteenth-century laissez-faire capitalism and free international trade.

These attitudes are given the lie by the Nazis' own testimony. It is frankly stated over and over again that the conditions of the last post-war era can never return; that in the coming "New Order" Germany will assume the role of "leader-nation" in a world forced to subservience on Nazi terms; that war is a permanent and desirable biological and social condition of mankind. The Germans say that war will continue as a "war of action" or as a "war of nerves" (war between wars) until the Nazi world state is established.

This blueprint for world control includes our own country and especially South America. Yet in spite of its apparent strength, the German program contains many weaknesses.

From the morale point of view, the Nazi leader-principle has grave psychological defects. Hitler possesses all power (what primitive man calls "mana" or magical potency) which may be delegated to others but which may also be withdrawn at the leader's wish or whim. This is a new form of the theory of the divine right to rule. This in itself gives rise to "leader-anxiety," such as a fear of arbitrary dismissal by an immediate superior without appeal, to say nothing of other more serious implications. Linked up to this is the long-established German thesis that the state is master, not the servant, of the people, embodied in Treitschke's famous phrase: "Der Staat ist Macht"—the state is power.

Our democratic ideology stands in sharp contrast to all this. Our national society is larger in scope and power than the political state. The democratic process provides a brake or check on the exercise of unlimited authority by government personnel, who at best are agents of the people, not their rulers. Our conception of individual dignity, integrity, and the place of personal merit runs counter to the Nazi thesis, and the material and spiritual history of democratic progress flatly contradicts it.

The Nazi manipulation of the individual and mass also contains essential weaknesses. Although considerable attention is given to conditioning soldiers to carry out a specific task in co-ordination with their comrades, this training is highly specialized and is directed not to the whole personality but largely to the particular job on hand. There is no evidence that the individual is trained as a "total citizen" to make up his own mind and choice on public issues or on vocational, marital, or other matters. The state ideology completely conditions his whole outlook and, while he may be a relatively free agent with reference to a specialized task, on all wider issues he is thoroughly controlled by the Nazi system.

Thus, while the present régime in Germany recognizes the importance of some rational training, it tends to be limited to special skills. On all larger, especially nationalistic, matters, the emphasis is put upon absolute emotionalized faith in the state and its leader. True, a place is given to material, moral and religious interests, but these are subordinated to the worship of the state which is whipped up by hysterical enthusiasms, hatred, revenge or else by coercive measures invoking fearsome obedience.

This may bring about external conformity and compliance, but does not create an inner strength that will fortify the individual (within the mass) for hardship, defeat or for assimilation to a kind of world other than the Nazi type built around actionism and overt aggression.

Thus the Nazi system would construct a personality that revolves around violence, aggression, and a doctrine of racial superiority divinely determined through the Aryan genes. This personality pattern provides nothing for living in a peaceful world of ordinary competition and co-operation. Psychologically and culturally, this is a narrow, fixed and uncreative existence which holds that the average man is a degraded fool unworthy to rule or even to voice his opinions.

Nevertheless, we should not underestimate the effectiveness of the present German program. There is clearly a psychological campaign under way against us, and the initial step in countering such a "war of nerves"—for that is what it is—is to understand the weak as well as the strong elements in our own strategy.

First, our point of view toward military psychology is decidedly ineffective, shortsighted and unrealistic. We may too easily consider the German treatment of many psychological problems as useless or as sheer quackery. We tend to underestimate the aims and practices of their psychological warfare and we hesitate to construct a counteroffensive because we feel it is unnecessary, or for fear we may fall prey to totalitarianism ourselves by so doing. These views stem in part from our long-standing attitude of over-confidence and isolationism.

Our Survey shows that the Germans had begun morale-building and the psychological amplification of military strategy long before Hitler rose to power. Germany today is still the only major nation which, in its training and practice, stresses the need for "mental elasticity"—that is, the courage and capacity to devise and execute new ideas. The Germans take particular care that their leaders exploit every field of knowledge to further the efficiency of military and political tasks. Associated with this mental elasticity is the readiness to borrow freely of ideas from others and to encourage research in all lines.

An important innovation of German military psychologists was their eschewing of "psycho-technics" in the final selection of officers and specialists. The Germans consider a man's social-emotional qualifications as an important basis for determining future performance as a leader and as a fighter. The analysis of intellectual and emotional attitudes, as well as uncovering psychological deficiencies and discovering capacities, determines the norms for finding "fighting spirit" in conscripts, specialists, and officers.

It is particularly important for our military authorities and co-operating psychologists to realize that mere intelligence-testing is inadequate in modern warfare. The Germans, despite a certain aura of mysticism in their concepts, properly recognize the central significance of "character"—that is, social, emotional, and temperamental qualities that are not adequately determined by the usual paper-and-pencil testing.

In certain other matters we have failed to employ important tactics. For example, the Germans have long recognized that new political and military programs should be preceded by psychological conditioning. In contrast, this country was psychologically rather unprepared for mass conscription. Our plan was largely built around the experiences of the last war. Our leaders ignored the intervening twenty-year period in which a new generation had grown up exposed to a variety of factual and propagandistic analyses of the first World War. This new generation came to believe that war is merely a "racket" created by munition makers and international bankers, that we Americans had been "suckers," and that consequently it was none of our concern what happened in Europe or the Orient. In addition, many people suffered from what I call the "Green Pastures" illusion about the glories of Soviet Russia and Fascist Italy (the particular belief depending on the person's income). All of this contributed to a tremendous loss of faith in our own way of life and in a representative democracy as we were working it out. The present survey should help Americans to realize, as the British people finally have come to realize, that the present war is an outgrowth of the Nazi program which was consciously cultivated and built up into an ambition for material, moral and cultural domination of the world, *not excluding the Americas.*

Unlike our haphazard procedure, the Germans studied all aspects of conscription for two years after Hitler came into power. True, the Nazis held back on conscription partly for fear of political consequences abroad; but it is a fact that the problem of conscription was thoroughly explored before the program was actually launched. In fact, the preparatory character of the German war effort needs to be underscored all down the line. This is true for their psychological enterprises as well as for their economic and military preparations.

Regarding morale-building among troops, the Germans have much to teach us. It is clear that morale-building does not consist merely of providing recreation and fun for the boys in camp nor in protecting them from vice on the outside. A soldier's morale is based on community, familial and religious values, and our survey indicates how thoroughly the German Army has taken these factors into account.

It is quite possible that a study of our survey of German psychological warfare may lead to a conviction that we are up against something which cannot be successfully combatted. Those who come around to this thinking neglect the fact that American culture has nurtured a strength which is vastly superior to the Nazi totalitarian spirit. We have had 150 years' experience with a democratic form of government and we should be loath to let it slip away from us.

Our superiority is backed up by tremendous technical skill and industrial capacity which in themselves constitute a powerful support for our psychological strength. Further, our individual initiative and strong sense of independence of action, if tempered and developed, are essential components of stable leadership. Our sense of team play, coordination of tasks, and *esprit de corps*, witnessed all through our everyday living, are also virtues of high importance. Our consciousness of mass strength, although it tends to be overboastful at times, provides us with self-assurance and self-appreciation. Although our democratic ideology cannot be said to match the "attack attitude" stressed by Nazi military psychologists, we have a sticking quality that can be aroused to a genuine "fighting spirit" if our basic values are threatened.

Finally, the crucial American faith in the common man, in his integrity, in his capacity to join his fellows in policy-making and execution of plans, and in his ability to combine individual responsibility with personal rights and liberties constitutes the foundation upon which a strong national morale may be built and sustained.

NEW YORK, MAY 15, 1941.

KIMBALL YOUNG

PART ONE

EXAMINATION AND CRITIQUE OF PAST WARS

I
GERMAN RATIONALIZATIONS OF DEFEAT

When Germany recovered from the shock of defeat in 1918, politicians, military writers, historians, philosophers, psychologists, and the people at large embarked on a frantic search for the most plausible, as well as the most expedient, explanation (38).

1. Why did the Germans think they lost the First World War?

Five main themes have appeared in the German literature of the past twenty-two years.

> a. The "stabbing of the army in the back by the November criminals." Germany was not beaten on the battlefield, but on the Home Front by defeatists, cowards, traitors, and revolutionists (20, 26, 48, 384).*

> b. Deficient co-ordination of military and political leadership (27, 34); the Kaiser's failure to run true

---

* The origin of the "stab in the back" legend was vividly described by John W. Wheeler-Bennett in his *The Wooden Titan*. Also see *Germany and a Lightning War* by Fritz Sternberg for more details.

29

to form as a leader (32); and the political confusion of the Reichstag (31).

c. Complete absence of psychological preparedness
of soldiers and civilians who were thus fatally exposed to increasingly effective enemy propaganda
(18, 454).

d. Inadequate military and economic preparations
for a prolonged war leading to a premature material
exhaustion of German resources (31, 367).

e. The collapse of Ludendorff's offensive in the
spring of 1918, and the subsequent success of
Foch's counteroffensive (40).

Hans von Hentig (17) was in a class by himself. Defeat was
caused, he maintained, not by the psychological collapse of the
military or home front, but by the nervous breakdown of General
Ludendorff, the mastermind of the German Supreme Command.
Von Hentig was contemptuous of the emotional debate raging in
Germany: "We must be able to discard the arguments of the generals that they could have won the war without the politicians, and
the contention of the politicians that they would not have lost the
war with other generals," he wrote.

Militarists and extreme nationalists, however, suppressed such
realism. They advertised their own rationalizations without attempting to validate them on a factual basis. Weniger (209), nevertheless, admits that their main concern was to salvage the army's
prestige by categorically refusing to acknowledge the strategical
mistakes and shortcomings of the Supreme Command. Freytag-
Loringhoven (255), a Junker military expert, revealed that at the
end of the war "the overwhelming majority of the troops was in a
far better psychological shape than was appraised by the military

authorities," (a fact confirmed by the orderly return of the troops to the amazed Fatherland which expected to welcome a motley band of beggars instead of the still smart remnants of the Imperial Army). Thimme (454), while blaming enemy propaganda for defeat on the one side, published documents on the other, showing that there was merely a slight deterioration of German military morale on the eve of the Armistice.

Thus the militarists confessed the truth to themselves while exploiting their rationalizations of defeat as a propagandistic measure. This, in fact, was the earliest stage of psychological rearmament.

When Hitler's advent to power enabled the militarists to carry out Germany's rearmament full blast, the promulgators of the "stab in the back" legend dismissed their opportunistic rationalizations. They were anxious to explore the genuine causes of defeat in a critical, unbiased manner.

Among these investigations was the one conducted by the German Society of Military Politics and Military Sciences under Simoneit (42). Military psychologists and physicians were assigned to the task of determining the share of psychological factors in the collapse. According to Simoneit, this investigation showed that the Reich was not psychologically exhausted at the end of the last war, but that it was the failure to exploit the nation's entire psychological resources which contributed to ultimate defeat.

2. What attitudes were derived from these rationalizations?

Whatever the cause of defeat, the Germans concluded that Germany must undergo a long process of physical and mental reconstruction for a second world war (13, 38).

    a. The critique of military strategy and tactics inspired the Blitzkrieg, an acceleration of the speed

of battle by introducing mechanized and motor-
ized forces, an expansion of the sphere of military
operations by use of parachutists and air-borne
infantry, and an increased efficiency by perfect
co-ordination of various combat units (346).

b. The lessons of war economy necessitated the
establishment of a separate economic staff to
mobilize industry and agriculture for mass production, to regulate the labor market, to organize
self-sufficiency and an Ersatz program, to store
raw materials and food supplies (367).

c. The critique of military psychology led to the advocacy of the morale-mobilization of the whole
nation and to the use of psychology as an instrument of politics, diplomacy and military strategy
(18, 356).

The German attitude toward war was formulated by philosophers and social scientists. Binder (4, 5) relegated moral justification of war to a "superhuman tribunal free of temporal influences."
Juenger (23) advocated the adoption of an "heroic-realistic attitude" which regards life as the "basically *peaceless* reality of our
milieu charged with permanent tension and struggle." Steinmetz
(46), a Dutch sociologist, became popular in Germany when he
described war as an inherent phenomenon of human nature which
cannot be eradicated. Such views were carried to an extreme by
radical reactionaries like Ruppert (281) who presented war as the
"fulfillment of human existence," and Banse (339) who saw in war
the "everlasting yea of the active warlike man." Simoneit (243)
advocated general militarization as the German way of life, while
Haushofer (15) and Banse (2, 3) demanded a popularization of
military science.

Ludendorff (27), Hesse (18), Nicolai (356) and others clamored for a supreme commander whose genius would solve the problem of a unified military and political leadership. Bonin (181) longed for a leader whose tremendous personality would be capable of erasing the memory of defeat (*Nichtgeschehenmachen der Niederlage*).

Juenger (23) "solved" the conflict between Prussianism and Socialism as the two main spiritual forces of the century by merging them in a "German Socialism" patterned after Spengler's (43) and Sombart's ideas. Superimposed on these attitudes were Rosenberg's (35) Blood-and-Honor "philosophy," Haushofer's "living space concept" (15, 16), and Guenther's* pseudo-scientific race theories.

The realization of all these goals was envisaged in Hitler's (20) total state. Binder (4), Dolberg (9) and Forsthoff (12) provided totalitarianism with a philosophical scaffold, reviving and streamlining Machiavelli's system of might and right.

---

* Hans Guenther, the "forgotten man" of Nazi racism, laid the foundation of his so-called Nordic race-theory in his three books: *Rassenkunde des deutschen Volkes*, *Rassenkunde Europas*, and *Rassenkunde des jüdischen Volkes*. In the first edition of his first-named volume, Guenther printed a picture of the Swedish swindler, Ivar Kreuger, presenting him as the "prototype of the honest Aryan merchant."

II
SEQUENCE OF REARMAMENT BETWEEN TWO WARS

3. What was the sequence of rearmament between two wars?

Psychological rearmament (433) preceded all others, followed by political (355) and economic (367) rearmaments. Military rearmament (348) concluded the list.

The Germans began psychological rearmament immediately after the war. The main reason, as Nicolai (522) puts it, was that "morale building agencies were not hit by the disarmament imposed on us by the Versailles Treaty; thus propaganda replaced military considerations and became a political weapon." (Also see Gutterer, 433.) The second principal reason was the newly found German awareness of the enormous importance of psychological factors in offensive and defensive warfare (348).

Economic rearmament began in 1926 with the establishment of the Economic General Staff camouflaged as a Statistical Society (367).

Military rearmament in its actual phase of munitions production and military conscription was carried out only under the Third Reich.

This sequence of rearmament was held logical because psychological preparation takes the longest time, involving, as it does, new patterns of education, indoctrination, and habituation (10).

War economy, on the other hand, must gear the economic machine for its immediate switch over to military needs at a moment's notice. Actual production for war must begin only when

conflict is imminent, since implements of war rapidly become ob-
solete and new inventions are quickly discovered by the enemy.
(This obviously places the United States, with its gradually expanding war machine, in a rather advantageous position.)

4. Why is psychological rearmament important for total war?

Blau (343), Foertsch (348), Pintschovius (329), Soldan (287),
Metzsch (29), Hentig (17) and Bircher (342) were all mindful
that total war is no longer a struggle between armed forces, but
between entire populations. Total war entails fast campaigns with
seemingly peaceful intervals when the war of nerves dominates
the national and international scene. In the Blitzkrieg, perfect
co-ordination is imperative, leadership and responsibility must
be highly developed, every means of disintegrating enemy morale
must be exploited so that the "Blitz" continues with a minimum of
organized resistance on the part of the enemy and the least possible confusion within the ranks of the attacker (346).

The demands of modern technological war are a terrific strain
on the nerves of soldiers, particularly in the army's special services:
parachutists, tank crews, aviators, and others (329). Between the
Blitz campaigns, while the military forces organize troops and
supplies for the next onslaught, the "war of nerves" continues as a
carefully planned psychological offensive intended to confuse and
divide the enemy's military leadership and civilian population.
(See a statement by the German "official spokesman," reprinted in
the *New York Times*, June 15, 1941, for a typical example of what
newspaper argot calls "plant"—a confusing and deliberately misleading statement coming from semi-official or official quarters,
"planted" in some neutral newspaper with the intent to keep the
enemy guessing, thus compelling him to disperse his forces instead
of concentrating them at the very spot where the blow is most
likely to fall. The technique of such misleading information was
fully described by Nicolai [356].)

PART TWO

PSYCHOLOGY IN TOTAL WAR

III
MOBILIZATION OF GERMAN PSYCHOLOGY

Psychology played a small role in German preparation for the *first* World War. While the French examined the psychological causes of their defeat in 1871, subsequently developed their conception of a "nation-in-arms" as an early theory of total war, and included LeBon's mass psychology in the curriculum of the École Supérieure de Guerre (18), the Germans confined their investigation of the various psychological factors in war to the sending of the Pfuelf (328) mission to study problems of panic in the Russo-Japanese war.

Other than Keller (349), only a few German militarists recognized the importance of morale on the military, and none on the home front. The Prussian drill system still dominated military training and education (192), while civilian morale was haphazardly "bolstered" by a flood of patriotic literature supporting German imperialism, repeating the "encirclement" bugaboo and the Kaiser's claim to a "place in the sun" (356, 458).

5. What was the origin of psychological work in the German Army?

During the *first* World War the conduct of "political warfare" was largely taken away from the civilians in the Foreign Office and entrusted to Section III-B (Intelligence and Politics) of the Imperial General Staff. The utter inefficiency of this department was admitted even by its chief, Nicolai (356). The German Admiralty maintained its own propaganda department (*Nachrichtenabtei-lung*), but it confined its activities to distributing Admiral Tirpitz's own propaganda policies. After the war broke out, the bulk of German propaganda was assigned to this agency (419).*

During the war, Ludendorff (28) issued several memoranda outlining the necessity for the establishment of a morale service, and urged "patriotic education of the troops" to counteract enemy propaganda. No psychologist was called in to advise Ludendorff or to implement his plans.

The High Command, however, invited a few psychologists, among them Dessoir (250) and Hirschfeld (259), to observe positive and negative factors in combat—but showed no interest in the psychologists' reports and recommendations. Plaut (261) reveals that the High Command refused to circulate a questionnaire which was drawn up by a special committee of the German Society of Applied Psychologists under Stern and Lipmann to determine the role of psychological factors in warfare.

Not until the middle of the war were industrial psychologists called in to help the High Command select specialists, a necessity raised by the rapid progress of technical and chemical warfare. Moede (172) and Piorkovski (59) describe several aptitude tests given truck drivers, and Rieffert (60) gives a comprehensive account of tests prepared for aviators.

6. What was the progress of psychological work in the army after the war?

A group of young officers, inspired by Bircher's (249) pioneering outline of military psychology, gathered around Hans von Voss

---

* For detailed accounts of political warfare during the last war see Frank P. Chambers' *The War Behind the War*, and G. G. Bruntz's *Allied Propaganda and the Collapse of the German Empire*.

(54) and advocated the introduction of aptitude testing into the professional "nucleus army" (Reichswehr) and the immediate psychological implementation of military training and education.

Voss (54, 66), a retired colonel with good connections in the Reichswehr, became the lobbyist of the group, receiving his scientific data from Simoneit (63), a student of Ach. He was practically the only professional psychologist in Voss's inner circle. The others were unemployed former officers whose chief qualifications were their newly found interest in military psychology and the study of LeBon's *The Crowd* (18). They adopted a mass-psychological approach to their subject matter, because—as Linnebach (58) puts it—they found it easier to understand and handle.

In April, 1929, Voss finally succeeded in persuading the Reichswehr to use psychotechnics on an experimental and limited scale, beginning with a skeleton psychological laboratory for research and seven testing stations (54). Voss was appointed military commander of the institute, and Simoneit was made its scientific director. They were assisted by only seven professional psychologists. The methods adopted were those suggested by Rieffert on the basis of his wartime experiences (106).

While the army experimented with psychology, the following psychological laboratories and testing stations had already been established in Germany (50):

    a. RAILWAYS ADMINISTRATION
       3 laboratories,
       25 testing stations, employing a total of 6 professional psychologists and 76 assistants.

    b. POSTAL ADMINISTRATION
       1 laboratory,
       80 testing stations, with 1 professional psychologist and 80 assistants.

c. School of Commercial Aviation
1 laboratory and testing station, under Reichswehr supervision.

d. Labor Exchange Agency
21 professional psychologists and 21 assistants.

e. Bureau of Statistics
1 laboratory with 1 professional psychologist.

f. The Police had 4 testing stations, and various municipalities, 25, with a total of 31 professional psychologists.

g. Scientific research was conducted in laboratories maintained by 13 universities and 9 institutes of technology.

7. Why did the Nazis mobilize German psychology?

With the Nazis in the saddle, the whole conception of national life and aims underwent a rapid transformation. Total war became a conscious goal and a master plan was drawn up to insure victory (19). To exploit all energies within the state and to accelerate the break with Germany's short-lived democratic past, the Nazis regarded psychology as their most effective weapon. E. R. Jaensch (56), representing a new psychological school with certain mystical conceptions of human types and countertypes, was very much in favor because of his early membership in the Nazi party, and became the Pied Piper leading German psychologists into the Nazi orbit.

8. How are German psychologists mobilized?

Academic psychologists were designated to provide scientific research (59), while army psychologists were commissioned, first, to examine the psychological problems of the army, and second, to solve them by the application of the findings of the academic school (64). The total cooperation of both groups led to the gradual development of military psychology as an independent discipline, which, at its highest point, matured into the strategy of psychological warfare.

Even at present, the actual nucleus of Germany's psychological mobilization is not particularly imposing. In 1939, there were only about two hundred psychologists on the army payroll (54), and there is no reason to believe that their number increased during the war. The overwhelming majority of psychologists remain in the universities, research institutions and factory laboratories. Nevertheless, their intellectual and emotional approach to psychology and their research methods have changed (55). Today every German psychologist finds his place in the war machine, specializing in details of psychological warfare. A psychological "laboratory" maintained by the High Command co-ordinates them by serving as a transmission belt for their ideas and findings, translating them into practical use.

Ach (68), for instance, is investigating problems of leadership; E. R. Jaensch (55) is indexing and "typing" the character and capacity of the "new German race"; Hellpach (396) studies the psychology of other nations for the use of military intelligence in framing morale offensives; Poppelreuter (358) examines the psychology of political activities; Bock (216) delves into the problems of homesickness among conscripts; others are studying the effects of the war on civilian morale, the nation's religious-ethical attitude in war, and the problems of political faith. Others contribute to the manipulation of popular opinion through propaganda, press, radio, and film.

Army psychology, it must be remembered, has gradually come to include the study of all psychological problems in total war on both the military and the home fronts. Simoneit (65) was fully justified in cautioning against mistaking army psychotechnics for military psychology.

9. What are the tasks of German Military psychology?

Simoneit (63) describes the main tasks as follows:

a. Psychological problems within the military organization, army, navy and air force;

b. psychology of military "work" and special services, (marching, driving, flying, signaling, wirelessing, shooting, ambushing, range-finding, etc.);

c. psychology of equipment and symbols;

d. psychology of selecting army personnel;

e. psychology of indoctrination and training for war;

f. psychological factors disturbing communal life and comradeship in the army;

g. psychology of propaganda;

h. psychology of actual conduct of war.

Army psychologists also advise the Nazi party and the state on (a) selection of political leaders, (b) molding of community spirit, (c) nationalist education for a heroic life and (d) manipulation of public opinion (63).

In addition, Blau (388) and Pintschovius (329) consider "comparative national psychology" as an integral part of the German psychologists' activities, providing psychological profiles of outstanding personalities, drawing up the characterological picture of foreign nations especially seeking out their strong and weak points, and collaborating with the military in analyzing and interpreting war reports and such news from abroad which may be of importance for shaping the Fuehrer's policy (52). The execution of these tasks is assigned to the psychologists employed by the High Command.

10. How are army psychologists selected and trained?

This can be best summed up by quoting the official decree issued by the High Command over Hitler's own signature (51), making a psychological department within the armed forces a permanent fixture of the German war machine.

The decree was signed on April 1, 1937, as part of the general civil service regulations. It contains rules on the previous educational requirements of applicants, preparatory training and examination of candidates, as well as their place in the civil service after successful passing of the examination.

    a. EDUCATIONAL REQUIREMENTS. The applicant must be a graduate of a German university with the degree of Ph.D. He must have majored in psychology with any of the following minors: pedagogy, history, history of literature, history of art, anthropology, ethnology, biology, mathematics, and physics.

    b. PREPARATORY TRAINING. Before admittance, the academically approved psychologist must personally appear for an interview at the Psychological Laboratory of the High Command. Later he is notified to apply in writing and state his preferences, if any, for either the army, navy or air force.

    During the training period the applicant may receive funds for living expenses if he has no other source of income.

c. GENERAL PRINCIPLES OF PREPARATORY TRAIN-
ING. The applicant is trained in practical and independent psychological research. He must also
have an opportunity to complete and deepen his
knowledge of the theoretical principles of psychological work by self-study. Preparatory training is
designed to promote formation of character and
to mold the applicant into a soldierly prototype.
Mentally, the applicant must be thorough and
lucid in his thinking, self-disciplined, imperme-
able to corrupting influences, and have intellectual versatility and many-sided interests.

A talent for psychology is essential. This must
express itself in gregariousness, sensitivity in
thinking, and self-control of sympathetic and anti-
pathetic feelings encountered in everyday life. A
social sense and community attitude, warmheart-
edness toward youth, justice, self-domination, and
complete devotion to psychological science are indispensable personality characteristics of practical
psychologists.

d. LENGTH AND DIVISION OF PREPARATORY TRAIN-
ING. The candidate is trained for three years:

    i. 3 months in the Psychological Laboratory of
       the High Command;
    ii. 24 months in one of the army's psychological
       testing stations;
    iii. 6 months military training in the branch of
       service to which the candidate will be assigned
       eventually as an army psychologist;
    iv. 3 months additional training at the Psycho-
       logical Laboratory;
    v. further training at other psychological institu-
       tions to be decided in individual cases.

e. DISMISSAL FROM PREPARATORY TRAINING. If the candidate shows himself unworthy or unsuited to the army's needs and does not achieve satisfactory progress, he is summarily dismissed.

f. ARMY TESTS FOR PSYCHOLOGISTS. To insure the candidate's suitability as an army psychologist, his whole personality is investigated—his professional and general knowledge, his practical talent in completion of psychological research work, as well as his characterological and other personal qualities.

The judgment of a candidate's merits must take into account his psychological work with youth and his ability to project himself into youth's experiences and educational problems. An all-embracing knowledge of German history and cultural heritage must be exhibited in the tests.

g. EXAMINATION BOARD. The Board of Examiners consists of one officer (general's rank of the army division to which the candidate will be assigned), acting as chairman, the commander of the Psychological Laboratory, the scientific director of the Psychological Laboratory and his deputy, and a university professor of psychology.

h. TEST IN GENERAL. The test begins with the preparation of a thesis on typology. The completion of the thesis is followed by a psychological test given by the candidate to three future officers or non-commissioned officers. The oral examination begins with an exhaustive round-table discussion of the test reports turned in by the candidate and gradually leads to a discussion of general theoretical questions of all branches of psychology.

i. ORAL EXAMINATION. Subjects discussed are: candidate's performance in psychological tests, general methods of making test reports, general psychology and its history, practical characterology, psycho-characterological typology, psychological diagnostics, particularly the science of expression. Occasionally the scientific and philosophical principles of the candidate's outlook on life are also examined. Finally the candidate must show a complete knowledge of the history and organization of the German Army including army laws as well as civil service regulations.

J. REPETITION OF TESTS. If the candidate fails to pass his examination, he is allowed to re-enter preparatory training for not more than twelve months and not less than six months. The second test is final. Repetition of the examination is banned if the results of the first test indicate a second to be hopeless.

k. DESIGNATION OF ARMY PSYCHOLOGISTS. If the candidate passes, he is assigned to his specific branch of service: army, navy, air force, or as psychological adviser to the government. He is a civilian employee of the High Command personally appointed by the Fuehrer with the title of *Oberregierungsrat* (chief governmental counselor) or *Regierungsrat* (governmental counselor) and works together with the army officers specially assigned to cooperate with the army psychologists.

Twice every year, the Central Psychological Laboratory conducts postgraduate courses for army psychologists and officers. Voss (67) reports that one of the courses held in 1938 was attended by 114 army psychologists and 17 officers. This may be accepted as the average pre-war attendance.

Scientific work is also carried out at the semi-official German Society of Military Politics and Military Sciences, Department of Military Psychology, in which the works of academic and military psychologists, as well as those of medical specialists are co-ordinated for the benefit of war-psychological research. In general, this organization, headed by General Friedrich von Cochenhausen of the Air Force, should be regarded as a division of the psychological section of the German General Staff.

11. What is the relationship of the psychologists to the military?

In actual practice as of today, the army psychologist is definitely subordinated to the military. He is regarded as an adviser whose recommendations may or may not be accepted by the officers. Such recommendations are by no means binding on the commanding officers, usually colonels of regiments.

This limitation is somewhat philosophically admitted by German army psychologists (64, 91, 112, 133), who thus reveal a still existing rift between the army's own psychological laboratory and the army at large. Such conflict is not at all unusual; neither is it confined to the German army.

While armed conflicts were confined to opposing military machines, and as long as army psychologists were recruited from among civilian scientists with no, or but slight, understanding of peculiar military problems, the officers' opposition to academic psychologists was understandable and, to a certain extent, even justified. Today, however, total war has expanded the sphere of conflict to include the civilian population as well, which has become the active and passive participant of wars no longer confined to professional armies.

In Germany, particularly, the army psychologist is compelled to undergo a strict military training parallel with his equally strict scientific education. He is required to combine the important qualifications of the "good soldier" in a practical and efficient manner. There is ample evidence, however, that, even under these changed conditions, army officers are still not fully convinced of the psychologist's usefulness within the army and they continue to try to find their own solutions for most of the psychological problems of war.

Weniger (209), when reviewing the influx of psychological research into military sciences, traced the origin of recent antagonism to General von Seeckt, the organizing genius of the Reichswehr, the defunct nucleus of the present German army. Writing in 1929, practically on the eve of the establishment of the first German military psychological laboratory, von Seeckt acknowledged the overwhelming importance of psychology in military matters, but denied the necessity of establishing an independent service for the handling of psychological problems. His line of argumentation is highly illuminating; therefore a short condensation of his article follows:

The most difficult material the officer has to deal with is man himself. Military leaders and sub-leaders must be fully aware of these difficulties. Recent (1929) military literature discovered the *War-Lord Psychologos.**

The art of government and warfare is unthinkable without psychology. In fact, psychology is the most complex ingredient of government and the most important part of military leadership. Its proper application may lead to success, while the inaccurate

---

* This is a reference to Hesse's much publicized book (18) which, in the opinion of certain army circles in Germany, tended to overemphasize the importance of psychology at the expense of strict military thinking.

judgment and management of men is certain to result in failure. The leader's commands must be psychologically correct and effective to dispel all doubts and smash all possible mental resistance of spiritual weaklings. The will of the military leader—an important psychological factor—must extend to and inspire everybody serving under him. The will of Frederick the Great and Napoleon lived in every single one of their soldiers.

The selection of collaborators is a complicated task, and is often incidental or accidental. Their uselessness is often found out too late. Disappointment in collaborators is the daily bread of the war lord. Therefore, he must be a good judge of men to detect their strength or weakness, and to apportion the responsibilities he assigns to them. His collaborators must be imbued, if not with his spirit, then with his indomitable will. They must execute his orders, no matter whether their motivation is conviction, obedience, or fear (62).

As it may be seen from this condensation, von Seeckt refused even to consider the advisability of artificial selection and classification through scientific test methods so highly developed by industrial psychology. He was not alone in his opposition. General Marx (115) and Admiral Hansen (104) both argued that commanding officers, through long experience and training, are the best psychologists within the armed forces.

The controversy was carried into the open when the 1935 regulations made the largely independent psychological services a permanent fixture within the armed forces. The semi-official *Militaer-Wochenblatt* published a series of articles written by proponents and opponents of psychological services as an open admission of the controversial character of the subject.

On June 11, 1935, the magazine published an article by an anonymous writer (52) who advocated the immediate establishment of independent psychological services on the largest possible scale. The author was cognizant of the widespread opposition to his idea and conceded that the "future of military psychology is still shrouded in doubt." But he argued that the oversight or wrong solution of psychological problems, the erroneous treatment of the soldiers' and civilians' minds, had brought Germany to the abyss in the last war. Despite this realization, he found a majority among veterans of that war who denied the necessity of applying psychology to military problems. The first task he considered to be the winning over of the opponents to the side of the military psychological school, after which a practical solution of the problems could be undertaken.

The author maintained that the psychologist's cooperation with the officer is essential when, and if, it comes to a scientific analysis of factual reports or actual events and to the drawing of proper conclusions therefrom. Infantry schools, he held, should introduce psychology into their curriculum, to be designated as "The Soldier as Leader and Follower on the Basis of Wartime and Peacetime Experiences." In such courses the young-officer generation should be taught to regard and treat the soldier as an individual and a member of the greater community with a mind of his own.

The army's answer to this article was published on October 18, 1935, under the by-line of Major Schack (61) whose views may be accepted as characteristic of the officers' general attitude toward psychology in the army. The author repeats the familiar argument that psychology is, and remains, an ingredient of paramount importance in the military mind ("Napoleon was the greatest psychologist of all times"), but maintains that its practice must be confined to army officers rather than to outside academicians and theorists. Tradition is said to be more important than "newfangled psychological theories." Despite the progress of psychological research, the author questions that it will ever succeed in turning men without leadership qualities into leaders. The lack of judgment and management of men was, within the army, only a by-product of the general decay of German life. If such decay can be halted, the shortcomings will be remedied without, and even despite, the use of psychology.

The author took a position of firm opposition to the inclusion of psychology in the curriculum of the officer's education. The future officer must remember but one dictum of Frederick the Great: "You must die stalwartly!" His understanding of this dictum will help him more than long-winded psychological theories. The army regulations are permeated with psychological considerations, and the new school of military psychology will realize that it can add nothing to this existing structure.

The controversy ended in what may be described as a compromise. A psychological "annex" was added to the existing military organization, with the military retaining the upper hand by having the power of decision over the recommendations of the psychologists. Today, however, it is generally admitted that German psychologists have made invaluable contributions to a psychological amplification of military strategy, and have, in this way, accelerated its adaptation to the nature and requirement of total war. Thus the army psychologist comes into his own and is a really indispensable adviser in all matters pertaining to "characterological selection" (with all its inherent shortcomings) and what is called psychological, or intellectual, warfare.

12. What is the organization of the psychological section of the general staff?

As may be derived from largely circumstantial evidence, the psychological section of the German General Staff is organized in four divisions:

  a. Psychological research is concentrated in the High
     Command's Central Psychological Laboratory, at
     present called "Inspection for Aptitude Testing in
     the High Command of the Armed Forces" (66). It
     is composed of twenty scientific departments (54),
     housed in quite palatial headquarters of their own
     in Berlin (56).

b. Psychological selection is decentralized in sev-
enteen army and two naval testing stations. The
army's testing stations are at Berlin, Muenster,
Muenchen, Breslau, Kassel, Hamburg, Koenigsberg, Stettin, Dresden, Stuttgart, Hannover, Wiesbaden, Nuernberg, Wien, Salzburg, Magdeburg,
and Jena. Those of the navy are in Kiel and Wilhelmshaven (54).

c. Special staff for the prosecution of psychological
campaigns, as part of the High Command's own
press department and attached to Section III-B
(Politics and Intelligence) of the German General Staff. This division is known to be closely collaborating with the Propaganda Ministry, Foreign
Office, Secret State Police (Gestapo), and the numerous party organizations (421, 426).

d. Psychological intelligence service specializing in
the study of the political, social and intellectual
attitudes of foreign nations and personalities
(387). This division, by its very nature, is closely
linked to the other existing intelligence services
and is not believed to have an independent status.

After the conquest of France, the psychological laboratory was
given the partial use of Strasbourg University for the conduct of
large-scale investigations into the psychological problems of war.
(*Das Reich,* 1941).

Head of the Inspection for Aptitude Testing in the High Command of the Armed Forces is General Hans von Voss, who was recalled to active service at the outbreak of this war. Officers known
to occupy high positions in the various psychological services are
General Folttmann as chief of staff (66), General Fellgiebel as expert of propaganda and communications (429), and Colonel Blau

in charge of intellectual warfare (344). The present size of their staff is not known.

Even this truly elaborate psychological section of the German General Staff has no independent status, but is closely co-ordinated with other departments. With them it shares the task of "preparing the mobilization, deployment of troops, and planning of military operations; observing foreign armies; gathering all kinds of intelligence data; and cultivating military sciences and topography"—as it was laid down by the Elder Moltke in his classical plan of a Greater General Staff (*Grosser Generalstab*). The latter is composed of a combat, an economic, a political, and a psychological section.

According to information which the Editors of this Survey accept as authoritative, the political and psychological sections of the German General Staff are not themselves conducting political and psychological campaigns. They merely indicate to other existing agencies of the Nazi state what line of general action is required to prepare and support military operations. The execution of the campaigns is then usually left to the agencies among which the Propaganda Ministry, the Foreign Office and the Secret State Police figure most prominently.

It is known, however, that the army retains full supervision over the execution of its indirectly conducted campaigns by having liaison officers delegated to the agencies to which their execution is assigned. For example, Colonel A. Wrochem represents the army in the Propaganda Ministry as chief of a considerable delegation of army and navy officers. Today, army representatives can be found in practically every organization in all branches of Germany's public life.

Typical of this supervision is the army's control over war correspondents, now organized by the High Command of the armed forces in so-called Propaganda Companies (*Propaganda Kompanie* or PK for short). This organization is patterned after a similar pioneering Soviet system which the Germans had an opportunity to study prior to 1933 and during the Spanish Civil War. War correspondents and photographers, although working under the nominal jurisdiction of the Propaganda Ministry, represent an actual division of the German armed forces, even having commissions from second lieutenant to colonel.

The Editors have been informed that such an organization of war correspondents serves a dual purpose. First, strict army discipline is extended to the formerly civilian war correspondents' corps, preventing it "from becoming a nuisance or working contrary to army interests." Second, the army is now free to utilize their activities for its own good. This is especially useful in the case of photographers and motion picture cameramen who may be ordered into action, thus obtaining invaluable pictorial records for military analysis. Superimposed on these incidental advantages and duties is their task as propagandists, as distinctly expressed in the name of their organization. While nominally still aloof from propaganda, the German army thus maintains a direct avenue to German public opinion no matter how muzzled it otherwise may be.

All its direct and indirect approaches to political and psychological activities taken into consideration, the gigantic organizational structure of the German army's psychological section becomes obvious even though its functional arm is naturally subordinated to the one and only General Staff which is jealously guarding its traditional privileges and prerogatives.

13. Is this system efficient?

The main deficiencies are (a) the conflict between objective research and Nazi suppression of free intellectual discussion; (b) the quackery arising from pseudo-scientific Nazi theories and the sudden influx of amateurs to military psychology; (c) the careerist scramble to please the new masters and the deficient qualifications of job-hunters with good Nazi connections; (d) lack of intellectual contact with foreign scientific bodies; and (e) the familiar German metaphysical approach and obscure style of writing.

These deficiencies, however, are largely weeded out by the psychological section of the General Staff which frequently shows a high degree of independence and courage in defying and even refuting Nazi policies. Blau, for instance, rules out the totalitarian press as a reliable guide to public opinion and national sentiment. None of the army psychologists is above using the findings and methods of Jewish scholars like Bergson, Freud, Lazarus, and Steinthal (388). In fact, the Central Psychological Laboratory has a special department for the study and application of psychoanalysis.

Thus the system of mobilizing psychology for the war effort is fundamentally efficient because of its machinery of checks and balances. The tremendous participation and the mass of material produced by German psychologists, moreover, provides an opportunity for selecting the truly valuable contributions.

IV
PSYCHOLOGICAL PROBLEMS OF LEADERSHIP*

"The form of state best suited to the German character is sovereign power centralized in the hands of one supreme leader."

Thus, in 1920, Gottfried Feder, author of the Nazi party program, introduced the leadership principle into present-day German political philosophy. The idea was picked up by Hitler (20) who envisaged the "true Germanic democracy of a leader obliged to accept all responsibility for what he does or does not do."

14. What is the Nazi leadership principle?

The German totalitarian state in personal union with the Nazi party is based on the selective leadership principle and the doctrine

* The question of leadership was perhaps the first among the many psychological imponderables of war which engaged the full attention of American military circles as well. In fact, American army officers responsible for the abstract psychological work within the U. S. Army long maintained that leadership being a "short-cut to morale," its cultivation may be accepted as the primary task of morale-building. For a professional officer's study of leadership and an illuminating little book revealing the army's attitude to this vital military problem, see Leadership, by Colonel E. L. Munson, a brilliant young officer attached to the Special Services (Morale) Branch of the War Department. The book was published by The Infantry Journal. It goes without saying that both the book and the American army reject the Nazis' mystical and mythical approach to the problem.

of national community (Volksgemeinschaft). This means the division of authority and responsibility in the hands of consciously selected leaders of a theoretically classless German society.

The leadership principle is applied in international relations by contending that Germany is to be the leader nation as envisaged in the slogan the "New Order."

Psychologically, the leadership principle revolves around Der Fuehrer who delegates authority to subleaders in the form of a person-to-person mandate. The personal interrelationship between Der Fuehrer (Adolf Hitler) and his followers (Germanic people everywhere in the world) is the psychological basis of the whole Nazi political system (77). To establish and solidify this personal interrelationship, the Nazis apply all weapons of psychological warfare (indoctrination, propaganda, terror, intimidation) to the German people themselves.

The Nazi hierarchical pyramid, consisting of the leader, subleaders, praetorian guards, uninitiated masses of Germanic people, and the uninitiated masses of the subjugated slave peoples, is remarkable in its similarity to the organizational structure of the League of Assassins, a secret religious sect, first heard of in Persia in 1090. The propaganda and political methods of both groups, as well as the unlimited power assigned to their respective leaders, is practically identical, even though the Nazis have cleverly chosen a less suggestive name to designate their party. As a spectacular outward evidence of this resemblance, both the chief of the Assassins and the leader of the Nazis live in mountain-top hide-outs to symbolize their exalted status. The Assassins called this castle of their chief the Vulture's Nest; its streamlined Nazi replica is called the Kehlstein. There is a very obvious psychological kinship between the two political organizations, both medieval in character and power. Those who are interested in the study of the psychological roots of this kinship should read The History of the Assassins, by J. v. Hammer-Purgstall (London, 1840) and The Ansyreeh and Ismaeleeh, by S. Lyde (London, 1853).

15. What is the Nazi psychologist's approach to the problem of leadership?

German psychologists, suddenly confronted with the task of exploring the implications of leadership when the Nazis came into power, undertook a dual approach to the problem. First, they endeavored to determine the psychological components of 'leader-genius" (71), and, second, they devised means of selecting a new generation of leaders for the German state and army (64).

Their analysis (71) of the leader-genius ended in a scientific cul-de-sac. Jaensch alone argued that the composite of his J1 (artistic), J2 (natural masculine vitality), and J3 (tough-minded idealism) types makes up the leader-genius. On this basis Jaensch is now supposedly engaged in "recreating mankind."

The consensus of opinion among other psychologists, however, was that leader-genius cannot be typed—since its historical appearance and impact follows no established norms. Neither can its leadership methods be canalized, because they are exclusively formulated by the individual's personality released to its full effectiveness by the circumstances of the era in which he lives, his environment, and his supposed or real historical mission (71, 84).

The study of former leaders failed to supply clues to a prognostic analysis of leadership. It merely demonstrated the appearance of two different types of leaders, of whom the purely spiritual leader (Jesus) was rejected, while the conqueror type (Caesar and Napoleon) was accepted as a model for German leadership.

The psychologist's second problem was to create norms for finding "subleaders" to receive authority from the leader-genius. These subleaders are not required to possess creative genius, but they must conform to the political principles of the Nazi state and be capable of adjusting their personalities to community interests. It was decided that even their leadership qualities cannot be prognosticated by experimental performance tests, but only through the study of their behavior, character and temperament.

16. What are the specific requirements of leadership?

"A perfect leader exists only in theory," wrote Frederick II of Prussia in his General Principles of War.

"The most important qualification of the general," said Napoleon, "is a clear head that estimates situations correctly, is not easily dazzled, and cannot be paralyzed by good news or bad."

To the time-honored question: are leaders born or made?— Schaefer* gives an unequivocal answer: Training, the appointment to office, and even experience are not enough; the qualities of leadership must be innate. He quotes the sarcastic remark of Frederick the Great: "The mule that carried Prince Eugene's packsaddle through ten campaigns did not thereby become a better tactician. To the shame of mankind, many grow old and gray in otherwise honorable professions without making greater progress than that mule."

The Germans are inclined to agree with Napoleon when he said: "A great general requires that well-nigh miraculous combination of gifts, the free, prophetic view of genius and a keen, intelligent appraisal of the practical." Moltke stressed the union of intelligence and character, and was again instrumental in influencing the ideas of German military psychologists.

These, then, are the criteria which, according to German army and academic psychologists, make a good leader:

> a. POSITIVE WILL (69). In Nazi psychological jargon, will is a habit of voluntary response to the command of the superior leader. This will princi-

---

* Schaefer, T. v., "Feldherr und Feldherrntum," Handb. d. neuz. Wehrw. (Berlin: de Gruyter, 1936), I, 69-73. Theobald von Schaefer, a colonel on the retired list, is undoubtedly present-day Germany's greatest and most objective military historian. For another brilliant essay on the art of war, see his "Kriegskunst," ibid., I, 181-227.

ple is exemplified in the dynamism or actionism of the whole Nazi movement. Its prime motivation is devotion to the cause and unconditional faith in the supreme leader. Will is considered the most important requisite of the leader personality. Thus a great part of psychological research is concentrated on ways and means of examining and testing the capacity and strength of an individual's will. Professor Ach in his report (69) on the "new will-theory," enumerated some of these tests, while Kreipe (110) presented a critique of accepted will theories from the Nazi army point of view.

b. DETERMINATION. Ach (68) considered the achievement of a goal and the creation of means to achieve the goal, both basic principles of determination psychology, as the prerequisites of leadership. The law of specific determination, according to which the increased specification of the goal accelerates and insures its achievement, he held to condition the realism, tempo and organizational ability of the leader.

c. OPERATIVE THINKING (88): Intellectual capacity must be coupled with will capacity. This means reasoning, not per se, but for the planning and executing of a preconceived action.

d. MENTAL ELASTICITY. This is the ability to live up to any situation in a manner most expedient for the accomplishment of a given goal. Nuber (81) says that modern leaders particularly must be endowed with mental elasticity, since modern communications have speeded up political and diplomatic processes, and warplanes and tanks

have accelerated military operations. In the Third
Reich, mental elasticity is interpreted as being an
indigenous German capacity to deviate from accepted values and to assimilate new ones. (It may
be pointed out that the lack of "mental elasticity"
in the French army and political leadership contributed heavily to France's defeat.)

e. MATHEMATICAL THINKING (83). In Germany, it is
held to be an important part of the high military
leader's whole formal reasoning.

f. CHARACTER (71, 84). Integrity, selflessness, idealism, and well-controlled self-esteem are considered important components of the "leader-char-
acter."

17. What are the psychological pitfalls of leadership?

In their study of the possible pitfalls besetting a leader's path the
Nazis foresaw two chief dangers. They were:

a. FATIGUE produced by great responsibility and ac-
cumulation of work due to the centralization of
deciding power (79).

b. OVERESTIMATION OF ONE'S OWN PERSONALITY
which may lead to a fatal interruption of the "psychological contact" between leader and followers
and thus to despotism and petty tyranny replacing leadership by the consent of the governed (71,
77).

18. What psychological precautions are used to protect leaders?

Lufft (79) says that "all the outstanding gifts of the leader-genius are of no use if and when he reaches a state of fatigue. The genius then ceases to be a genius."

Fatigue can be caused by lack of sleep, by sustained creative work, and by the monotony of the leadership routine. In the best interest of leadership and its continual effectiveness, "individuals with great responsibilities must be given an opportunity to regenerate their mental efficiency." Lufft cites the tragic example of General Ludendorff and agrees with von Hentig (17) that the utter mental and physical exhaustion of this key officer contributed heavily to German defeat.

a. LACK OF SLEEP. Lufft maintains that leaders must be habituated to six to eight hours of sleep in their daily cycle of "work-and-rest," if possible without artificial stimulation. His period of absolute rest should be respected by his staff and he must not be disturbed too often, since such interruptions, as well as too much sleep, are held to be more harmful than lack of sleep.

b. SLACKENING OF CREATIVE GENIUS. Fatigue caused by mental enervation must induce leaders even at the apex of the political or military hierarchy to take a vacation no matter how greatly their absence may influence the course of events. The transition from work to rest should not be too sudden. During a transitory period, the leader must indulge in sporting activities which engage him sufficiently to divert his attention from his accustomed work, even though they may demand considerable physical strain. Mountain climbing without guides is held to be the best transition to complete rest; skiing, hunting, sailing, or deep-sea fishing are also suggested. The period of "genuine rest" should be devoted to extensive sleeping, rich meals and friendly gatherings. After one or two weeks of such rest, the spirit of enterprise and longing for return to work usually reappear.

c. MONOTONY OF THE LEADERSHIP ROUTINE. This results in a gradual blunting to external stimuli. It is rare with leaders and, if it occurs at all, is usually caused by the recurring necessity of making decisions or by regularly meeting the same people. In this case, the regeneration may be confined to lighter sports, such as tennis with frequently changed partners of equal strength. Complete rest is unwarranted, nor is remaining within the family circle advisable. The study of an unfamiliar scientific subject, no matter how difficult, is held to be the best means for regaining mental energy.

19. How do problems of leadership affect military psychology?

The army, realizing that superior leadership is the surest way to victory in the quickest possible time, hopes to solve its leadership problems by carefully selecting military leaders (104).

The High Command distinguishes between the selection of leaders (officers) and supreme leaders (generals). Graduation from a German Gymnasium is generally considered sufficient for an air-force officer, but an engineering degree from a technological institute is required for commissions above major, and a doctor's degree in engineering (the hardest to get in Germany) is said to be a prerequisite of generalship in the Luftwaffe.

The unification of political and military leadership in war still has its opponents within the German army. General Wetzell (86,

87) is the spokesman for a group which advocates "splendid political isolation in the army." Since he is the editor of the army's official weekly, it can be assumed that his opposition to the political supervision of the army by Hitler (never openly voiced but an underlying implication of his criticism) has the official approval of high army circles.

While Wetzell concedes that the political leadership must have an insight into military matters, he insists upon keeping military leadership within the army, leaving ultimate responsibility, however, to the head of the state—Hitler.

This attitude may be regarded as the generals' on-the-record absolvency from blame should military matters go astray. Their seemingly futile "opposition" to the political leader's interference with military matters may enable them to salvage the army's prestige from a possible second collapse.

V
SELECTION AND TESTING OF PERSONNEL*

"The selection of men qualified to become leaders . . . must occupy first place among all measures taken by the state to insure the maximum development of our people's fighting spirit and striking power." Thus the German Admiral Hansen (104) defines the primary task of psychology in the preparation and efficient prosecution of total war.

* On the basis of all known facts including very recent information from Germany, it may be stated with complete assurance that the American system of selection and testing, called classification by our War Department, is far superior to that of the German army. This is natural indeed if one knows that most of the German tests are merely teutonized imitations of methods developed in this country. A basic difference between the American and German system is that enlisted men are not tested in Germany, while they undergo ingenious psychological tests in the United States. The crushing superiority of the American classification system is most evident in the tests given to aviators, both army and naval, while tests given to other specialists have proved to be valuable aids. Classification in the army is one of the many duties of the Adjutant General's Office whose head, Major General Ulio, has a group of scientific advisers headed by Dr. Walter V. Bingham, in improving tests and other methods of selection.

20. Why was scientific selection introduced in the German army?

The gradual disappearance of the Junkers as a military caste and the revolutionary changes brought about by the progress of technological warfare necessitated the use of scientific methods of selection rather than that based on class and educational privileges and competition.

Prior to the first World War, officers were drawn from the landed and financial aristocracy and the upper middle classes— main props of the Imperial Reich. All others were conscripted on the basis of physical fitness. This system proved deficient in many instances, especially where leadership was required. General Marx (115) reports that only two commanders of the eight cavalry divisions fighting in the Franco-Prussian War of 1870-71 were able to stand the test of battle. During the period of 1860-71, the failure of Generals Wrangel, Vogel von Falkenstein, Schmidt, Bonin, Steinmetz and Tuempel also showed the inadequacy of hereditary selection.

The tremendous demand for officers during the last war led to the expansion of a reserve officers' corps selected on the basis of higher education and proven ability in battle (255). As the war developed into a struggle of machines requiring skilled specialists and a new type of leadership capable of independent action and initiative, a makeshift system of selection was introduced with test methods borrowed from industrial psychology (53, 59, 60, 172).

After the war, when the Versailles Treaty limited the German army to 100,000 men and the navy to 15,000 men, the militarists proceeded to build up this skeleton force into a "nucleus army of leaders" for the future war (192). The most intricate form of psychological selection now became inevitable, first, to find the best human material among the immense number of volunteers flocking to the "nucleus army," and, second, to choose the right man for the right place in the war machine, thus effecting the highest possible efficiency and co-ordination in the army as a whole (106).

The comprehensive preparations for the second World War under the Nazis resulted in a conscious intensification of all these selection processes, partly to discover outstanding leaders and specialists as quickly as possible, and partly to conform to the general organizational principles of the Nazi state (133).

While selection was largely neglected during the early and easy stages of the present war, the increasing strain on German manpower, caused by immense losses in Russia, again necessitates an acceleration of selection by means of the various scientific test methods. (Cf. answer to Question 36.)

21. What are the general military principles of selection?

Hansen (104) states that masses of technical weapons are not sufficient to decide victory or defeat in total war: "Our only hope for victory is based not on material but on mental superiority achieved in the planned preparation and organization of all human forces to multiply the fighting spirit and individual spirit of each soldier." Mental superiority is contingent on the characterological make-up and practical efficiency of leadership in high and low places.

Hesse (192) emphasizes that leadership must be firmly anchored, not only at the top of the military hierarchy, but in the whole army. The army needs men capable of becoming leaders if emergency and circumstances so require. The psychological effects of new weapons, especially warplanes, tanks and antitank guns, require personnel "with never failing nerves." Therefore, the selection of specialists must go beyond the mere examination of intellect and skill and concentrate on the analysis of the whole personality. Thus a characterological approach became the criterion of selection, despite its apparent shortcomings.

22. When does selection begin?

Selection actually begins long before the young German is called to the colors (129). Boys (and girls organized in the Alliance of German Girls) from six to eighteen are closely observed in school, in the Hitler Youth, Storm Troops, Black Corps and Labor Front. All these organizations have their own selective apparatus set up in their respective race-political bureaus, while the selection in schools is organized and supervised by the Bremen Institute for Youth Study (Institut fuer Jugenkunde) under Dr. Valentiner (140).

Selection within and for the Nazi organizations is made on the basis of physical, characterological, mental and racial examinations, including aptitude tests given to students in schools and apprentices at their places of work (123).

Members of the Hitler Youth are specially examined to determine their general conduct in service (punctuality, orderliness, reliability, subordination), attitude toward superiors and comrades, adaptability, diligence, will power, skill, sensory perception, intellectual capacity, practical and special talents, and leadership qualifications (131). The records are tabulated, analyzed and filed. Thus when the German youth enters the army or political service, his complete record of character development, behavior and accomplishment is available to the army psychologist.

23. Who is selected for what in the army?

Psychological selection in the army is confined to the testing of officers, noncommissioned officers and specialists (91).

Prior to this war, officers (156) were selected from applicants whose preference for branch of service was usually respected. The application had to be submitted, while the applicant was still in school, to the colonel of the regiment with which he intended to serve. Thus his future commanding officer had both the first and last words in his acceptance as an officer-candidate.

On reaching the conscription age of eighteen, the applicant was called to present himself before a board of medical and a board of psychological examiners. His future colonel was always present at both examinations, retaining the power of final decision with the psychological examiner acting only in an advisory capacity and merely supplying scientific opinion of the applicant's character and aptitude.

Since the outbreak of the war, officers have been selected on the basis of demonstrated ability in actual service with the armed forces at the front. Their psychological examination is now relegated to second place and is usually carried out only after they have been sent back from the front to attend one of the officers' schools and to receive additional theoretical training as officer-candidates.

Noncommissioned officers (158) were also given psychological tests before being fully inducted. Previously, "noncoms" had been selected from among volunteers who had enlisted in the army to become noncommissioned officers and who had agreed to serve a period of twelve years after a two-year training period. Today, however, their selection, too, depends on demonstrated ability, the testing being a formality rather than a decisive factor in their promotion.

Specialists (167), including aviators, observers, radio operators, antiaircraft observers and gunners, drivers, tank crews, antitank gunners, submarine crews, parachutists, flame-throwers, motorcyclists, range-finders, signal corps men, and spies, are largely selected from among the masses of conscripts by the private's own preference, backed up by the recommendation of his commanding officer. Members of the music corps are selected for their later use as stretcher-bearers, intelligence agents and possible bearers of the flag of truce (Parlamentaer) (310).

The acceptance of an applicant as an officer-candidate or specialist, and the promotion of a private to noncommissioned rank is not always contingent on the passing of the psychological examination. The final decision rests exclusively with the commanding or induction officer (52, 91).

Conscripts are not given formal psychological tests. They are, however, psychologically appraised at the time of their medical examination and subsequent induction into the army.

24. How are conscripts psychologically appraised?

Schimrigk (130) reveals that this appraisal is formed by the first impression (98, 108), the conscript's life history and a brief written test to be completed within fifteen minutes on any subject the commanding officer (always present at the physical examination) deems appropriate to the conscript's educational level and social background. This test is intended to furnish characterological indices of the conscript's will power, ability to concentrate, intelligence, reasoning and adaptability. No questionnaires are used and no army psychologist is present at these tests. The paper submitted by the conscript is filed for future reference in case he becomes eligible for the special services or for promotion to noncommissioned officer. Only in cases of exceptional merit are conscripts promoted to officers.

The psychological appraisal at induction is confined to questions about the conscript's civilian occupation, his ambitions in private life, his likes and dislikes, and his preferences within the army. Due to the great influx to special services, examining officers are instructed to persuade conscripts to express a preference for the infantry which must be eulogized both at the medical examination and at the induction as the most important branch of service despite the progress of mechanized warfare and the importance of special weapons.

Thus the army psychologist confines his activities to the examination of what may be described as a select few within the war machine. While an average of 2,500 applicants was examined in 1930-32, the number of psychological tests had passed the 100,000 mark in 1939 (54). The number of persons tested since the outbreak of the war is not known.

25. What are the psychological principles of selecting officers and specialists?

In line with current political and military considerations, all performance tests are subordinated to comprehensive characterological examinations; "Technical skill must naturally be tested—but the prime requisite is the search for soldierly qualities which can be determined only through the study of the whole personality" (167).

The Germans are mainly interested in the soldier's readiness to apply his will to a certain act (an imponderable of military action called Einsatzbereitschaft), rather than his ability for performance which can be objectively tested (112). Since no direct methods are available to measure the future application of will and courage, the Germans depend on a characterological examination of the whole personality to supply a reliable clue (122).

Even performance tests are so designed as to furnish indices of the testee's will power (136), mental energy, sustaining power, and readiness to act to the limit of physical capacity, coupled with clear thinking and planned behavior—in addition to formal knowledge, skill and aptitudes. Formal knowledge is explicitly stated as being of secondary importance to the spiritual qualities and emotional attitudes of the soldier (63). Scoring, therefore, is rarely used. In the examination of certain specialists who must possess considerable mental alertness, attention is given, however, to the candidate's intellectual capacity (162, 167).

Physical fitness, including sensory perception, is judged by the medical officer whose observations may be implemented by the psychologist, especially in the case of aviators. Only the psychological implications and effects of physical handicaps (such as shortsightedness, deafness, and bodily defects) are left to the exclusive analysis of the army psychologist (102).*

* Cf. Simoneit, M. Der Psychiater auf der psychologischen Prüfstelle, Der deutsche Militaerarzt, 1939, 5, 201-5; Tiling, E. ibid, 205-6.

26. What techniques are used to select officers and specialists?

The estimation of character and aptitude is left largely to the observation and interpretation of the examining psychologist who formulates his opinion upon analyzing the candidate's life history, expressive movements, mental capacity and performance (93).

LIFE HISTORY. The chief biographical data contributing to the appraisal of a candidate's personality are the influences of environment, schooling, youthful experiences and inspirations gained through reading and trips, attitude toward parents, teachers and national heroes. In the course of several interviews designed to implement the candidate's biographical file, his political and social outlook, personal ambitions and his general attitudes toward life are also ascertained (109).

EXPRESSION ANALYSIS (100). It includes the study of facial expressions, body movements, appearance, voice and speech, handwriting and writing style.

> a. Facial expressions are studied by a device developed by Lersch (113). A movie camera is concealed from the candidate by a wall chart. While the test is being given, the candidate is seated in a chair, requested to answer specific questions, subjected to unexpected and painful stimulations like electric shocks of varying intensity, and instructed to work an ergograph. His face is photographed throughout the test, and the film is later studied, the psychological evaluation of the various expression forms being based on Lersch's norms (127, 128). (This and other tests were described by Dr. Pryns Hopkins in Occupational Psychology, London, 1939, 13, 56-63. Dr. Hopkins, in an article

entitled, "Psychological Tests in the Army and Air Force of Foreign Countries," reported on his observations in Germany, Hungary and Japan. For additional information see 146 in Bibliography.)

b. Body movements, such as involuntary gestures like scratching behind the ear or the position of the lips while thinking, are observed and analyzed along lines suggested by Strehle (138, 139).

c. Voice analysis is described by Dach (96), Volkenborn (141) and Zeise (144). They distinguish between phonetic and formal expression in voice and speech. The former is differentiated in respect to loudness, pitch, melody, clang timbre, articulation, accentuation, tempo and intermittent pauses, the latter in respect to the divergent selection of words, sentence development and idiom.

A combination of warm melody, softness of timbre and accentuation is held by Dach to indicate a person capable of strong sympathetic and emotional participation. Monotone, hard timbre and staccato accentuation (characteristics of the Kommandosprache) are considered indices of calm and determined will power. In a similar, rather commonplace, manner, army psychologists claim to be able to determine active-impulse, meditative, melancholic, practical, choleric, sensitive-excitable, vain, and timid-uncertain characters and temperaments.

d. Appearance analysis is described by Eckstein (98) and Kreipe (108), who both proceed from the psychology of the first impression.

i. Behind physically weak appearance, they detect hesitation and meekness, occasionally developing into strong mental resistance, permanent tension, high excitability, stubbornness,
lack of sense of humor—a personality altogether difficult to handle if his character is not
tempered by intellectual capacity or special
talents.

ii. Physically robust appearance usually shows
energy, power of endurance, considerable
physical resistance to strain and hardship,
light-minded, careless courage—but also
"mental vacuum," superciliousness, a high degree of egoism, pretentiousness, and scornful-
ness. If not properly recognized, such persons
once commissioned may become harmful to
the service.

iii. Neat appearance may indicate carefulness,
reliability, parsimony, with vanity added as a
usually harmless side product—but such positive characteristics may be diminished by the
person's inclination to bluffing, and an overdeveloped desire for recognition. Kreipe remarks
that such people "hate to play the role of the
unknown soldier."

iv. Untidy appearance may conceal valuable positive characteristics such as precision in special
tasks, but is tempered by a strictly rational approach to all soldierly duties.

e. Handwriting analysis (119) is given much attention in Germany, chiefly through the influence of

Klages (107) whose pupil, Renthe-Fink (120), is the army's chief graphological expert. The study of writing style is also used as a medium of personality analysis (98).

MENTAL CAPACITY. It is determined by intelligence (92) and interest tests (143), some of which were adopted from American psychology with slight variations. An original test is described by Hesse (106). The candidate is presented with a picture and asked to describe it in writing. The description is claimed to reveal his power of observation and imagination (145). In a sort of completion test, described by Zilian (147), thirty-two objects of varying degrees of difficulty are arranged. The candidate's task is to continue finishing the series once he has begun. Scoring is hardly used, since the tests are expected to be qualitative rather than quantitative indices of the testee's character and not of his formal intelligence.

ACTION ANALYSIS (132) is obtained by testing choice-reaction in the conventional manner, and by the use of two test methods devised by the Germans specifically for military purposes. They are called command series (Befehlsreihe) and leadership test (Fuehrerprobe) (63, 106).

a. The command series are described by Hesse (106). "The candidate receives a series of orders to be carried out during the day. He may be ordered to report at certain periods, to state the correct time, to mail a letter, to pack his knapsack, rifle, belt and helmet, to attach a rope to hooks fixed at certain intervals and, finally, to climb a smooth escalade with full equipment. The examiner frequently changes the tone of his commands and intentionally censures minor mistakes to determine the effect on the candidate. Physical dexterity, alertness, quick thinking and memory are tested in this manner."

   b. The leadership test is described by Hesse and Simoneit (63). A group of infantry soldiers is placed under the command of the candidate who must explain and then supervise the execution of some manual task, like the making of a clothes hanger out of a piece of wire, or the assembling of a prefabricated bridge. During other phases of the same test, the candidate is called upon to lecture to the group about a picture or a subject for which he shows particular preference. The effects of his leadership qualities are determined by observing and questioning the soldiers in the group.

In a frequently used choice-reaction apparatus described by Simoneit (63, 132) and Hopkins, a number of levers are placed at the disposal of the candidate, who depresses them in response to different patterns of red, white and blue lights, and to lights with circles and squares which are successively lit. The candidate's errors and speed of response are automatically recorded.

The psychologists use additional criteria to implement the tests and facilitate their interpretation. Kuenkele (112) suggests the analyses to be based on Rohrer's morphologic face index, skull indices, the study of psychosomatic appearance based on Kretschmer's and Jaensch's types. Craniology, anomalies of poise, cutaneous reactions, deformities, stigmata of degeneracy and anomalies of sensory perception may also be studied (114).

27. What is the actual procedure of the psychological examination?

The examination (91) is conducted at one of the testing stations of the armed forces by a board of examiners consisting of an army officer usually with the rank of a colonel, a medical officer and three psychologists. The tests require two full days in the army, and two and a half in the air force, during which the candidates are confined to the testing stations. The general tests are given to groups of four and five at a time, while the interviews are conducted individually by delegated psychologists.

The actual sequence of the tests is the following:

> FIRST DAY. Intelligence test—voice analysis—choice reactions—photographic record of mimetic expressions—command series.

> SECOND DAY. More intelligence test—study of capillary reactions—leadership tests—examination of handwriting and speech—another choice reaction test to auditory stimuli with the falling rod apparatus of Rupp—exploration of life history, attitudes and interests—round-table discussion (106).

During the one day rest between the two days of examination, the candidate remains under constant observation.

28. What are the general principles of selecting specialists?*

The main principles, for selecting all types of specialists are formulated in respect to one fundamental consideration: experience

---

* A detailed description of several German tests used for the selection of specialists (including workers in aviation factories) is printed for the first time in the Appendix on page 171. For some of the descriptive material the Editors express their gratitude to Dr. H. L. Ansbacher of Brown University, one of the outstanding experts of German military psychology. His comprehensive bibliography of German military psychology appeared in the *Psychological Bulletin*, while *The Infantry Journal* published part of his survey.

and occupation in private life does not necessarily qualify a man for service with similar duties in the armed forces (130.) The Germans found that good chauffeurs do not make good tank drivers, and that good commercial aviators do not make good combat pilots, when their technical skill is not complemented by "soldierly qualities."

It is, again, evident that the characterological approach dominates German military psychology even for the selection of the most skilled specialists.

Thus the army psychologist's task is to find and recommend for special services men who possess natural inclinations for such work in addition to inborn zeal, devotion, national pride, effective will power and a readiness to accomplish any given task (167).

The Germans believe this type of man can be trained for special duties in the shortest possible training period and is likely to achieve best possible results in actual combat. Among the general principles regulating the selection of specialists, the following seem to be the most important:

AVIATORS (169). The Germans consider the prime requisite of a military aviator to be his ability to adapt himself completely to his machine and to regard the individual components of a plane as he does those of his own body.

The indices for selection of such men are obtained through the study of eyesight, static sense of equilibrium, capacity of muscular strain, glands and other inner organs which have a highly developed susceptibility to stimulation.

The aviator must also possess characteristics which facilitate his habituation to permanent mental tension, dangers, perseverance and sudden impulses, as well as a tenacious feeling of duty.

TANK CREWS (175). Characteristics looked for are a high degree of individualism and ability for independent action, a mechanic's devotion to his machine, a readiness to sacrifice and an absolute devotion to the national cause. *Esprit de corps,* the feeling of belonging to a privileged service, develops a marked self-appreciation in the tank driver's and gunner's personality and endows the tank itself with a "morale quality."

Tank crews must be able to perform simultaneously different functions with both hands within split seconds despite the tank's jerky motions. They must be able to habituate themselves to continuous darkness, extraordinary heat, cramped quarters and the difficulty of intercrew (and outside) communication. They must also possess what the Germans call the "instinct of terrain" (spatial perception and sense of direction), which enables them to retain their course toward a fixed goal even after detouring around tank traps and other obstacles.

The selection of tank crews is especially strict, since the tank's efficiency and co-ordination with other units exclusively depends on the crew's morale. (Also see 172 for the description of Moede's test apparatus used during the last war for the selection of automobile drivers, and reportedly still in use.)

LISTENING POSTS (aircraft detectors, submarine detectors, 162, 167). The qualification for this work is not necessarily dependent on auditory acuity but on the ability to differentiate intensity and quality of sounds and to locate them. In addition, capacity for sustained wakefulness and concentration, considerable physical endurance in adverse weather, and a highly developed consciousness of responsibility are indispensable. Intelligence is required for the correct observation of plane formations and designs, and for the quick and concise drawing up of written reports, as well as for the accurate estimation of their observations. It is interesting to note that the Germans consider men in their late twenties and early thirties more suited to this important work.

The system used in Germany in testing gun crews of the Flak-artillery, and spotters of enemy aircraft (who are, in contrast to England and the United States where civilians are widely used, members of the armed forces), has been copied from the French. This again proves that the Nazi claim to originality in this branch of military psychology is—just another Nazi claim.

RADIO OPERATORS (161, 165, 170): For the task of receiving, identifying and transcribing radio signs, the candidate must possess emphatic adaptability, acoustic comprehension and discrimination, and intellectual capacity.

The requirement of these qualities complicates the problem of selection, since intellectually developed city dwellers, exposed to urban noises, are usually blunted to delicate acoustic stimuli, whereas rural persons whose acoustic sensitivities are better developed lack the intellectual versatility for the work.

The examination determines:

a. whether susceptibility to acoustic perception is free or wilfully inhibited;
b. whether acoustic or visual orientation predominates;
c. whether discrimination of acoustic reception is sustained even at an increased rate of incoming signs;
d. whether the reception, transcription and retention of rhythmical sounds is assured;
e. the candidate's conscientiousness and reliability under all conditions.

Special attention is devoted to the candidate's ability to differentiate between similar sounds, such as b and d, and his ability to execute simultaneous multiple performances.

It has been found that musically talented persons show better qualification for this type of work.

Naval radio operators must be able to receive ninety letters per minute over a consecutive period of four to six hours of duty; radio operators on warplanes must be able to receive eighty letters

per minute under considerable physical strain and special circumstances; radio operators attached to the signal corps must be able
to receive seventy letters per minute in actual combat conditions.

29. How is the prognostic accuracy of tests secured?

German army psychologists, mindful of the limitations inherent
in their characterological approach (99), caution against the indiscriminate application of these methods and analyses to professions
in general. Simoneit (133) says that the "system of prognostic personality study" is applicable only to professions where certain vital
stimuli can be properly foreseen, such as the army with its fixed
ultimate aim of combat. Nuber (118) remarks that such methods
can be used successfully only in strictly co-ordinated units, again
like the army where uniformity of motivations and aims prevails.

The final efficiency of the characterological examination depends on the "psychological instinct," soundness of judgment and
psychological training of the examiner (99, 112). Care is taken,
however, to assure the psychologist's scientific knowledge being
blended with a practical understanding of human nature, and the
examination taking place under circumstances closely resembling
natural conditions. Performance tests, in contrast to the characterological examination, are validated in the generally accepted manner. The methods of validating characterological examinations,
however, are only occasionally referred to in German publications.
Masuhr (152) presented a paper on the subject in a postgraduate
course for army psychologists, but censorship prevented the publication of actual data. Another one of the rare attempts at validation is contained in one of Eckstein's papers (98). No serious and
large-scale attempt at validating these tests was ever made, probably because some of the charlatans of German army psychology
were fearful of results. Final validation was left to the war itself
which has fully confirmed the tests both in a strictly functional
and in a wider characterological sense.

30. What is the psychologist's technique of making out test reports?

Since characterological test reports are prepared for army officers not familiar with the language of psychology, they must first of all be short and to the point, avoiding, as far as only possible, the use of the cumbersome lingua franca of academic psychology. This primary condition is stressed over and over again, most often in articles by Simoneit, who himself is the least capable of fulfilling his own condition. But as a warning it should be heeded by our own scientists now assisting the military men in the more efficient prosecution of the war. Some of their reports lose much of their effectiveness because of the language used and rejected by the sobersided officer as "pure scientific doubletalk" (142).

Generalities like "straightforward and honest" or "he has an impeccable character," or such ratings as "good, very good, excellent" must be avoided. The quality of personal characteristics must be described with careful choice of words so as not to convey misleading interpretation.

For the actual making out of test reports, Guenther (103) suggests the following principles: The report should begin with a general appraisal of the soldier's intelligence and performance, the latter being especially important in the case of specialists. This report includes information on the candidate's reading (technical, military, political books, or mystery novels), memory, manner of thinking, attention, orderliness. The data must be related to the estimation of other characteristics.

Then the candidate's "will disposition" is described—his power of decision and determination, with regard as to whether it is sustained, spasmodic, rational, sensitive or automatic.

The third section describes the candidate's self-consciousness, feeling of self-importance and capacity of subordinating himself while retaining a certain degree of independence. Then follows the description of emotional attitudes and sentiments, such as temperament, tendencies toward vanity, boasting, ambition for power, inferiority and superiority complexes. (Also see 124.)

Summing up, it must be repeated that the primary aim of all tests and examinations is to establish an accurate picture of the candidate's whole personality with an eye on his qualities for leadership.

And again, the reports must be written in a style understandable to the psychologically untrained staff or field officer.

VI
PSYCHOLOGY OF MILITARY LIFE

"The driving motive of the Hitler Youth is to produce a new type of militant young German . . . and to make one militarized corporate body of the whole nation."*

Thus military life in Germany does not mean merely army service. It is intended to be the way of life of the entire German nation. Simoneit (243) states that the "most noble task of military psychology is the indoctrination of the German people with traditional soldierly virtues."

This reorientation of German life grew out of the conviction that victory in total war is contingent on a people's positive attitude toward war. Planned effort is held to be capable of promoting and preserving such intellectual and emotional attitudes, and Bonin (181) says that the peacetime activities of Nazi leaders must, therefore, center on the "proper mental preparation of the entire German nation for the Hour."

To achieve this goal, the Nazis replaced all existing educational principles with what they call *Wehrerziehung* (military education), a grandiose project aimed at the mental, spiritual, and physical preparation of Germans for war (186). Pedagogy was thus revolutionized to meet the aims and needs of the Nazi master plan.

---

* Koerber, W., *Young Germany: The Hitler Jugend.* (Berlin: Terramare, 1933). Koerber is head of the Press and Education Department of the Reich Youth Leadership.

31. What is the role of pedagogy in Germany today?*

Pedagogy has been made the servant and transmitter of the philosophical and political principles of Nazism. This end was achieved, first, by a radical departure from all accepted educational ideas, and, second, by a merger of pedagogy with Nazi psychology. The psychologist was called in to advise in the selection and presentation of the new educational material. Krogh (199), describing the process, calls this co-operation of educationalists and psychologists "psycho-pedagogy in the service of total education."

32. What is total education?

Total education is the mental, spiritual, and physical conditioning of all ages, sexes and classes *to act* according to the principles of the Nazi state. All media of education thus serve the goal embodied in the slogan, "One Reich, One People, One Fuehrer."

This implies the indoctrination of military spirit, physical culture, military sports and rifle practice (195). It expands education beyond the sphere of traditional institutions (family, school, army), to include all Nazi organizations (Hitler Youth, Storm Troops, Black Corps, Labor Service, Labor Front and others) for participation in the educational program (184, 210).

* A detailed description of the new German pedagogical approach to the problem is far beyond the scope of this survey. The role played by educators and philosophers like Krieck, Schmitt and others is of considerable importance but has no immediate bearing on the basic subject matter of this book. For those interested in this particular aspect of the problem, the Editors recommend *Educational Philosophy of National Socialism*, by G. F. Kneller, *The German Universities and National Socialism*, and *German Youth and the Nazi Dream of Victory*, both by E. Y. Hartshorne, *German Youth Movements*, by C. B. Schmid (Ph.D. Diss.).

In school (203), subjects are adapted to the specific require-ments of military upbringing. German studies concentrate on the dramas, epics and novels of Germanic heroism.

History is presented generally as the "development of an idea," namely, the political, spiritual and ethnic unity and destiny of the German people. It emphasizes the political and armed struggles conducted to accomplish this unity (185).

Arithmetic is taught in terms of military science, including ballistics, military geometry, naval mathematical problems, and calculations of airplane mechanics.

The curriculum also includes lectures by high army officers, visits to the War Academy and other military establishments, and tours of historic battlefields in the company of military instruc-tors.

The Nazi organizations implement the program of the schools and continue to indoctrinate patriotic spirit after the Nazi pattern, to preserve the will-to-fight, and to organize means of insuring the perfect physical condition of individuals (204, 240).

33. What do the Germans think is the importance of total education?

First, total education is designed to give German youth a firm and logical intellectual and emotional sequence throughout life. In contrast to the democracies, where young people gradually alienate themselves from early ideas, Nazi total education claims to effect the youth's transition to other age groups without the confusion of conflicting ideas, and to fortify the continuous de-velopment of leadership qualities, loyalty, and faith (78).

Second, total education prepares for army service by imbuing young people with those soldierly virtues which General Franke (186) lists as self-discipline, secrecy, loyalty, readiness to sacrifice, courage to acknowledge guilt, resolution, willingness to share re-sponsibility, and national pride.

Third, total education is held to develop courage in young men even when not inborn (182).

34. What are the principles of indoctrination in the army?

Today service in the army is considered the climax of a youth's total education (193).

This attitude is in marked contrast to the views which prevailed prior to the first World War when drill, military skill and blind obedience were the essential principles dominating military education.

Previously the soldier was trained to handle his own weapons and obey orders. He was not supposed to be a free agent. This system was adapted to the military tactics of the time which demanded that a soldier act in company always within earshot and view of his superior officer.

The first World War broke up the company formation and required a sense of initiative and independent action for which the individual soldier was not psychologically prepared. Changed requirements necessitated a "transformation of the soldier" and induced the Germans to evolve a new educational principle to "create a new type of warrior who is able and willing to subordinate himself while yet capable of independent action" (192).

This transformation was skillfully adapted to the day-by-day requirements of Germany's armed forces. During the Reichswehr period (1919-33), its primary aims were the development of leadership qualities and military skill in each individual soldier, and the preservation of "honor and devotion to the Fatherland as the sacred heritage of a glorious past."*

The introduction of compulsory military service under the Nazis for the purpose of ultimate war marked the second and final stage of the "transformation of the soldier." Responsibility and

---

* From General Hans von Seeckt's decree of January 1, 1921.

manly defiance became the basic principles of military education with "devotion to the Fatherland superimposed on each of these elements." Instead of emphasizing a will-to-die, the new education infuses a will-to-live in order to accomplish given tasks, blended with a readiness-to-die when the accomplishment of the task so requires (202). Individualism is considered a prerequisite, but it must always be in harmony with basic community interests.

The High Command's new Service Regulations define the fundamental principle of present military education in these words: "The individual soldier must be educated so that he is able to accomplish his tasks in battle even if left to himself. He must know that he alone is responsible for all his acts and failures (180)."

Since the combination of discipline and independent thinking contains dangerous elements, the Regulations offer this solution: "Readiness for responsibility is the foremost leadership quality. It should, however, under no circumstances lead to arbitrary action which disregards the interests of the army as a whole. A brash feeling of knowing-it-all should not replace discipline, and independence must not develop into arbitrariness."

Hesse (193) contends that army education is devised to co-ordinate the conscript's training with the ideas of Nazi total education, and Braun (182) to complete the transformation of the peacetime conscript into a full-blooded warrior. There is, however, one basic difference between the German Army's and the Nazi party's educational principles. The latter tends to emphasize the party's overwhelming importance as the controlling organ of the New German State. The prime motivation recognized by its educational system is unconditional loyalty to the Party Leader and his subleaders. The army, on the other hand, bases its indoctrination on the principle of undivided devotion to the Fatherland, patriotism being the main motivation.

Certain observers in the United States and abroad claim to detect a distinct rift between the army's and party's educational principles in this apparent difference between their respective aims and motivations. They even describe the army's basic educational principle of undivided patriotism as a camouflaged attempt at taking the conscript away from the party's educational spell, at least for the period of his service. For such an interpretation of a somewhat complex situation no evidence was found in the available German literature.

The army is actually held to produce better results in both men and efficiency than the educational organs of the Nazi party. Such a comparison was made possible by the party's attempt at directly participating in the army's military training program as well as in actual combat. The Nazis now have several divisions of Schutzstaffel (SS, Black Corps) in what is known as the *Waffen-SS*, a huge, fully militarized unit developed out of what first was Hitler's bodyguard and later became the Nazis' own private army.

These SS-troops represent what Himmler (552) called the "wish-picture of the Nordic prototype" and are bred in the Nazi test-tube manner devised by the Black Corps' own Race-Political Bureau. The originally extremely rigid conditions were considerably relaxed in the wake of the immense blood-letting of the Russian campaign during which practically all the initial SS-regiments were wiped out. A recent recruiting campaign to replenish the ranks of these black-uniformed, ruthless young men promised a lot in privileges, but requested surprisingly little in duties. It is possible that these recruits were needed, not for the front in Russia, but for Hitler's own civil war army to fight on the Home Front.

At the outbreak of the war, Himmler insisted that since members of these regiments were fully imbued with the aggressive Nazi ideology, they provided the ideal human material for shock-battalions. He then placed his troops at the disposal of the army, and several battalions were reportedly used in Poland, Greece, and Russia. Authentic reports, however, describe the fighting capacity of these super-elite shock troops as being below the average performance of regular troops, which the army takes as an indication of the superiority of its own traditional educational principles.

The progressing "nazification" of the German army that reached its climax in Hitler's assuming actual supreme command of the army in December, 1941, resulted in the allocation of more spectacular though, in the final analysis, easier assignments to the rapidly growing *Waffen-SS*. Moreover, their officers were given glamorous military ranks instead of their drab SS titles. Thus, for example, one of Hitler's early henchmen, a bibulous rowdy of Beerhall-Putsch fame, was made a full general together with a peculiar assortment of Nazi blackguards who were made major generals and lieutenant generals.

The *Waffen-SS* is usually kept in reserve while regular troops "soften" enemy positions. Only when a sufficiently softened enemy bastion is about to fall, are these Sunday-soldiers of the Nazi party sent into "action" which usually consists in the mere occupation of a town or village. Nevertheless, the communique issued by Hitler's Headquarters is able to announce that Fort X, or the village Y was "occupied by detachments of the *Waffen-SS*"—giving the impression that the same troops participated in their storming as well.

This trick is part of Hitler s psychological campaign which he wages against the population on the German Home Front. But in this respect at least, he is waging a losing battle. The easy parades of the *Waffen-SS* are getting to be known in Germany and create antagonism against these "pluckers of phony victories." Within the army, too, from field marshal down to buck privates, hostility against the *Waffen-SS* is steadily mounting, a fact probably kept from Hitler.

35. What are the techniques of indoctrination used in the army?

As far as the psychology of military training is concerned, the Germans inject realism into the drill by stressing danger-elements (*Gefahrsmomente*) during maneuvers. This practice accustoms troops to battle conditions and averts monotony in training. Grunwaldt (188) refers to the Japanese system of distributing one live bullet during maneuvers, the soldier never knowing when he may be hit, but we have no evidence that such practices were introduced into the German Army. In fact, American military observers frown upon the whole idea. The one live bullet may kill anybody including the commanding officer, a risk which is out of all proportion to the slight advantage inherent in the system.

The *ideological* conditioning of soldiers is considered of equal and often of greater importance than technical training. It is explicitly stated that "work on the drill-ground, although indispensable for the practice of military action and for the habituation to orderliness, smartness, and discipline, should take up only limited time" (188).*

* In line with the democratic principles of the British and United States armies, informative education takes the place of indoctrination and intellectual conditioning. In Britain, a daily discussion of political events was introduced shortly after the first edition of this book arrived there and, indeed, the Editors were informed that the decision was largely influenced by the present Survey. The United States Army found an even better solution of the problem when it introduced the so-called orientation courses. These are talks prepared by the War Department's Bureau of Public Relations for our new soldiers. They are clear, non- controversial synopses of the events that led to the war, our problems at home and in South America, and the ten major campaigns since the Japanese took Mukden in 1931. The success of these orientation courses surpassed even the most optimistic expectations. It is the consensus of expert opinion that these lectures, augmented and amplified with the guest appearance of prominent speakers from all walks of public life, notably famous foreign correspondents recently returned from overseas assignments, succeeded in making the average soldier understand *for* what and *against* what he is called upon to fight, while the civilian population is still largely groping in the dark. For the benefit of the latter group, the lectures were published under the title *The Background of Our War*. Another series of orientation lectures, sponsored by General Ben Lear of the Second Army, is on a somewhat higher plane. Entitled *School of the Citizen Soldier*, it has been published in book-form, another example the magnificent intellectual care with which our citizen soldiers are treated in the army.

The keynote of military indoctrination is a sort of habituation to patriotism, deliberately and carefully stressed on every possible, and even impossible, occasion. Officers are obliged to include patriotic references in every one of their addresses to their men, and always end their critiques of individual problems with an appeal to the patriotism of the German soldier. Among the means of army indoctrination, Heeren (191) lists the following:*

   a. DISCUSSION OF DAILY POLITICAL EVENTS. For an hour every day, officers gather their men for an explanation of the political acts of the Nazi leadership so as "to give every soldier an immediate participation in the decisive events of the functions of state and race." These discussions are reported to be very effective.

   b. PATRIOTIC EDUCATION. Although such education is in accord with the principles of Nazism, Heeren cautions against the haphazard continuation of formal Nazi education in the army, since the tasks, aims and program of Nazism are already thoroughly drilled in the premilitary indoctrination. Therefore, patriotic education in the army concentrates on the presentation of historic military examples to develop the soldier's sense of duty and desire for emulation.

---

* Also see Die Freizeitgestaltung in der Wehrmacht, *Deutsche Wehr*, 1939, Suppl: Truppendienst, 19; Captain Roesler, Vaterlaendische Geschichte, *ibid.*, 1939, Suppl: Truppendienst, 22; Merker, Geschichtsunterricht im Heere, *ibid.*, 1939, Suppl: Truppendienst, 15; Gedanken ueber den Unterrieht ueber politische Tagesfragen, *ibid.*, 1938, Suppl: Truppendienst, 32; Schmidt, Das kriegsgeschichtliche Beispiel als Mittel der Erziehung, *Militaer-Wochenblatt*, 1940, 144-6; Die Geschichtskenntnisse der Rekruten, *ibid.*, 1939, 2282-83.

c. Social Evenings of Comradeship. Carefully prepared on the basis of voluntary participation with common soldiers running the show.

d. Weekly Hour of the Company. Cultivation of music and community singing, particularly German classics and folk songs. Political, scientific and cultural lectures. (These lectures are presented by the German Labor Front as "the gift of the German worker to the German soldier.")

e. Festive Hours. Commemorating historic events to give soldiers direct contact with German history. They are usually held in connection with visits to national shrines and historic battlefields.

f. "10 Minutes Front-Spirit." Ten minutes are set aside every day to whip up a militant spirit in the conscripts. Officers who participated in the last war tell about their own experiences in combat (182).

g. Planned Recreation. The entire recreation period is given over to further the soldier's cultural education and additional physical training. Tours are conducted to public institutions, historic monuments, libraries, galleries, theaters, and movies. There are dancing, singing, swimming lessons, hikes, and mountain climbing in free time (197).*

---

* After a somewhat confused and rather spasmodic start, planned recreation in the United States Army, Navy and Marine Corps developed rapidly, until today it may be regarded as superior to that of Germany both in quality and quantity. This is largely the result of a unique co-operation between military and

36. How are officers indoctrinated?

The basic aim of the officer's indoctrination is the formation of his personality (194). His training is concentrated on bringing out his leadership qualities by developing his sense of responsibility and determination. The sense of responsibility must make him feel like a "father to his company"; determination must endow his orders with an irresistible quality of evoking immediate voluntary response (196).

The officer's army education is designed to develop his intellectual power, his positive political attitude toward Fatherland and Fuehrer (Fatherland being much more important than Fuehrer), and his absolute conviction in the Greater German idea.

Nuber (154) and Hesse (194) maintain that in the new German Army the officer's origin and family background are not considered important factors in success in the army. This obviously inspired assertion is clearly contradicted by practice, even though no published evidence can be cited that would directly refute Nuber's and Hesse's sweeping statements. The fact that the colonel of

civilian agencies, and of the population's genuine concern for the material and spiritual well-being of its own soldiers. In this as in many other respects, the free citizens of this country reveal a better understanding of the specific needs of the military than the regimented subjects of Nazism, Fascism, and Nipponism whose conditioned hero-worshiping still leaves a gulf between the army and the people at large. Civilian participation in the recreational activities of our armed forces helps to maintain their character as a people's army. Germany, on the other hand, may be regarded as the army's people.

These recreational activities have but an indirect bearing on what is generally known as military morale. Indeed, morale presents a series of more complex problems than those of sheer entertainment. The fighting spirit of a tank destroyer unit cannot be raised by a visit of Miss Ann Sheridan to a military camp. The fact was partly responsible for the War Department's decision to change the name of what used to be the Morale Branch to Special Services Branch.

a regiment retains the right to veto any applicant's final acceptance in the officers' corps, is calculated to endow him with the power of selection on the sole basis of strictly social considerations. This discretionary power is known to be exercised to keep the officers' corps a class by itself, an essentially aristocratic clique, and, indeed, to preserve the Junkers caste within the army.

When officers were urgently needed for the new army in 1934-35, the temporary shortage was partly solved by enlisting "reliable" police officers in the armed forces. In the German Army's closely knit aristocratic setup, these newcomers represented the lower middle classes, a stratum of the population previously barred from the officers' corps. These police officers, despite their loyalty to the new regime and previous experience in the half-militarized German Police, were never recognized as full-fledged officers by the masters of the German Army. As soon as a new crop, bred and brought up along traditional lines, became available for service the police officers were discharged or returned to their former duties.

It is also known that despite statements to the contrary by Eickemeyer (184), Schmidt-Logan (204, 240) and Schmuck (205), officers of Nazi party organizations such as the Storm Troopers, Black Corps and Hider Youth—again members of the lower middle classes, and of the upper lower classes—find it practically impossible to climb the ladder of the aristocratic German officers' corps with its still very potent Junkerism.

The peacetime practice of the officers' indoctrination is this: It begins during his term (six months to one year) in the compulsory Labor Service, where he is brought in contact with all strata of the German population, and where he is supposed to learn subordination and manual labor. His military indoctrination starts out with his entry into the army as an officer-candidate. During this period, though having the status of a private, he enjoys special privileges such as dining in the officers' mess. His progress is closely followed by superior officers who keep a record of his character and conduct.

During this early period he is given a "father-adviser" (*Faehnrichsvater*), usually an elder officer with the rank of captain or major, with whom he may discuss all his private and professional problems, and whose example he is expected to emulate.

This preliminary training of character-building lasts one full year, at the end of which the officer-candidate is promoted to noncommissioned rank. The next eight to ten months are spent in one of the five officers' schools in Dresden, Hannover, Munich, Potsdam or Wien. Four additional months may be spent at one of the several arms schools (*Waffenschule*). After two and one-quarter to two and one- half years in the army, and after passing two examinations, he is commissioned as second lieutenant and is admitted as a member of the officers' class, usually by Herr Hitler himself. Officers to be assigned to the General Staff must take an additional three-year course in the War Academy (193, 194).

Since the outbreak of the war, officers are not preselected but are chosen on the basis of demonstrated ability. Each candidate must obtain his promotion to noncommissioned rank, not in a garrison, but at the front, after which he is sent back to attend the officers' school, arms school and/or War Academy. The training periods in these schools have been considerably shortened, and officers now return to their units after a period of four to six months in the educational institutions.

The immense blood-letting of the Russian campaign necessitated the broadening of the principles by which selection and indoctrination of officers were regulated. In addition to the ordinary procedure of receiving in the armed forces young men with special qualifications as officer candidates (those qualifications including family background and such educational requirements as high school or junior college grade), now enlisted men may be selected by their commanding officers to become officers, on the front or of the reserve, without possessing these qualifications.

This what may be considered revolutionary change has been promulgated in a special order of the High Command, on April 19, 1942.*

---

* Reported in the German press on April 21, 1942.

According to this emergency decree, enlisted men must now as before undergo their basic training period of not less than two months during which they are carefully observed by their commanding officers to ascertain their character and special aptitudes. If men show qualities of leadership and other character features of a strong positive nature, the commanding officer may recommend them to be accepted as officer candidates or, in exceptionally meritorious cases, may even appoint them.

Upon receiving this appointment the men become *Kriegs-Offizier-Bewerber,* called KOB, abbreviation standing for War Officer Applicant. They are then transferred to a KOB course of three months, at the conclusion of which they are appointed private first class and are sent to the front where they are given command of a squad, or acting command of a platoon. Their schooling is then continued on the front by individual officers specially assigned to this task within each regiment. These officers are called *Faehnrichsvater* (cadet adviser).

After a period of at least two months on the front and not less than one year in the army, the men are again transferred to an *Offizier Anwaerter Lehrgang* (Officers Candidate Course). Completing this course within two to three months, the KOB are appointed second lieutenants and are sent to the front.

The importance of this emergency decree is twofold. First, it emphasizes the selecting power of the commanding officer whose psychological instinct rather than the army psychologist's academic training thus becomes the dominant factor in officer selection. Second, from the political point of view, the army attempts to retain the final word in selecting a young generation of officers by reserving this privilege now more than ever for commanding officers, usually colonels in charge of regiments, or major generals in charge of divisions. While the decree may appear as a step toward the "democratization" of the German Army, in reality it is intended to preserve the aristocratic character of the officers corps, even though the Junkers may gradually disappear from the ranks of a new German "aristocracy," Nazified in spirit but traditionalistic in its ultimate allegiance to the army as a state within the state.

37. How are noncommissioned officers indoctrinated?

The Germans found the perfect "noncom" to be a simple, straight-forward, unsophisticated type with the latent qualities of pains-takingness, conscientiousness, industry, orderliness and reliability, intellectually and emotionally limited to complete devotion to his family and job. The task of selection is to find men with these latent qualities, and the task of indoctrination is to develop them (187).

The ideological education of the "noncom" is intended to eliminate all disturbing factors in his relationship with privates. This training is considered particularly important by the Germans, since they maintain that present-day youth is more sensitive and more critical of his superiors, and thus more likely to have disdain for the "noncom's" practical knowledge and simple way of thinking.

The first difficulty in the ideological training of a "noncom" is his generally lower intellectual level, which causes him to judge his subordinates by their actual performance rather than by their character and temperament. The education of the "noncom," therefore, includes the principles of elementary psychology so as to enable him to appraise his charges from a characterological point of view and to develop his own personality with which to impress his subordinates instead of resorting to disciplinary measures (189).*

* The special task of developing a class of sub-leaders (Unter-fuehrer) within the German army was treated in a series of more recent articles not listed in the Bibliography. Some of the more important are: Ausbildung der Unterfuehreranwaerter in einem Ergaenzungsbatallion, *Militaer-Wochenblatt*, 1939-40, 350-1; Der Unterfuehrer in der Gefechtsausbildung, *ibid.*, 1938-39, 1643-44, 1864-65; Die Vorbereitung und der Ersatz der Unter-fuehrer und Unteroffiziere, *Deutsche Wehr*, 1939, Suppl: Trup-pendienst, 31, Nov. 3; Major Totzer, Wie sage ich's meinem Rekrutenausbilder, *ibid.*, Suppl: Truppendienst, 32, Nov. 17. Also see Der Unteroffizier des deutsches Volksheeres, by First Lieutenant Hans Flemming, Oldenburg: Stalling, 1940.

38. What psychological problems were raised by conscription?

The universal problem was the people's attitude toward compulsory military service after having been accustomed to peaceful pursuits and to a professional army where soldiering was regarded as a way of "making a living."

There were two other vital problems of more immediate importance, the solution of which was partly left to the army psychologist (126, 144).

1. Young men entering the army in 1935 were not yet psychologically prepared for military service. The idleness of long unemployment, the democratic principles and pacifist movement of the German Republic still retained their marks on the outlook of the new conscripts. There were sharp religious, regional and class prejudices among the recruits, as well as the reluctance of the civilian to subordinate himself and the fear that the army would divest him of his personality (241).

2. The army's problem was directly related to the conscript's. Outside of the immense task of selecting and classifying millions of raw youths for their proper place in the military organization, the army realized that the conscript's civilian personality was wholly unsuited to the military needs of the Nazi state. Egotism, avarice, selfishness and class consciousness were considered incompatible with the "community spirit of the army."

Civilian ties of family, profession and church also had an unfavorable influence on the conscript's assimilation into the army. These emotional bonds could not be eradicated, but the army resolved that the conscript must be sufficiently removed from them so as to make him think along military and nationalist lines. It was seen that he must be induced to put army interest above personal desires, that he must become accustomed to live under constant supervision, and that the changed mode of living, eating, sleeping and sexual habits would force the conscripts to undergo initial mental suffering (183, 226).

This transition from civilian life to army life meant that the big problem was to replace the conscript's civilian personality with the "soldierly personality and will" (234).

39. What solutions to these problems were suggested by army psychologists?

The universal problem of the nation's attitude toward conscription was solved by general propaganda and indoctrination to the effect that military service is a "sacred duty to the Fatherland," endangered and threatened by foreign enemies (186).

For the solution of the two specific problems the army psychologists had two approaches. The first was a consciously brutal deindividualization of the conscript by deliberate criticism of his performance, conduct and attitude. When applied indiscriminately, this practice was found to have an adverse effect on the conscript's efficiency and morale. It was suggested, therefore, that each conscript be judged and treated according to his character and temperament (183, 226).

The second and more satisfactory approach is to make military service attractive to young men. Their habituation to army life is gradual and subtle. Their masculine pride in competition, brawn, and aggressive spirit is applauded. An understanding for army regulations is consciously cultivated, and the men are encouraged to emulate the example of comrades and immediate superiors. This system ultimately develops conviction and enthusiasm.

Punishments and prohibitions, which are held to impede military training and to have bad effects on both the individual and the company, are avoided. Conscript morale is thus based on the system of "military honor," a feeling of trust in the conscript's conduct and an appeal to his professional pride and ambition.

To alleviate other tensions, the psychologist suggests the creation of "room-comradeship," for which conscripts of similar professional, educational, regional and common neighborhood interests are thrown together in companies and living quarters.

Measures carried out on the psychologist's suggestions are constantly supervised and are remedied if they do not work out smoothly (241).

40. What are the chief psychological problems of the soldier and the company?

Since young soldiers are in a stage of hyperactive bodily development, their immediate problems are related to appetite and sex. The psychological consequences include crises of companionship, homesickness and suicidal tendencies. Individual problems also arise from the divergent intellectual level of conscripts, from their social, religious and regional differences, and from the psychological effect of physical defects and mental abnormalities. Superimposed on all these problems is the relationship of men to their officers (213).

The psychological problems of the company, the immediate solution of which is held to be indispensable for the company's highest physical and mental efficiency, grow out of monotonous routine, harsh and unreasonable treatment, inadequate handling of promotion and furlough, and defective living, clothing and food conditions (214). The psychological results of these defects are found to differ with officers and men. The former are likely to grow nervous, exhausted, utterly disgusted with their duties. The latter lose their discipline, become ill-humored, disgruntled and inclined to desertion (214).

It is the commanding officer's duty to detect such problems and eliminate their causes. The final suggestion toward a solution, however, is left to army psychologists.

41. What are the problems of companionship and how are they handled?

The heterogeneity of a conscript army makes the smooth creation of good companionship a difficult task, especially in peacetime when the absence of combat experiences retards the natural formation of comradeship.

Good companionship is held to be contingent on the "consciousness of a fateful belonging to one another, creating a feeling of responsibility, sense of duty, and marked consideration of others." This is dependent on self-criticism and self-discipline, usually wanting in young soldiers (232).

Thus certain crises of companionship must be expected, especially during the early months of military service when the conscript's "civilian personality" still dominates his outlook. Pallokat (234) finds that these crises occur when the first attraction of the new mode of life wears off, when military realism shatters all preconceived ideas, and when too short a time has been spent in the service to make the conscript "feel at home in the barracks." Pallokat calls this period a "hybrid state of depression" which demands special attention from the army psychologist.

At later stages, crises of companionship are usually caused by the monotony of military routine (the conscript being surfeited with seeing the same faces and doing the same type of work day after day). Other disturbances are caused by the presence in the company or barracks of egotists, cynics, critics, skulkers, grumblers, go-getters, bullies, or conceited, arrogant, frivolous, inconsiderate, obstinate or capricious persons. Intellectuals and newly-wed conscripts also find it difficult to fit into the army's comradeship pattern (232, 234).

The formation of good companionship begins on the day of the conscript's arrival at his army post, since the first impression, good or bad, is held to have a lasting effect. It is suggested that new arrivals be welcomed with music and with an intimate man-to-man talk. Intellectual, religious, social and regional differences are eliminated by quartering together conscripts of the same educational level, social origin, professional interest, and religion. The elimination of disturbing influences caused by individual conscripts requires individual handling and great care, and is left to the commanding officer who usually acts in co-operation with the army psychologist.

The formation of permanent comradeship which requires the cultivation of "community spirit, self-discipline, and consideration of others" is left to education and indoctrination designed to shape and fortify these characteristics in the individual conscript. *Thus, planned military education is considered to be the first and final formative influence on companionship* (241).

42. What is the relationship between officers and men?

The present relationship between officers and men of the German Army is said to be excellent as the result of policies consciously cultivated along lines of army regulations (180).*

The officer is reminded throughout his training period that he must act as a teacher of his men rather than as their superior (196). Their relationship must be based on the soldier's confidence in the officer's intellectual capacity and character (239). To maintain this intimate relationship, the officer is required to stay in constant touch with his company or regiment, and he must be

* Also see Friedel, Wie sage ich es meinem Rekruten, *Artilleristische Rundschau*, 1939, 9, 477-84; Der Kompagniechef beim inneren Dienst seiner Kompagnie, *Militaer-Wochenblatt*, 1940, 423-26; Die Rekrutenbesichtigung, *ibid.*, 1939, 2565-69.

given sufficient time to acquaint himself individually with every one of his soldiers, even if this requires considerable time as in the case of regiment and division commanders. It is explicitly stated that officers should not be frequently transferred.

Among the means suggested for the cultivation of good relationship, the following practical hints seem to be the most relevant:

a. The officer must inspect his company or regiment every day. A casual atmosphere should prevail during these inspections, the officer looking into the eyes of his men to detect personal problems in their looks. He is expected to be present at mess as often as possible. His visits to living quarters should not be too frequent, but in these trips he should notice and show genuine interest in the flowers and knickknacks brought in by the soldiers to enliven the usually barren rooms. (Such embellishment of living quarters is encouraged to promote individuality in the soldier.)

b. The officer must never expose his soldiers to ridicule, and the scolding of individual soldiers should never take place before the whole company. He must try to unearth positive qualities even in "bad soldiers" and attempt everything to promote such qualities.

c. He is expected to congratulate his soldiers on their birthdays, the clerk being assigned to furnish the date. To accept congratulations, the soldier should be requested to appear in his dress uniform at the officer's quarters, the officer also wearing his Sunday best. Moreover, it is advisable to send birthday congratulations to members of the soldier's immediate family (father, mother, or wife). The dates should be secured from the files rather than directly from the soldier.

d. The officer must never make a soldier responsible for the officer's mistakes, or censure the company for the mistakes of individual soldiers. Admonition or appropriate punishment should be the final word, and no grudge must be borne afterwards.

e. At conferences with noncommissioned officers or soldiers, the officer should create a casual, friendly atmosphere, inviting his men to join him sitting down and offering cigarettes to loosen the usually stiff atmosphere of such meetings.

Behind all this friendly attitude, the officer must have a strong will and firm personality. He must impress his soldiers as a man who can punish as well as praise. Above all, he must subtly create an atmosphere in which immediate and unconditional response to his commands is absolutely secured (238).

43. What are the psychological problems of command and obedience?

The psychological appeal for obeying a command is directed to both the intellectual and emotional attitudes of the soldier. In Germany, general indoctrination and specific military education are intended to assure a voluntary obedience based on the soldier's faith in the cause, confidence in the leader, and his readiness to participate in the execution of the state's political decisions (231).

The Germans make a fine distinction between this type of "intelligent obedience" and "unconditional blind obedience." In peacetime, intelligent obedience of carefully conditioned soldiers is considered sufficient. In war, when the individual soldier is not cognizant of the military plans as a whole and is unable to follow commands rationally, unconditional blind obedience is still required (229).

Commands must be simple, short, and reasonable. They must always be adapted to specific situations. Mueller-Roemer (80) supplies two interesting examples. In one case, an officer succeeded in overcoming a mental paralysis of his troops by immediately responding to his own command and thereby effecting the mechanical reaction of his troops to his own explosive action. In the other example, panic and inefficiency in fighting were avoided when the officer gave orders in a calm and simple manner to troops suddenly awakened by a Cossack attack.

Pintschovius (329) cautions against long-winded orders, and Lau (316) finds that command by word of mouth is more effective than commands given over the telephone which is, however, preferable to written commands.

44. How is homesickness handled?

Since homesickness causes a soldier to be indifferent to his own fate, impairs the fulfillment of his duties and is a bad influence on others, the Germans have given the problem much attention. Bock (216) suggests extensive search and development of a special homesickness therapy, but there is no evidence that this has actually been accomplished.

Bock's suggestion for a temporary alleviation of homesickness is to grant frequent furloughs to troops not actually engaged in military operations. The Germans have evidently put this advice into effect. It is known that after the conclusion of the western offensive in the summer of 1940, forty full divisions were sent home on extended leave.

After long investigation the conclusion was reached that professional soldiers suffer no homesickness. Therefore, the solution, it is proposed, rests in the thorough habituation of conscripts to the military way of life which in itself excludes all distracting influences.

45. How are suicidal tendencies dealt with?

Soldiers who attempt to commit suicide are not treated according to their apparent motives (mental depression, sexual deprivations, disappointments, fear of punishment, inferiority feeling). Professor Wuth (246) advises a thorough examination and analysis of the attempted suicide's background, disposition and physical impulses.

He is placed under the observation of a neurologist whose findings and recommendations are given to the military authorities who decide the soldier's fate. Often the soldier's motive for attempting suicide is given satisfaction as part of the therapy, but care is taken to prevent the soldier from considering this as a reward for his act.

According to the Nazi system of morality a soldier suicide deprives the state of his services which he owes to the community, and thus his act amounts to a felony. The Military Code provides severe punishment for attempted suicide, and even more so for its simulation.

Baumbach (215) says that officers and "noncoms" should prevent the possible emergence of suicidal tendencies by referring to it in terms of ridicule, contempt and satire. Wuth, on the contrary, questions the value of such tactics, and advises confining therapeutic education to officers who should eliminate causes of suicidal tendencies.

46. How are sex problems dealt with?

The first few weeks of military service are filled with heavy labor to diminish the sex desires of conscripts who have been separated from a sweetheart, fiancée, or wife. Later, as the soldier's sex interest gradually drifts away from a specific person, dangerous elements of jealousy and despondency on the part of the woman become a problem to both the army and the soldier. The commanding officer and army psychologist must attempt to gain the confidence of the soldier and counsel him on his sex life.

More complicated are the dangers of homosexuality which is described by Grunwaldt (222) as being frequent, particularly in the case of officers who abuse their position and exploit their "tender bond" with the soldiers. The only solution suggested is the denunciation of men who are even slightly suspected of homosexual relations.

47. What is the problem of the intellectual from the army point of view?

Army authorities in Germany generally dislike intellectuals. They consider them physically too weak and mentally too strong for army needs. Their cultural education endows them with contrariness and hypercriticism of the army's educational program.

Eichberg (219) distinguishes between three types of intellectuals:

a. "BORN INTELLECTUAL." This is considered to be the most valuable type. Although frequently lacking physical strength, he is usually found to be willing to overcome his innate disinterestedness in, and to adapt himself to, army needs. He is also held to be more capable of mingling with soldiers of lower intellectual level.

b. "GENUINE INTELLECTUAL." This type has specialized his knowledge to such an extent that he has become narrowminded in all matters not pertaining to his specific intellectual interests. He remains

an outsider in the army and there is little that officers or education can do about it. Schulz suggests
that these "genuine intellectuals" (as well as conscripts whose political orientation is suspected)
should be placed in special companies by themselves. In this way, they will not be able to endan-
ger the community spirit of the army, and their
supervision is made easier.

c. "FALSE INTELLECTUAL." This type, the half-edu-
cated, self-proclaimed "coming genius," is comparatively easy to assimilate once his self-conceit
is broken by harsh treatment and unending tasks.
If, however, he is not recognized he may exert the
worst influence of all the intellectual types.

These three types of intellectual are obviously difficult to distinguish accurately. Kreipe (108) determines their classification by
observing their orderliness, obedience, and general conduct.

Eichberg (219) cautions against confusing intelligence with
intellectualism. Soldiers with native intelligence and common
sense are held to be exceptionally valuable.

48. How are "eccentrics" handled in the army?

Since physical fitness is the only criterion for army acceptance,
mentally abnormal persons often find their way into the conscript
army. Among "imbeciles" Geegener (217) lumps together "morons,
simpletons, semi-Aryans, habitual criminals, intellectual pacifists
and conscientious objectors, former Communists, atheists, and
egotists who are incapable of understanding the Nazi conception
of national community and hanker for the better income and
living conditions of civilian life."

The morons and imbeciles are termed "incurably dull" and conscripts suffering from "mental illusions and intellectual attitudes" are described as acutely and incurably "uninterested" in army ideals. Their open or disguised opposition to the military way of life induces them to look for some sort of escape from military service, or to revolt against regulations and instructions, thus causing considerable harm to the company or regiment as a whole.

No education, friendly advice, nor punishment can help. Thus the psychologist's only task is to find such men, report them to the military authorities who remove them from the army at once, since it is not "the number of soldiers, but the quality of human material that is decisive in modern armies."*

49. What is done about clumsiness?

The psychologists caution officers against the common belief that "awkward fellows are good sports." In reality, they are found to be incapable of even the simplest military work. Timid, fearful, lackadaisical, overpolite, overcourteous and kowtowing, they are "misanthropists by experience" whose hatred of their comrades expresses itself in kleptomania and frequent outbursts of rage.

Eichberg (218) distinguishes between two types of awkward persons, positive and negative. Since the "positive type" can be made a valuable member of the military community, the army psychologists must determine the presence of each individual type.

The *positive* type, in which Eichberg counts Scott, Swift and Napoleon, has grown clumsy through the fault of educators without psychological training and through the fault of a family apparently unable to appreciate the young man's real qualities, branding him a "black sheep, moron, or block-head." Such unjustified

---

* Also see Eichberg, A Der nervoese Mensch als Soldat. *Deutsche Wehr*, 1939, Suppl: Truppendienst, 28, July 28.

prejudices awaken in the "positive type" a feeling of persecution, turning him into a moody, suspicious and antisocial person. He can, however, become an excellent soldier by virtue of his desire to prove himself in his new environment. His army education warrants special attention, and the granting of slight privileges (called "Ersatz-affection" by Eichberg), will aid him in gaining self-confidence and a positive attitude toward his future.

The *negative* "clumsy" type is a "spoiled child for the rest of his life" because of early pampering. He is mentally and physically backward, weak-willed, and utterly lacking in drive and energy. His negative attitude may be aggravated by harsh treatment which makes him defiant and revengeful, expressed in exaggerated awkwardness. Since therapy for this type requires several years of psychological treatment (psychoanalysis is hinted at, but not openly suggested), he must be weeded out as a hopeless case before he can do any damage to the company. Transfer to a mental institution is recommended.

50. How are "recluses and individualists" handled?

As the army is based on a mass-psychological community spirit, recluses and marked individualists have no place in the army. They are considered "germs of destruction" and a continuous prey to desertion. Their character is revealed by an overdeveloped ego, lack of a desire for participation, the inclination to sleep and dream, and by an ever-present attempt to build up an emotional and intellectual barricade behind which to hide. A man of this type is always reading and writing a diary or letter. His reading matter is usually confined to radical or spiritualistic literature and he is often found to be a member of some quaint religious sect.

Punishment is not a remedy since it will only increase animosity toward the community. The recluse or individualist, therefore, if he belongs in the category of the well-meaning passive type, is referred to the army psychologist who endeavors to gain his confidence and an insight into the causes which made him a recluse. Here again Gerathewohl (221) suggests psychoanalysis as most advisable even though the term is never explicitly used.

If shyness is found to be the main cause of the conscript's seclusion, his performance should be highly praised, thus developing his "will-to-performance." The psychologist should discover his special talents, pointing them out to the commanding officer who may then assign him to duties best suited to his capacities.

The other type, incapable of adapting himself to army life—and using the community merely to achieve his personal ends—is held to be unfitted for military service and should be discharged.

51. How are courage and cowardice handled?

Courage and cowardice are held to be psychological imponderables whose measurement and promotion still await final solution. Braun (182), however, finds that certain elements of courage may be concealed even in seemingly timid and unsoldierly persons, and proper education may be capable of developing these hidden elements into positive attitudes. Indoctrination is also expected to break down certain inhibitions which lead to cowardice.*

The army needs "born soldiers" with so-called natural courage, and it is left entirely to the field officer to find such men among the conscripts, while the psychologist's task is to detect "natural cowards" and recommend their elimination from the forces as "incurables" (224).

* For an interesting experiment see Simoneit, M. Mutuebungen. Wehrpsychologische Gedanken ueber die seelische Kriegsbereitschaft. *Deutsche Infanterie*, 1935, 18-20.

52. How is the problem of desertion handled?

Desertion is handled by the judge-advocate rather than by the army psychologist. Desertion is held to be caused by the deficiencies described above. It is believed that the elimination of the causes, as well as education and indoctrination, may on the whole prevent desertion.

No recent paper was found on the subject. It seems that "desertion" is one of those terms which, as Grunwaldt (188) points out, are consciously excluded from the official Army Regulations along with "defeat." It is interesting to note that the education of the Nazi soldier excludes the possibility of defeat or the necessity of retreat. Tenacious stick-to-itiveness is hammered into every German conscript. The indoctrination of an unwavering sense of duty and mental resistance makes the German soldier theoretically invincible and rules out the possibility of his "deserting his comrades or duty."

A paper from the last war deserves mention. The author (291), a psychoanalyst, disregarded the belief that deserters are defiant men who refuse to subordinate themselves or that they are cowards who run away from danger. He points out that desertions for the most part occur in barracks or in the hinterlands rather than at the front. Desertion is not a coward's escape, since it means enduring hardships greater than those encountered in the ranks. Deserters are usually "mental cripples": epileptics, escapists, neurotics with acute anxiety neuroses due to libidinal inhibition. Political motives and a lack of interest in war aims or the military way of life may also lead to desertion. Thus "mental cripples" should be rooted out of the army.

53. What is the situation of the German conscript with respect to religion?

This rather complex question seems to be the least "solved" by the Germans. The army's attitude toward religion is affirmative and thus deviates from the attitude of the Nazi party which is largely negative.

The conflict is being solved by subterfuges such as Ruppert's (237) attempt to present soldierdom as a religion in itself emanating from "the German's eternal fighting spirit." According to this interpretation, "Wars are inspired by God to separate the weak from the strong, the worthy from the unworthy, the chaste from the unchaste." Christianity is not the "aid of the weak, but the aim of the strong." Lonicer (228), an army chaplain of high rank, presents the same idea when he describes war as the best means for "leading a nation from chaos to order." War is held capable of purifying a nation, purging it of all unworthy elements and retaining only those who are capable of religious devotion. Army service is compared to divine service: "The soldier knows that there is a superior will, a greater power, a Master who disposes of him and commands his devotion."

Such extreme views are generally censured within the army, and Simoneit goes so far as to criticize (in a belated review of Rosenberg's book) the Nazi party's negative attitude toward religion and its concept of "man's self-identification with God," which refuses to recognize the Christian principle of neighborly love. "The really stalwart man," he writes, "will certainly be able to marshal enough strength for the defense of his honor and still have sufficient power for neighborly love."

Feeser (10) indicates that the army has succeeded in overcoming the party's opposition to religion, and chaplains are again functioning on both the front and in garrisons. In fact, they are considered to be important morale-building agents, particularly needed in bolstering "fighting spirit" for actual combat.

VII
PSYCHOLOGY OF COMBAT

Every young German is expressly trained and conditioned for war. Hoelter (195) points out that Nazi Germany "is building valorous men always ready to go to war for the National Socialist idea." The official Army Regulations (180) explicitly state that "the preparatory task of the army's educational program is to mold wartime heroes out of peacetime soldiers." Lucke (201) emphasizes that "offensive war, and not merely defense, is the fulfillment of the officer's professional ego. Defense is the civilian's attitude toward war, a conception summarily rejected by the German officer."

Thus combat is the centripetal force of German military psychology, centering its attention on the solution of war's psychological problems.

54. What are the psychological problems of war?

Plaut (261), whose catalogue was later endorsed by Mierke (279), believes that modern war raises acute psychological problems accruing from the following attitudes, sentiments and habits:

>   a. the nation's and the individual's attitude toward war in general, and toward the enemy in particular;

b. national and individual attitudes toward danger and "killing in battle";

c. attitudes toward hardships, sufferings, casualties;

d. the soldier's attitude toward invisible superiors, professional and reserve officers, comrades; the civilians' attitude toward the military and political leadership; their attitudes toward command and obedience;

e. attitudes toward war prisoners of various nationalities and races;

f. the soldier's attitude toward the civilian population of his own country and enemy country;

g. his attitude toward other people's property;

h. his attitude toward relatives at home, and the civilians' attitude toward soldiers;

i. his attitude toward his own civilian interests and convictions;

j. his religious devotion and political faith;

k. recreation;

l. sexual habits.

The attitudes and sentiments toward these problems may be positive or negative, and it is up to the leadership to condition them to fit the requirements of war.

55. How are these problems generally solved?

The Germans work out the general solution of these problems by advance indoctrination, habituation and conditioning of the individual soldier and the nation at large. Indoctrination exploits emotions of patriotism, sense of duty and the "soldierly spirit of adventure" to create a *positive* attitude toward war. Conversely, it generates hatred of a specifically identified opponent to create a *negative* attitude toward the enemy.

The proper balance of positive and negative attitudes produce "positive morale," which can be promoted and maintained by natural and artificial stimuli.

56. What is the German conception of morale?

Foertsch (348) says: "The final word regarding victory and defeat rests not on arms and equipment nor the way in which they are used, nor even on the principles of strategy and tactics, but on the morale of the troops." The German conception of morale implies a positive state of mind of the individual and the mass toward a uniform goal.

According to Altrichter (295, 296), an army's efficiency depends on its equipment, its training, its physical strength, and, last but not least, on its morale.

Morale, although but one of four pillars on which ultimate victory rests, is of decisive importance.

First, it expresses itself through all the elements of the military organization and releases their working efficiency to its utmost capacity.

Second, war itself is a struggle of morale forces in which victory means the eventual shifting of the moral equilibrium of the opposing parties. This is in line with Clausewitz's classical definition which described the primary aim of war as the desire to impose one's own will upon the opponent.

Third, morale is capable of equalizing existing physical differences, such as discrepancies in numerical strength and in the quality of equipment.

Fourth, morale is an automatic defense against panic and other disintegrating influences.

57. How is morale promoted and maintained?

"War calls for courage and vigor, pertinacity, and skill, enthusiasm, steadfastness, obedience, and the spirit of teamplay. To foster and promote these qualities is not the province of military art, but of educational policy" (348).

Therefore, it was left to civilian and semi-military organizations to foster and promote morale in preparation for war and it is now the military leadership's task to "maintain and nurse this morale as the most precious of military tools."

A great part of the preparatory morale work was done by the Military Political Bureau of the Nazi party (*Wehrpolitisches Amt der NSDAP*) under General Franz Ritter von Epp. The avowed aim of this organization was to "clarify military-political questions, to conduct propaganda campaigns for the purpose of creating a belligerent spirit and a better understanding of military matters among the people, and to control all activities in the fields of military politics and sciences."

The organization was dissolved after the introduction of compulsory military service in 1935. Its functions were then assigned to the German Society of Military Politics and Military Sciences under General von Cochenhausen, the Propaganda Ministry, and to other Nazi organizations, with the Secret State Police playing a prominent part in all of them. Today, organizations functioning under the Woman-Leader have the special task of fortifying the morale of mothers, wives, daughters, sisters, and sweethearts. The Labor Front replaces the former Socialist leadership of the working class whose pacifistic tendencies were held to have contributed to the weakening of Germany's war spirit in 1914-18. (Cf. *Handbuch der neuzeitlichen Wehrwissenschaften* and the publications of the German Society of Military Politics and Military Science.)

These organizations, in close co-operation with army authorities, maintain morale in the armed forces and develop it in the civilian population by the skillful manipulation of individual and mass.

58. What is the German Army's approach to morale promotion?

German soldiers are drafted from a crowd which, especially insofar as the now active military classes are involved, has been infused with an overall external motivation. This is composed of an unholy trinity of sentiments: pseudo-religious as represented in Nazism, moral as represented in the idea of Greater Germany, and material as outlined in the chimerical "New Order" (249).

The basic use of mass psychology by the Nazis is the source of a common belief that the German soldier is a robot. Indeed, the Nazis intend him to be exactly that in his attitudes and sentiments toward the rigidly demarcated national community dominated by them. But the conditioning of the individual is considered more important in the long run, being the ultimate defense against setbacks, hardships, pain, and in all kinds of abnormal circumstances.

As far as the German army is concerned, it has two fundamentally divergent approaches to morale promotion.

Both approaches accept spirit and discipline as the fulcra of military morale.

Spirit is the sum total of the soldier's sentiments generated by his attitude toward the army's ideological motivations and toward the ideas by which his community is ruled.

Discipline is the soldier's will to subordinate himself to the ideas, decisions and rules of his community. It involves the temporary or permanent restriction of the individual's own personality, and a willingness to sacrifice, even one's own life if it need be.

Spirit and discipline are conditioned by the national character and by the teachings of the existing political order. In an ideal military community envisaged by Altrichter (296), the army must think and act in accordance with the nation of which it is an integral part. Spirit being the dominating motive of morale, it must automatically animate discipline. The latter then acts as the functional organ to invigorate the troops and to ensure the prompt execution of strategic plans in general, and tactical commands in particular.

Down to this point, German psychologists follow the line of academic military psychology. It is, however, at this juncture, that their subsequent explorations and interpretations fork out in two directions.

The mass-psychological school, represented by Altrichter (295, 296) and, to a qualified degree, also by Freytag-Loringhoven

(255), emphasizes the army's character as a crowd in the LeBonian sense. In the crowd, morale is anchored to unconditional subordination, and is maintained through coercion.

The rational-individual school, elaborated by Pintschovius (329), recognizes progressive rationalism and individualism as primary morale-producing factors.

Altrichter rejects the haphazard combination of artificial and natural impulses to promote morale. He recommends planned effort to build morale in a largely synthetic manner. Morale in the military crowd is founded on community spirit and applied discipline. The latter must be the result of habituation of every detail of behavior.

Pintschovius proceeds from the realization that changes and progress made modern armies dependent on technologically skilled specialists who are, in an overwhelming majority, provided by the urban population. Traditional influences lose much of their morale-promoting effect if pitted against the rationalism of modern man whom technical training and urbanization accustomed to independent and critical thinking. Instead of accepting traditional impulses at their face value, the modern man, even in the crowd, searches for causes and possible effects, and feels competent to demand explanations.

Moreover, urbanization tended to diminish courage, while the enlightened man rejects bravery as a detached, self-evident stimulus of morale. Here, too, he weighs the "practicability" and "sense" of his action against its possible returns.

As a matter of course, the individual's rational approval of an action or a situation is an integral part if not the dominating stimulus of his will-to-co-operate. This very will-to-participate must be the ultimate goal of enlightened morale promotion.

The fulcra of this enlightened morale are, first, spirit conditioned by the convictions of the individual, and, second, discipline as the result of voluntary and rational subordination. Coercion can have no plane in promoting this type of morale. The spirit should be formed and preserved by morale appeals. Discipline should be obtained by appropriate education in contrast to mere habituation.

While Altrichter's approach to military morale is explicitly totalitarian, the second approach is implicitly democratic. Indeed, Pintschovius and his sponsors within the High Command* are fully aware of this apparent similarity and are careful to conceal it behind a smoke screen of ambiguous phrases.

The existence of two opposing theories may be accepted as a basic weakness of Germany's whole policy of military morale. It is indeed possible that a future clash between the two schools will contribute to the eventual undermining of German Army morale.

The High Command, or at least those generals who survived Hitler's recurrent purges, is mindful of the potential danger inherent in these contradictions. To avoid a clash between the two, they are regarded as parallel rather than conflicting schools, and handled as alternative solutions of fluid problems. It is left to the judgment of individual officers on the spot to pick the one which seems better fitted to a given situation.†

For a description of the fundamental difference between the army's and the Nazis' approach to morale, see our answer to Question 77.

---

* Pintschovius' book was brought out by an Oldenburg publisher close to the generals prior to Hitler's purge of von Fritsch, Beck and others of the old school. Its devastating criticism of Nazi methods appeared as a bold challenge to the political party in power and was tolerated only because of the support it received by men like General Wetzell, editor of the *Militaer-Wochenblatt,* and General von Metzsch, in charge of the whole army's educational system and, indeed, morale promotion.

† Cf. The official review of Pintschovius' book in the *Militaer-Wochenblatt,* 1936, 34, 572-573; and *Der einzige Schutz gegen die Niederlage,* by General von Metzsch. The latter regards positive morale as the only protection against ultimate defeat.

59. What are the principal positive factors in stimulating military morale?

According to the rational-individual school (329), morale can and should be stimulated by positive intellectual and emotional factors, just as negative intellectual and emotional stimuli may lower and destroy morale.

The intellectual stimuli must convince the soldier of the necessity and the reasonableness of all military and political measures; create a thorough understanding for all kinds of military eventualities; introduce safety measures without softening effects; awaken confidence in the absolute qualifications of the political leadership, supreme command, and immediate superiors.

Emotional stimuli are the cultivation of reinforcing sentiments and attitudes, sharing of responsibilities, and avoidance of monotony.

According to the mass-psychological approach, positive factors to stimulate military morale are traditional influences, hero worship, discipline (cf. question No. 43), consciousness of mass strength and superiority, confidence in leaders and the influence of leader-personalities, equipment and supply adequate in both quality and quantity, symbols, promotion, rewards, and, of course, the external and internal motivations derived from the German ideology in general and the Nazi ideology in particular (258, 295, 296).

Tradition is considered the most important element, both by itself and in every single one of the above factors. To cultivate this spirit, each new German regiment is assigned to carry on the tradition of an old Imperial regiment. Outstanding German artists were commissioned to paint historic scenes from the past glory of the old regiment. Their pictures embellish the officers' mess, and contribute to the perpetuation of the traditional element in German army morale-building.

The keynote of German military morale is, first, the privilege inherent in being selected a soldier and thus permitted to join the sacred fellowship of military men, and, second, personal pride derived from a feeling of superiority by having achieved military training.

This is said to be the Alpha and the Omega of German military psychology, the motive power of all psychological work insofar as building of morale is concerned. *

The German soldier is considered by himself, as well as by the nation at large, a member of the privileged brotherhood. It should be mentioned in this connection that no guardhouses are maintained by the German army. The very idea of one soldier watching over another with a gun is repugnant to the basic German military ideal. The lack of guardhouses is based on the fundamental consideration that, if a soldier commits a criminal offense which requires his imprisonment, he has no right to remain a soldier. Nor can his fellow soldiers be subjected to association with a criminal. The offender is summarily and dishonorably discharged from the army, to which he can never return, and he is turned back to the civilian authorities. The Germans impose no degrading penalties, even for minor offenses. Work in the kitchens, the despised KP duty, is never required as punishment.

Next to tradition and the overall feeling of superiority, equipment, and symbols play a paramount role in building military morale in Germany.

60. What is the role of equipment and symbols?

Good equipment in sufficient quantity† and a continuous flow of adequate supplies obviously enhance military morale. They

---

* For this and the immediately following invaluable information, as well as for advices and critical suggestions, the Editors wish to express their gratitude to a competent American military observer whose intimate knowledge of the German Army helped to correct some of the shortcomings of the first edition.

† We know of at least one case when *lack of equipment* had a tremendous morale-building effect. Prior to her rearmament, Germany used dummy tanks mounted on small BMW-automobiles during local maneuvers at Doeberitz. The officers lost

promote a feeling of pride, strength, and superiority, and a sense of belonging to a specific branch of service—in short, an *esprit de corps.*

According to Grunwaldt (310), and an article published in *Charakterologische Arbeiten* (an intramural publication of the Psychological Laboratory, edited by Simoneit prior to the appearance of *Soldatentum*), military officers, army physicians and psychologists collaborate in the design of equipment. When combat uniforms were designed for German soldiers in 1934, officers advised on their military practicability, medical officers on the hygiene involved, and army psychologists on the psychological effects of their appearance. The same collaboration was observed when experiments were made with new steel helmets, and helmets for parachute troops.

Symbols are held to be the "visible manifestations of sacred German blood and heroism." They produce morale through their emotional bond with loyalty, heroism, *esprit de corps,* honor, unselfish sacrifice, tradition, comradeship, and memories of past combats. Such symbols include: the uniform and all its trimmings, the flag, medals, shields, oaths, martyrs (Horst Wessel, Schlageter, the student-soldiers of Langemarck), patron saints (St. Barbara of the artillery). Symbolic acts are elaborate ceremonies of victory or surrender (receiving the keys to conquered Warsaw; negotiating the Armistice with France in the legendary railway carriage at Compiègne, an effective symbolic act skillfully exploited by Hitler, while utterly played down by Foch).

The military salute as it is given in the German army is among the most effective morale-building symbols. *Today, all German soldiers, whether on or off duty, are compelled to salute, not only*

(† cont.) no time in pointing out to their soldiers that Germany had observed faithfully the articles of the Versailles Treaty which prohibited the use of actual tanks. The tiny tanks built of papier mâché were thus used as symbols of Germany's enforced disarmament, as well as harbingers of her imminent rearmament.

their superiors but one another as well, thus promoting the spirit of comradeship among all ranks. Nobody outside the armed forces is permitted to use the military form of salute, which thus becomes a privilege rather than a duty, strictly in line with the basic and all-important military ideals described in our answer to Question 58. In fact, the independence of the German Army from the Nazi party is once more demonstrated in the fact that members of the armed forces use the traditional military salute instead of the party's "German Salute"—the outstretched arm and the resounding "*Heil Hitler*."

The salute's present importance as a morale-building factor is said to go back to feudal times when it was a privilege reserved for free men who thus signaled that, although they were permitted to bear arms, they approached their acquaintances as friends. This prerogative perpetuated in the military salute the German soldier's right to bear arms as distinguished from the unarmed civilians.

Military bands, too, are used as symbols. The current importance attributed to them by the German Army is manifested in the fact that full-sized bands are taken to the front line. The bugler has never been given up by the Germans, and the impressive tattoo of the drums (*Zapfenstreich*) is described by Grunwaldt as one of the most inspiring symbols of the German army.

The Germans also have supersymbols (Blood Flag of Munich) which are endowed with mystical elements. Grunwaldt (310) relates a story of the last war which is characteristic of the German attitude toward symbols. A British colonel, who happened to be a soccer fan, often discarded the Union Jack in ordering his men to go over the top and instead threw a soccer ball toward the enemy lines, shouting, "After it, boys!"

Grunwaldt's comment on this incident is: "The German does not consider war as a sport but as a sacred duty—in which the flag can never degenerate into a soccer ball."

The morale force derived from equipment and symbols endows the soldier with what the Germans call "the highest form of individual voluntary participation in military action—fighting spirit."

61. What is meant by "fighting spirit"?

According to Article 265 of the German Infantry Regulations, fighting spirit is the soldier's application of his innate aggressive impulses to the command: "Forward against the enemy no matter what it may cost!" Simoneit lists the psychological elements of "fighting spirit" as masculine defiance, the longing to advance, the will-to-conquer and the urge for adventure (286).

The cultivation of fighting spirit is a task of military psychology, particularly in the present war where the army requires a specific type of "fighting spirit" from members of individual services. Thus the fighting spirit of the infantry, the aviator, the tank crew, the antitank gunner, and other specialists requires specific training (190).

62. How is fighting spirit promoted?

First of all, aggressive Nazi ideology (exemplified in the name of the Berlin Nazi organ—*Attack*) indoctrinates young Germans with what Simoneit (286) calls "an heroic outlook adapted to offensive spirit." Later, military training exploits the natural competition and other drives of youth, encouraging pugnaciousness, enthusiasm and intensifying both impulsive and temperamental energy. Soldiers are carefully habituated to danger by difficult maneuvers closely imitating battle conditions, prearranged inconveniences, and sports.

The fighting spirit of tank drivers and aviators is promoted by developing their mechanical knowledge, versatility, sense of distance, and "driving instinct" into "artistic perfection" so that their professional skill by itself becomes an impulse that drives them into action. They are not expected to be reckless, light-minded daredevils, but men who are capable of releasing all their impulses when circumstances require; "fighting spirit" being an added latent quality of their character (293).

"Fighting spirit" is especially important in antitank gunners whose job exposes them to attack from superior equipment. They are specially selected elite troops, soldiers with "iron nerves," mental elasticity, and absolute will power. Seemingly passive while waiting for the onrushing tanks, they are, however, trained and habituated to danger by developing what Engels calls their "permanent aggressivity." Their task is presented as "attack against the tanks" rather than "defense from the tanks" (303, 305).

Special care is being taken to prevent "fighting spirit" of antitank gunners from slackening by the expedient of transferring them frequently to other "aggressive functions" such as attack against fortified positions, especially steel bunkers.

63. What are the principal negative factors influencing military morale?

Among the principal factors impairing military morale are fear, isolation, exposure to protracted bombardment, adverse weather conditions and darkness, superstition, surprise, insecurity and uncertainty, deficiencies and changes in command, apparently idle waiting for enemy attack, fatigue, defeat, losses, and reorientation of the army's and state's ideology (296, also cf. Question 73).

64. What is the problem of fear and how is it handled?

Analyzing the soldier's attitude and disposition to fear, Mierke (322) distinguishes between real fear of external dangers, and neurotic anxiety or phobia. Soldiers suffering from neurotic anxiety are not necessarily cowards, as it was often found that the impact of actual combat repressed their complexes and opened the way to courageous action.

Fear is caused by the disturbance of the ego, releasing instincts of cowardice and cruelty. Thus anxiety is individually determined by the ego's strength and power of resistance which may again be impaired by fatigue and protracted tension. Moody and inhibited persons and pubescent youth are likely victims of anxiety. Other factors promoting anxiety are illness, privations, deficient leadership, inferiority complex, previous fear-experiences, consciousness of isolation, and an overdeveloped instinct of self-preservation.

Anxiety cannot be cured in the decisive moment of combat, but it may be eliminated through indoctrination of community spirit, duty and discipline. The psychologist's task is to solidify the soldier's ego by planned covering of his impulses with self-discipline, a spirit of comradeship, masculine defiance and readiness to sacrifice. Punishment or the threat of punishment are considered generally insufficient because the fear of imminent death is usually greater than the fear of punishment. Mierke, obviously conforming to the spirit of Nazism, rejects the use of artificial stimulants, such as medicine, alcohol or drugs—but it is known that such stimulants as well as better food are actually used in practice in an attempt to alleviate fear. (Also see 318.)

65. What are the problems of isolation and how are they handled?

Ludendorff (28), who developed the "defense in depth" idea, was the first to point out the morale problems in isolated advance outposts at the front. His solution, presented in a memorandum to the Supreme Command in 1916, was to keep in constant touch with isolated units by telephone communications, regular mail delivery and the dropping of supplies by parachute, completely disregarding the cost in men and material as a result of these tactics. Isolated outposts thus never feel abandoned.

Luederitz (319), describing the state of mind of soldiers in isolated advance positions, says that thoughts on the "meaninglessness of life" and the "uselessness of his own role" arise in the isolated soldier's mind. An ever-widening mental gulf develops between himself and the main units behind him. Eventually, he identifies himself emotionally with the soldiers in enemy outposts rather than with his own troops. He loses his sense of proportion, preoccupies himself with his own fate and personality, becomes disinterested in the military organization as a whole and thus neglects his specific duties within the army.

Isolation has only two advantages: it instills close companionship among soldiers in the advanced outpost and prevents certain disturbing elements like political agitation and community frictions from penetrating the advanced lines. Luederitz proves his point by describing how German soldiers in isolated positions during the last war were unaffected by army disintegration and retained their fighting spirit to the last.

Today, the problems of isolation are handled along lines suggested by Ludendorff with the advantage of amplifying them with modern communications to fit the extraordinary conditions of the war of movement.

66. What are the psychological effects of, and psychological defenses against, protracted bombardment?

The artillery drumfire of the last war which the Germans now describe as useless, has been replaced by protracted bombardment by aerial artillery and tank cannon. Its aim is not so much material destruction as the rapid disintegration of enemy morale through acoustic effects (screaming Stukas, bombs with sirens attached) and the tremendous terroristic impact of mass bombardment. The first effect on enemy soldiers is a marked lessening of will power rapidly developing into nerve paralysis and acute fear neuroses. This terror-stricken state of mind and body can be heightened by cutting off electricity and communication systems by bombardment of power stations, and by throwing down garish flares causing the sudden appearance of sinister light in the midst of darkness, all of which is further aggravated by the concussion and shock of explosions.

Aside from peacetime habituation to danger, Hesselmann (275) suggests for such emotional crises preventive measures of instilling calm by preoccupied activity in manual tasks, music, singing and the telling of jokes and stories. Since experience has proven that religious feelings are exaggerated during bombardment, officers are instructed to play up to these emotions.

67. What is the influence of superstition on military morale?

The soldier becomes intensely superstitious at the front, largely due to his separation from normal life and the anxiety and weakness due to his ignorance of events of which he is a passive participant. He seeks refuge in supernatural appearances, mystically interpreting meteorological and astronomical phenomena. Symbols of superstition are extremely contagious and soon engulf the whole army.

Nass (324) and Legius (227) suggest an education of enlightenment and sophistication against superstition during the peacetime training period. On the other hand, the Germans do everything in their power to generate and exploit the superstition of the enemy. It was authoritatively reported that during the 1940 fighting on the western front, the Germans spread emotional and symbolic superstition through secret agents, and used "magic lanterns" to project mirages on the face of drifting clouds during moonlit nights.

68. What are the role and importance of surprise?

The importance and the effects of the surprise element in warfare are generally recognized and require no explanation. References to surprise, found in numerous German publications, add nothing new to our knowledge. An anonymous author (297) of the *Militaer-Wochenblatt* formulated the current German principle in these words: "The efficient application of the surprise element should be the foremost task of peacetime maneuvers. The basic problem is to determine how the enemy can be surprised. Espionage, alone, is capable of finding means to surprise the enemy and to avoid surprise attack on our own troops. Reconnoitering will prevent our being surprised by the terrain."

General Erfurth (307) wrote an excellent historical book on the subject. General Wetzell's review of the book (336) may be considered as an essay by itself. The two reveal Germany's full understanding of the "streamlined" surprise element for the purpose of "strategic onslaughts"—the expression preferred by the Germans for the more popular but less accurate *Blitzkrieg*. (Cf. Question 75.)

69. What is the psychological effect of waiting for enemy action?

Despite the obvious psychological importance of this problem, no direct answer to the question has been found in available German literature. An indirect reference is contained in an article by Strauss (290) who examined the psychological implications of undermining enemy positions, a practice largely outdated with the possible departure from trench warfare.

The actual explosion of mines has, by itself, terrific psychological effects which, however, do not differ from the impact of other similar military actions like protracted bombardment. But in this case the effect of waiting for an imminent action is added to other psychological impacts.

During these periods of waiting, Strauss (290) suggests that soldiers engage in diversions. Monotony must be dispelled by improvising concerts, vaudeville performances, the publication of company newspapers, and especially through organized listening to the radio. At the same time, the commander must do everything to freshen up his troops mentally and to strengthen the individual soldier's will-to-live. Officers are said to be trained beforehand to meet such eventualities.

70. What are the psychological effects of gas warfare?

German literature on the subject terms poison gas a "weapon of secondary importance." Its chief shortcoming is said to be an adverse psychological effect on attacking troops almost identical to its effect on the attacked.

Soldan (287) is emphatic in describing gas as the greatest disappointment of the last war. The prolonged wearing of a gas mask causes gradual exhaustion until it results within eight hours in complete incapacity for fighting. Advance under gas is practically impossible, since the attacker loses his sense of direction and contact with others in the first hundred yards. Poison gas "destroys fighting spirit on both sides of the fence," and slows down the velocity of attack up to eighty per cent until it peters out entirely. Gas cannot be used in tank attacks, since it cannot be kept out of the vehicle and the tank crew cannot be expected to wear protective masks.

Hanslian (273), too, cautions against the overestimation of gas as a really effective weapon—a fact which did not prevent him from writing two weighty volumes on its use. He points out, however, that in certain cases, especially if the attack is directed toward the disintegration of civilian morale and in other actions not directly connected with immediate material offensive, poison gas may be used to aid long-range military operations.

More important than poison gas seems to be the use of smoke as camouflage and as an offensive weapon in itself. Its primary effect on the enemy is confusion, producing a situation where the surprise element can be exploited. Peacetime training under battle conditions with the use of mild gases (preferably tear gas) are held to be the best means of habituation to gas attacks.

71. What are the eventual psychological effects of these negative factors?

Negative factors affecting military morale may lead to a slackening of the individual soldier's "fighting spirit and morale resistance," culminating in his "active or passive surrender."

Any one or more of these negative factors, if affecting mass morale, may lead to panics.

72. What is the psychology of individual surrender?

The sudden collapse of morale resistance, if it does not lead to retreat, panic, or both, usually results in the cessation of military action on the part of individual soldiers, and in their subsequent surrender.

Fritzsching (270) describes this "reversal of the military conscience" as "perversion." He analyzes the psychological process leading up to surrender: The soldier goes to war with a definite attitude toward friend and foe. Education, experience, observation and judgment give him an understanding of his task and a concern for the fate of the Fatherland.

Suddenly, the negative influences of military service and combat begin one by one to cancel out these preconceived ideas. Anxiety and other negative factors, resulting in simultaneous physical disturbances, reverse his way of thinking and he becomes inclined to overestimate the enemy's power while underestimating his own strength as an individual and as a member of the military community. He reorients his thinking to that of the enemy and is being irrevocably drawn toward a state of mind where the thought of surrender is pleasurable and often an outright psychological necessity.

It is due to this frame of mind that the war prisoner is usually gay after his capture and willing to "tell everything to the enemy intelligence officer." The sudden relaxation of tension hatches high treason.

Fritzsching's advice is to explain this psychological process to soldiers during peacetime training and thus to expose to the soldier himself all the subconscious elements leading up to surrender. His knowledge of these factors usually immunizes him thereafter to voluntary surrender in combat. (Also 292.)

73. What is panic and what are its causes?

Panic is an "upheaval of the mass mind" (301, 337). It appears suddenly and spreads rapidly. The word itself is derived from Pan, Greek god of shepherds, who found pleasure in suddenly attacking unsuspecting peasants. Stark (334) thinks that panic itself is of Greek origin.

The individual usually loses his individuality in the mass. He feels and acts according to mass impulses and mass instincts, his own personality automatically adapting itself to the aggregate character of the mass (328).

The subconscious emotions of the individual mind—irritability, exaggeration, suggestibility, exclusion of intelligence and a lack of sense of duty—gradually obtain the upper hand. Thus the "man in the mass" is like a grain of sand; the slightest breeze can blow it at will.

This is the essence of the feeling of panic in its military sense. It arises from purely accidental or seemingly insignificant events. It may have a great or small effect, according to the troop's power of morale resistance.

Immediate causes of panic may be a feeling of insecurity in a fog or in the darkness of a wooded countryside, a real or imagined threat to the army's flank, rear or communications, a lack of information concerning the enemy's whereabouts, contradictory

commands and vacillating leadership, frequent alarms and repeated troop transfers, prolonged waiting at rail or road junctions due
to deficient organization, inadequate equipment and supplies,
unreasonable mixing of military units, loss of the leader, exhaustion in battle, high percentage of casualties, and retreats. The appearance of unexpected weapons (tanks and gas) may also lead
to panic. The danger of panic is particularly prevalent in cavalry
due to the excitability of the horses, and among troops going into
action for the first time (306). (A "typical" panic is vividly described by Hesse [18].)

74. How is panic avoided, alleviated, controlled and exploited?

Discipline, education, indoctrination, habituation to danger, and
outstanding leader-personalities among field officers are held to
be the best antidotes to panic. Education and training are of particular importance. To aid the field officer in handling panic situations, in detecting disturbing factors and eliminating the possible
causes of panic, official Army Regulations contain exhaustive and
minute instructions. Officers, moreover, receive special training
on how to act in panic (337).

Education and indoctrination strive to mold "men with never-
failing nerves" (18), automatically decreasing their susceptibility to fear and doubt. Habituation to danger includes extended
night drills (one third of all German drills are held at night, a
system copied from the Soviet Union), and prolonged maneuvers
in thickly wooded country and in terrain where vision is naturally
obstructed. If panic breaks out despite all precautionary measures,
the officers' duty is to "suppress it at once, by force of arms if
necessary" (306).

Panics are held to be advantageous if circumstances require the
acceleration of a retreat, if the military action is desperate, or if
the commanding officer hopes to obtain increased, albeit disorganized, efficiency for an attack. In such cases, "moderate panics

may be created with care." It is essential, however, in "synthetic panic" to keep in reserve some radical means of suppressing it at once. This may imply the release of good news previously kept from the troops, or the achievement of an immediate military objective (301, 306).

Before this war, the Germans conducted large-scale experiments of artificial panics among soldiers, civilians, and school children. The lessons derived from these experiments were utilized in making German troops as panic-proof as possible, and in generating panic among the enemy. Especially effective in the case of the latter is the spreading of news reporting an exaggerated defeat, or the sudden change of news from victory to defeat.

All these negative morale factors have offensive and defensive implications in present-day German strategy. They are, in fact, the military weapons of the Nazi's psychological warfare.

PART THREE

THE OFFENSIVE IN PSYCHOLOGICAL WARFARE

VIII
STRATEGY AND TACTICS OF
PSYCHOLOGICAL WARFARE

"In the past people migrated from place to place; today ideas migrate from people to people. We are in the midst of an ideological upheaval of unprecedented magnitude. Its common root is the universal yearning for a New Order, replacing the Old Order which has outlived its usefulness."

Thus at the 1937 Party Congress at Nuremberg, Rudolf Hess, then Deputy Leader of the Nazi party, defined the world-revolutionary character of the National Socialist movement. The same idea is presented in thousands of German publications, particularly those of the German Academy of Munich, the geopolitical organization of General Haushofer (503) set up to camouflage Nazi Imperialism behind a pseudo-scientific smokescreen. Ross (361) frankly calls for an "immediate redistribution of the earth," and Rupprecht (502) designates Hitler's Third Reich with the task of seizing the initiative to achieve this goal.

The Nazi revolution is taking place at a time when war itself is going through its own social and technological revolution. This process started in the last war which marked the final break with all traditional conceptions and techniques of warfare, ushering in a new era of "revolutionary wars."

Three factors lie at the bottom of this basic transformation. First, the invention and perfection of new military weapons are replacing flesh and blood with steel and oil on the battlefields. Second, the civilian population has become an active and passive participant as a result of the broadening of the sphere of military action. Third, war aims have been changed to include the settlement of ideological accounts in addition to material demands and the solution of supreme leadership among the nations.

These three changes have led to what is known as "total war."

75. What is the concept of total war?

Blau (343) describes total war as the collective effort of a co-ordinated nation to impose its will on other nations. This implies full active and passive participation of the entire population, the total exploitation of the nation's intellectual and material resources, and a totalitarian leadership tolerating no opposition (355).

Ringel (360) says that total war is primarily characterized by the absence of a dividing line between the military and the home front: "Its prosecution is not confined to the armed forces, but includes economic campaigns and the war of ideas, the latter being of decisive importance."

This is realized in what Blau (344) calls the "three-dimensional war," expanding into military, economic and political-psychological spheres.

In the military field, Germany developed a new type of warfare best suited to her limited economic and vulnerable morale resources. The most important phase of this warfare is the "offensive battle" (*Angriffsschlacht*)—the sudden onslaught of primeval fury which the world has come to know as the *Blitzkrieg*. We are informed that the word Blitzkrieg, although it has been adopted as a standard word in the English language, was not coined by the Germans, but by American newspapermen stationed in Berlin looking for a "snappy" journalistic translation of what the Germans implied with their *Angriffsschlacht*.

From the psychological point of view, the free translation turns out to be an unfortunate one. Blitzkrieg or "lightning war" implies a war complete in all its phases, from the outbreak to the conclusion of hostilities, conducted over an extremely short period.

Angriffsschlacht, or "offensive battle," on the other hand, represents but one phase of a long war. The short campaigns against Poland, Norway, the Low Countries, France, Yugoslavia, Greece, and Crete were but phases, lightning phases at that, of a war which is certainly no lightning war.

The indiscriminate use of the word Blitzkrieg tends to lead to an often fatal underestimation of Germany's innate strength when its campaigns fail to yield immediate and final results, such as in her struggle against the Soviet Union. This invasion is a gigantic phase of the greater war, composed of a series of "offensive or lightning battles," such as the storming and taking of Kiev, or the advance to cut off the Crimea.

Writing in the 1939 volume of the official *Militaerwissenschaftliche Rundschau*, General Geyer described the "offensive battle" at considerable length, revealing that it is composed of four interrelated phases. The first phase is the preparation for the battle itself, requiring the longest period of time, often from six to ten months. The second phase is the artillery preparation, now assigned to dive bombers, and directed against enemy morale rather than merely enemy positions. The third phase is the encirclement movement by pushing the flanks in order to make a full circle of the original crescent of the attacking troops. The fourth phase is what the Germans describe as the "annihilation of the encircled enemy," or, if such annihilation is thwarted by a successful and timely enemy retreat, the consolidation of whatever gains the offensive battle has yielded.

The operations are also called "strategic onslaught" chiefly because tactical considerations are largely eliminated, due to their usually costly character and delaying influence on the operations as a whole. In General Geyer's opinion, the "offensive battle" must yield decisive results within fifteen days, or else it must be concluded with whatever gains have been achieved, and then turn to the preparation of another "offensive battle," i.e., another phase of the war.*

* For a comprehensive account of German strategy and tactics see *The Axis Grand Strategy—Blueprints for the Total War,* another survey of the Committee for National Morale.

Braun (346) describes the "strategic onslaught" (*strategischer Ueberfall*) as follows:

The attacker disregards international law and starts the lightning offensive without a formal declaration of war. On the eve of the attack, fast mechanized forces in overwhelming numbers are deployed along the border. The attack begins at dawn with a driving fury, superior force and tremendous speed, eliminating all existing border defenses within the first few hours and penetrating deeply into the enemy hinterland. Concurrently, the air force attacks a single all-important vital point in the interior, destroying it within a short space of time. Parachutists and air-borne infantry are landed at other strategic points in the interior to destroy vital power stations, communication centers, bridges and government headquarters.

The *Blitz* must show decisive results within six to fifteen days, actually accomplishing all objectives and leaving mopping-up operations to the infantry. Prerequisites of a successful Blitzkrieg are suitable terrain, an absolutely assured surprise element, overwhelmingly superior attacking force with enormous reserves kept in the background, coordination of all combat units, uninterrupted supplies and favorable weather conditions. "Its ultimate success," writes Colonel Braun, "depends on one hundred per cent luck!"

Military action, however, is considered to be the last phase in the Nazi timetable of total war. Von Hentig (17) as early as 1926 predicted that the "leader of the future will be a military psychologist, a sort of aggressive pacifist withholding the use of armed force until all other means of warfare have failed to realize his aims." Pintschovius (329), adapting von Hentig's thesis to Nazi strategy, said that "future wars will be a conflict between opposing national cultures rather than a clash of arms and armies." He added that this nonmilitary aggression may bring victory without even the necessity of waging formal military hostilities.

The Germans believe that economic, political, and psychological campaigns are sufficient by themselves to win a war without resorting to military action. It must be emphasized, however, that none of these components of the Nazi total war is an isolated weapon in itself. Each works in conjunction with the other toward the realization of some particular objective. Each has its psychological tactics interwoven in one grand strategical scheme.

Political warfare, for instance, is the preliminary maneuvering to secure favorable political positions. It enhances the success of eventual military operations should diplomacy fail to eliminate a shooting war. Bonin (181) and Mueller-Loebnitz (355) point out that all preparations must be completed in peacetime through close co-operation between the political and military leadership. The military should receive not only instructions and orders but also their cues from the political leader. The latter must shape and conduct his country's foreign affairs in a consistent manner, so that the military will always know the identity of the prospective enemy and the time of the planned attack. After the outbreak of hostilities, political warfare takes the form of diplomatic offensives, aimed at a negotiated peace, at the breaking up of enemy alliances and scaring neutrals into "voluntary" collaboration.

Since 1935, the entire German diplomacy has been a peculiar combination of military and political operations in which the Germans applied political, economic, and psychological pressure to accomplish their ends without actual warfare in the conventional sense. But at no time did they apply such pressure without the necessary military force kept in readiness to be sent marching if the objectives could not have been achieved by "peaceful" means.

Moreover, it is interesting to note that at no time did the Third Reich concentrate a German army at some strategic point which did not cross the enemy frontier. In the case of Austria and Czechoslovakia, this crossing was achieved without actual fighting, while the Polish border was crossed as the result of a shooting war. Germany's show of force is coupled with unmistakable determination—this combination making the German war machine a truly menacing instrument.

76. What inspired the investigation and use of psychological factors in warfare?

Weniger (209) describes how the last war—as all former wars—revealed that purely military campaigns were in reality sequences of psychological phenomena. It became quite natural to look for the psychological imponderables behind military events, particularly defeat. It was found that fatal mistakes were made and serious frictions occurred because of the leaders' ignorance or underestimation of psychological factors (17).

Investigation showed that military psychological factors are subject to specific laws and rules which can be recognized in advance and solved accordingly. Frictions, for example, have their preliminary symptoms and are not as unpredictable as certain prewar theorists assumed. A knowledge of these laws and symptoms are held capable of enabling leaders not only to cope with frictions when they occur, but to forestall them or reduce their effectiveness by eliminating their psychological causes (329).

The solution of such problems became all-important when total war inevitably made man himself (his attitudes and sentiments), rather than arms and supplies, the focal point for determining ultimate victory or defeat.

Banse (339), a free-lance geographer, psychologist and military scientist, who is important only because his seemingly eccentric, incoherent and reckless ideas accidentally reflect the more carefully hidden plans of the German generals, classified all human beings in three distinctly different categories on the basis of their respective martial virtues. There were, according to Banse, the active warlike man, or stormer; the passive warlike man, or sticker; and the pacifist, or scuttler.

The active warlike man is the one who lives only to fight. "For him," Banse wrote, "the battle is the everlasting yea, the fulfillment and justification of existence."

The passive warlike man fights only to live. He rages at being compelled to fight, but once he is at it "he digs himself in with stoical determination and hangs on to the end."

The pacifist is timid, lacks organization, and is militarily incompetent. "Peace is the only state for which he is fitted," Banse wrote and added that the scuttler would rather endure humiliation, including loss of liberty, than go forth to fight.

Anglo-Saxons, on "both sides of the Atlantic," were ranged with the stickers; Frenchmen in the south of France and Italians were classified as scuttlers. But only a comparatively small minority of Germans, the Nordic elite already controlling the cadre army, was found to possess the characteristics of the stormers. Banse found certain other elements of the German population to belong in the category of scuttlers.

Therefore, as a result of such psychological critique of events and races, a reactionary clique with representatives both within and without the *Reichswehr* assumed as its first task the synthetic "unification" of the "Germanic" races by arbitrarily subordinating the "inferior" scuttlers to the will and leadership of the stormers.

With man as the ultimate center of all considerations, his morale became the prime concern of German warmongers. Indeed, civilian morale became just as if not more important than military morale.

It was at this point that a special role was assigned to Hitler's then up-and-coming Nazi party by the clandestine General Staff, already preparing for war. This task was to conduct a "psychological campaign" against the German people along the lines suggested by Banse when he wrote: "In the struggle between the German and un-German element . . . we are taking the sword in both hands and smiting the enemy' hip and thigh until we split him in two from top to bottom."

77. What was the origin of psychological warfare in Germany?

This so-called "struggle between the German and un-German element" was, in fact, the dress rehearsal of the German version of psychological warfare, conducted from behind the scenes by the reactionary generals of the *Reichswehr,* who hired Adolf Hitler and his radical Nazi party to do the "dirty work."

Strategy, tactics and weapons employed in this "psychological civil war" are of the utmost historical interest, since they are identical with those Germany used in the course of the present war to break the power of morale resistance of her foreign adversaries.

The strategy was the systematic disintegration of the Weimar Republic's political, economic and social structure. Six (449) describes this as the "National Socialist march into a divided nation."

The tactics were the planting of Nazi informers in government offices, the ridiculing of the Constitution and abuse of its symbols, provocations such as the holding of Nazi meetings in territories of political opponents, or the wearing of party uniforms in defiance of prohibitions, planned obstruction of law-enforcement agencies, intimidation, political murder. The whole tactical organization is frankly described by Six in his important book.*

The weapons were terroristic organizations like the SA and SS, slanted education along Nazi principles (35), and propaganda (431, 433, 435, 450).

The cruel test was carried to its extreme. By 1930-32, it developed to what may be called a total civil war in which Germans were pitted against Germans. It was anarchy—and yet, its conspicuous planning and visible controlling forces reminded one of a maneuver rather than a real battle.

Thus it was possible for Hitler to ride into power, not in the wake of a bloody revolution, but on the waves of terror. With his coming to power, the Nazi approach to civilian morale became exclusively dominant.

* For additional information see *Die Geschichte des Nationalsozialismus,* by Konrad Heiden; *Vom Kaiserhof zur Reichskanzlei,* by Paul Joseph Goebbels; *Die deutsche Revolution,* also by Goebbels; and *Mit Hitler an die Macht,* by Otto Diettrich. The memoirs of Hermann Wilhelm Goering and the late Ernst Roehm go into further illuminating details.

78. What is the Nazi approach to civilian morale?

As a militant national-revolutionary party patterned after a primitive form of Prussian absolutism, the Nazis designated spiritual militarism (*geistiges Soldatentum*, 186, 195, 199, 212) as the sole mode of life tolerated under their domination. Their immediate goal is to create and preserve "national unity" (*Volksgemeinschaft*) by subordinating the individual to the strictly regimented community and forcefully liquidating all political factions. Conflicting economic and social-group interests are balanced by a process of compulsory equalization.

The Nazis solved the problem of civilian morale by simply adapting Altrichter's theory of morale-within-a-military-community to the German people at large. (Cf. our answer to Question 58.) Thus civilian morale in Nazi Germany is the result of planned efforts which excludes natural and artificial influences as morale-producing factors.

The fulcra of German civilian morale are community spirit and enforced discipline.

Community spirit derives its motivation from the political and philosophical program of the Nazi party which exercises its influence through the simultaneous control of the state.

Discipline is the result of ruthless habituation.

79. How is civilian morale maintained in Nazi Germany?

Some of the most ambitious Nazi projects for fortifying civilian morale for war were purely physical in character although their psychological effects were considered highly important.

Pintschovius (329) reveals that the building of the Siegfried Line (Westwall), while primarily motivated by military considerations, had an immense psychological effect on the German people, imbuing them with a feeling of security and invincibility.

Grunwaldt (548) and Perignon (558) said that Germany's air-raid precautions were designed to increase this feeling of security and to create a "war consciousness" by enlisting the whole nation's active participation in rearmament. This explains the spectacular but rather superficial character of Germany's civilian air-raid precautions, a factor which adversely influenced civilian morale when large-scale British raids were unleashed on German cities.

The Nazis believe that civilian morale in wartime can be made impregnable by their elaborate system of education, indoctrination, and conditioning, a process that must be completed prior to the outbreak of the war. (Cf. *Total Education,* Questions 31ff.)

When these psychological walls are broken down, more overt methods are brought into play. Himmler (552) considers enforced discipline and intimidation the best means of preserving civilian morale during war. This is not a new Nazi approach. General Hartmann (551), an exponent of Bismarck's *Fuerstenpolitik,* declared that "whenever war breaks out, terrorism becomes a necessary military principle," since "terrorism is a relatively gentle means of keeping the masses in a state of permanent obedience."

Simoneit,* too, describes applied intimidation as an important weapon of maintaining civilian morale. "Political measures will have enduring effects only if they are psychologically appropriate. Psychologically correct are not only those measures which have pleasant effects, resulting in free devotion and love, but also those whose effects are distinctly unpleasant, resulting in respect for the state's overwhelming power."

The maintenance of civilian morale by intimidation is entrusted to the *Schutz-Staffel* (SS—Black Corps), organized along military lines and imbued with a "blind obedience that arises from the highest form of voluntary spontaneity." Himmler explains: "We teach our SS-men that there are many things which can be forgiven,

---

* In his introduction to *Wehrpsychologische Arbeiten,* No. 1, Berlin, Bernard and Graefe, 1936.

no matter how evil they may be. But disloyalty to the Fuehrer can never be pardoned."

Himmler also reveals that his private army is the ultimate guardian of German civilian morale. "I know," he writes, "that there are millions in Germany who become sick to their stomach when they see the black uniforms of our SS. We understand this and don't expect to be loved by too many. Those who cherish Germany should respect us. But those who have a bad conscience should fear us. For the latter, we have created an organization called State Security Service. We shall relentlessly fulfill our duty to maintain security within Germany just as our conscript army watches over our security from without."

Himmler later delivered a lecture to army officers where he enlarged his plans for sustaining civilian morale. "In the event of war," he said, "we must realize quite clearly that we shall have to place a very considerable number of people into concentration camps unless we are prepared to let them become sources of infection which might lead to unpleasant developments." He revealed the creation of a super-Gestapo called the "Skull-and-Cross-bones-Divisions" to operate in all districts throughout Germany in the following manner:

a. No unit will operate in its home district; i.e., a Pomeranian division will never operate in Pomerania.

b. Every unit will change its field of operations every three weeks.

c. The members of these units will never be used singly; for instance, a man with a Skull-and-Crossbones badge will never be on duty in the streets alone.

d. If it becomes necessary, these units will be used ruthlessly; no other way is possible.

He concluded: "The necessity for this new kind of organization must be recognized by every German, and you as officers must understand the significance of this new front, for if ever we have to stand the test of war Germany's fate will be decided on the Home Front."

According to the 1940 *National Socialist Year-Book*, there were 36 SS-divisions distributed all over Germany, each division consisting of 12,000 men. This means that Germany has at least 432,000 "morale-enforcing" agents, a veritable army of occupation functioning within Germany. On September 5, 1939, Himmler's plans were carried out by the establishment of a Cabinet Council for the Inner Defense of the Reich with fifteen Reich Defense Commissars in charge of areas roughly corresponding to army corps areas. The commissars are high SS-officers, working in close cooperation with the intelligence divisions of the armed forces and the State Security Service (520).

Their activities are not restricted by formal provisions of the law. Werner Best, legal expert of the Gestapo, warned that domestic enemies of the Nazi state outlaw themselves by their mere opposition to the existing political order. "We will employ the full, unrestricted force of the state against these native dissidents," he wrote in the 1939 *Year-Book of the Academy of German Law*.

Himmler's system of morale enforcement has its critics within Nazi Germany. Their spokesman is evidently Pintschovius: "In view of the terrible nature of total war," he writes, "it has become impossible to enforce the people's will-to-sacrifice indefinitely. It can be done perhaps in the beginning, but later on it is foolish to threaten men with court martial. Men who have become demoralized under the stress of total war are not afraid of court martials . . . The only thing which can save rational men from morale collapse and self-abandonment is an appeal to reason." He concludes with an ominous statement: "Total war is far more likely to prove our curse than our salvation."

For the time being, however, Himmler's plan of organized intimidation, silent terror, together with mass propaganda and individual conditioning, has proven sufficient to preserve civilian morale in Germany.

The Nazis are thus able to concentrate on a morale offensive against foreign countries in co-ordination with military action, economic warfare and diplomatic pressure.

80. What is the offensive application of psychological warfare in total war?

Hitler's victory in the Reich, as described in our answer to Question 77, his elevation to the office of Reichs Chancellor as the climax of a psychological civil war, furnished the military planners of the Reichswehr with the conclusive proof that their new strategy was practicable and efficient. On the basis of this experiment, Germany's psychological strategy was worked into its final shape, to be applied against Germany's foreign enemies as it was employed against the opponents of the Nazis.

In Franke's (341) definition, psychological warfare is an offensive war waged with intellectual and emotional "weapons" to destroy the power of morale resistance in the enemy's army and civilian population and to diminish enemy prestige in the eyes of neutrals. Blau (343) says that psychological warfare knows no limitations of space or time. It is conducted in the hinterland and on the military and home fronts of actual belligerents, and in the territories of neutral nations. It must, moreover, score its most decisive successes prior to the outbreak of armed hostilities.

The strategy and tactics of psychological warfare are described by, among others, Banse (339), Bircher (342), Blau (343, 426), Nicolai (356), Schumacher and Hummel (364). Banse says:

Applied psychology as a weapon of war means propaganda intended to influence the mental attitudes of nations toward war. . . . It is essential to attack the enemy nation in its weak spots (and what nation has not its weak spots?), to undermine and break down its resistance, and to convince it that it is being deceived, misled and brought to destruction by its own government. Thus the people will lose confidence in the justice of its cause so that the political opposition in those nations (and what nation is without one?) will raise its head and become a more powerful troublemaker. The enemy nation's originally solid, powerful and well-knit fabric must be gradually disintegrated, broken down, rotted, so that it falls apart like a fungus trodden upon in a forest.

81. What are the principal German agencies of psychological warfare?

According to investigations conducted by the Committee for National Morale, the agents of German psychological warfare may be divided into categories of troubleseekers and troublemakers.

Troubleseekers are the members of the innumerable German fact-finding agencies who ferret out what the Nazis call *Stoerungskerne,* kernels of disturbance in foreign nations such as: differences of opinion which divide political parties and minority groups, the frustrated ambitions of discarded politicians, racial controversies, economic inequalities, petty jealousies in public life and other cleavages. In the United States, these agents maintain contact with Americans of German origin and establish relations with native Americans of German sympathies and with those whose unwitting assistance to the Nazi cause can be exploited. Carefully chosen and specially trained for their jobs, members of this group form the personnel of Germany's psychological intelligence service.

Among the large number of Nazi troubleseeking organizations particularly interested in the United States are:

German Academy, Munich
Working-Community of Geopolitics, Munich, Heidelberg, Berlin
America Institute, Berlin

Academy of Foreign Politics, Berlin-Dahlem

German Institute of Foreign Countries, Stuttgart

Foreign Political Bureau of the Nazi Party, Munich and Berlin

Bureau Ribbentrop, Berlin

German Academic Exchange Service, Berlin

Foreign Organization of the Nazi Party, Berlin and Hamburg

Foundation of German Activities Abroad, Berlin

Society of Inter-State Institutions and Associations, Berlin

Institute of Political Geography, Castle Kroessinsee

Geographical Institute of the Technological Institute, Stuttgart

German Society of Geographical Research, Castle Marienburg

Ibero-American Institute, Hamburg

Institute of American Research, Wuerzburg

Ibero-American Research Institute, Bonn

Troublemakers utilize the facts discovered by the troubleseekers, exploiting and publicizing obvious and latent frictions in the interest of national demoralization, spreading Nazi ideology, discrediting refugees from Germany and her protectorates, and conducting material and psychological sabotage.

In addition to the agencies listed above, some of the "civilian" organizations in charge of troublemakers are:

Association of German Societies Abroad, Berlin

Alliance of Germans Abroad, Berlin

Alliance for the Protection of Germans, Berlin

Association of German Ethnographical Groups, Berlin

Alliance of Foreign Germans

A description of German political and military espionage agencies is beyond the scope of this Survey. A quotation from Nicolai (522), chief of German Military Intelligence during the last war, however, deserves mention. He states: "Into a dark future the intelligence service goes to investigate and spread influence far ahead of developments. This particularly concerns England and the United States. The structure of the British Empire and the immigration and race problems in North America directly provoke us to test our fine art of espionage. The secret power of this service will be far greater in the future than it has been in the past and present."

(For more references to Espionage and Fifth Column see Bibliography.)

82. What are the fields of psychological campaigns?

The primary objective of psychological campaigns is to influence and confuse public opinion. This is done through ordinary and extraordinary media of communications by rumors, illusions, suggestion, agitation, deliberate lies, and by the exploitation of superstition, national animosities, and prejudices.

The nature and importance of public opinion is exhaustively analyzed by Toennies (381), Bauer (371), Plenge (442) and Stern-Rubarth (452). An interesting analysis of mass-delusions along original lines is contributed by Baschwitz (369, 370), a German liberal opposed to the Nazis. The problems of agitation were studied by Endemann (373). For comprehensive abstracts of their books see Bibliography.

83. How is rumor exploited and guarded against?

Word-of-mouth spreading of news and rumor are recognized as valuable channels of Nazi propaganda. Schoene (380) believes that rumor and anecdotes have almost as great an influence on public opinion as the press. The dissemination of stories of personal experiences at Nazi party congresses and on Strength-Through-Joy trips are held to have greater and more lasting effect on the imagination of the people at large than official announcements and inspired articles.

On the other hand, rumor in its negative form may contribute to the undermining of faith in the regime. The administration must take notice of all current rumors and properly analyze them before deciding what measures, if any, should be taken. Neither denials nor silence are held to be adequate to countereffect rumors which are contrary to the state's interests. If investigation proves that the rumor has valid grounds, elimination of its causes is advised and frequently carried out.

The Nazis have various methods for detecting rumors and complaints which are objectively treated on the whole. Selected students in the *Hochschule fuer Politik* (formerly the Propaganda Ministry's political college where propagandists and party speakers were trained, now called *Auslandwissenschaftliches Institut* assigned to the exclusive study of propaganda abroad, while Berlin University is training domestic propagandists) are sent out as "political missionaries" (*politische Missionaere*) to various parts of the city to mingle with the people in restaurants, food queues, political demonstrations, theaters and other public places. Their observations are tabulated and analyzed. If it is found that the continued shortage of some particular food or consumer's goods is dangerously impairing morale and giving rise to rumors, that lack is remedied for a short period.

Rumors revolving around political events and personalities are analyzed to determine how far they have penetrated into the mass consciousness. If these rumors are considered dangerous, exemplary punishment with full publicity is made of one or more persons. The branches and cells of the Propaganda Ministry throughout the country also are instructed to make use of this subtle version of public opinion polls.

Several times the Nazis have swept away dangerous rumors by a lightning stroke of terror and violence, as advocated by Hadamovsky (434). Schoene cites the 1934 Blood Purge as a case in point: "All the extremely dangerous rumors which had been floating about for weeks were shattered by the Fuehrer's energetic action." Schoene also maintains that the Russian purges enhanced rather than damaged Stalin's prestige among the people, since the show of impartial force in dealing with high Communist officials is the best means of destroying contagious rumors.

Schoene also speaks of "directed rumors" put out by the propaganda apparatus of the state to serve some immediate purpose or, in its positive form, to establish the "general truthfulness" of all Nazi-inspired rumors. When such rumors turn out to be accurate, the people's confidence in rumors in general is bolstered and they may become important instruments in manipulating public opinion. The manipulation of negative rumors in psychological offensives is mentioned by Stark (334) and is described in our answer to Question 73.

IX

CULTURAL BACKGROUND OF PSYCHOLOGICAL WARFARE (PSYCHOLOGICAL ESPIONAGE)

The ultimate success of psychological campaigns depends on a "thorough knowledge of the country against which the campaign is to be directed and a basic analysis of its inhabitants' national character and temperament" (421).

Thus applied psychology is given another vital task in the German war machine. Blau (388) calls it "comparative national psychology." (For Blau's authority and present position in the psychological setup of the German Army see his detailed biography in the Bibliography, 343.)

84. What is comparative national psychology?

This academic terminology camouflages a "military science" (387) particularly expedient to military and political intelligence services. It specializes in the research and appraisal of the psychological and sociological factors and phenomena of foreign nations insofar as they may have a bearing on Germany's foreign political and military aspirations and plans.

The present German practitioners of comparative national psychology, among them Block (389), Goldenberg (392), Hellpach (396), and Keilhacker (398), take pains to emphasize that their discipline is of a strictly scientific character with considerable academic traditions. They refer to Hegel, Herder, Kant, Lazarus, Wundt, LeBon, Fouille, and others as its founders.

To obtain a systematic and balanced study of complex practical problems, the Germans have indeed adopted some of the methodology of physiological psychology, psychoanalysis, experimental psychology, social psychology, genetic psychology and cultural anthropology. These methods are used, however, to accomplish immediate practical aims and have little in common with the classic ideas which Hegel crystallized in his *Volksgeist,* Kant in his pragmatic anthropology, and Wundt in his folk-psychology. In fact, Banse (386) and Bessenrodt (387) frankly admit that the "characterology of foreign nations is intended to be a complementary weapon of war." Their approach to the psychological survey and appraisal of foreign nations is similar to their characterological approach to the individual's psychological evaluation.

85. What is Blau's own definition of comparative national psychology?

The task of comparative national psychology is to study intellectual and spiritual characteristics of foreign nations with which we have or intend to have peaceful or belligerent relations. We must appraise and understand these nations so that we can evaluate accurately the dynamic forces inherent in their national attitudes and sentiments inasmuch as they may affect our plans and react to our moves.

This may appear as an abstract scientific undertaking. The value of all scientific practices, however, is contingent on their ultimate practicability. In this respect, comparative national psychology has an exalted practical mission, since its findings are designed to benefit the leadership of the state. All political actions, belligerent or peaceful, affect man. Consequently, an exact and comprehensive knowledge of the people who inhabit neighboring and enemy countries must be regarded as a pre-requisite of a successful foreign policy.

The statesman as well as the soldier must know the peoples of foreign lands, their desires and aims, the strength of their faith and national pride, their characteristics, impulses and sensitivities, their domestic difficulties and cleavages (388).

86. What is comparative national psychology attempting to discover?

Comparative national psychology seeks a definite answer to the question: *What kind of nation is this?*

The composite answer to this question provides the clue to the conclusive question (*Zielfrage*): *What political acts and cultural achievements can be expected from a nation so constituted?*

In addition to examining and appraising the "character and temperament of foreign nations," comparative national psychology must investigate the following problems to obtain comprehensive answers to its questions:

a. the mental characteristics of foreign personalities;

b. the motivation of an opponent's will-to-war;

c. the spiritual and cultural currents which lie at the bottom of these motivations;

d. the morale of foreign troop contingents and civilian population both in enemy and neutral countries;

e. the extent to which various implements of war meet with the approval or disapproval of foreign armies, and the probable reaction of enemy populations to novel and unusual methods of warfare, air raids, gas attacks, tank offensives, psychological campaigns (329).

87. How is the "character" of a foreign nation analyzed?

The "character of foreign nations" is determined by the study of their folkways, their culture, their public institutions, and their political acts throughout history.

Specific national characteristics are analyzed through the study of a nation's reactions to cultural phenomena, natural catastrophes, economic and political depressions; through the analysis of its attitude toward the existing political and legal order, toward women and family; through the study of its general conduct under duress, such as occupation by foreign troops.

Several methods are used for the study of foreign national characteristics. Block (389) analyzed the character of countries in southeastern Europe by the "direct empirical approach": studying and appraising individual nations on the spot. Keilhacker (398) used the "indirect deductive approach" by analyzing Britain's national characteristics through the personality of Gladstone whom he believed to be the eternal "typical Englishman."

Keilhacker made some interesting observations of topical interest: "Anybody who has anything to do with England either as friend or foe must remember that he is dealing with a politically-talented and experienced nation. England calmly and thoroughly analyzes the power-politics and alignments of other countries from a long-range point of view, drawing its own expedient conclusions at the proper moment. As in the times of Gladstone, the English people are still profound observers of the shape of existing and coming things. This is the source and essence of their political success. Of course, England has made mistakes and suffered some political and military setbacks, but due to her accurate estimation of power-politics, she has rarely lost wars, and none at all in the last one hundred and fifty years. This fact should be borne in mind by everybody who wishes to acquaint himself with the English people and character as they really are and not as he would like them to be."

Other interesting studies of the English national character were made by Gauger (390, 391), Gramm (393), Banse (385), and Seeberg (408).

Similar analyses were made of the French, Russian and American national characters with special reference to their people's "soldierly qualities." Simoneit reveals that Lufft (42) made an exhaustive study of the United States during its transitory period from peace to war (from isolationism to interventionism) in 1916-17 the conclusions of which are said to be influencing present-day German policies. This report was prepared for the German Society of Military Politics and Military Sciences—but has never been made public. Walter Beck, an army psychologist now stationed in Breslau, analyzed the American's "soldierly qualities" while he was at Boston University (*Soldatentum,* 1936, 173-176). Scores of articles on American problems have been published in the *Zeitschrift fuer Geopolitik* (502), ranging from a study of CCC camps to the assimilation of Ukranians.

German psychological observers and geopoliticians differ widely in evaluating the American character. While Haushofer denies flatly that there is such a thing as an "American" ("the United States is a country, not a nation"), others have high regard for the moral qualities of the American people, particularly their puritanism and adventurous, pioneering spirit, which are held to be inseparable components of the American's national character. A study of German opinion on the United States thus reveals a peculiar duplicity: propaganda literature shows open disdain and distortion while serious studies and scientific journals are equally frank in voicing respect and regard for the American way of life and American personalities (446).

88. How are prominent foreign personalities psychologically appraised?

Nazi psychological intelligence is expected to draw up reliable detailed intellectual and emotional charts of political, economic and military leaders in foreign countries. These appraisals are largely based on biographies and a study of the personality's background. Dirks (74) obtained a psychological pen-picture of Poland's

Marshal Pilsudski by analyzing two of the Marshal's own books and other studies written about him. Schoenemann* succeeded in putting together an excellent mosaic of President Roosevelt's personality by studying his writings, acts, and by accompanying the president on a 1936 trip to Lincoln, Nebraska.

An intimate book on Churchill was published recently by one of his former secretaries, and the German News Agency in New York was ordered to telephone a long condensation of the volume to headquarters in Berlin, obviously to supplement available material on the British Prime Minister's personality in German files. Hitler's personal interpreter, Paul Schmidt, is reported to have an elaborate file on the personality and characteristics of every diplomat in Europe. Perhaps the most cherished property of Nicolai's (522) wartime intelligence service was a "morgue" containing personality analyses of over thirty thousand prominent foreigners.

On the basis of such personality studies, Leon Blum as French Premier was considered advantageous to the Nazi cause, while Churchill and Eden were regarded as extremely dangerous to German aspirations. Employing the findings of their psychological analysts, German political quarters did everything in their power to keep Blum in office and to prevent Churchill from becoming a dominating influence on Britain's prewar foreign policy. It is known that the German Propaganda Ministry instructed its press to refrain from attacks on the Popular Front government of France, and Hitler even permitted Hjalmar Schacht to pay

---

* Schoenemann, F., "Franklin Delano Roosevelt," *Z. f. Politik;* 1934, 7, 369-385.

"Franklin Delano Roosevelt, Praesident der Vereinigten Staaten von Amerika," *Hochschule fuer Politik, Jahrbuch,* 1939, 386-415.

Halfeld, A., "Von Roosevelt zu Roosevelt," *Z. f. Politik;* 1937, 1-2, 33-40. The author is one of Germany's outstanding diplomatic correspondents specializing in American affairs. His headquarters are at Hamburg.

an official visit to Blum as his personal envoy, thus creating the impression in France that Blum was *persona grata* with the Nazi régime. Simultaneously, however, French reactionaries were encouraged in their opposition to Blum so as to secure his prompt overthrow the moment he outlived his usefulness. Such tactics are in line with the policy of German psychological campaigns as outlined by Pintschovius (329): "It would be erroneous to fight against a Socialist regime abroad without permitting the Marxist virus to show its effects to a certain degree."

Germany is not the only country, however, which makes use of personality analyses. Binder (458) reports that, prior to the last war, the French Second Bureau made a comprehensive study of the younger Moltke's character and temperament, the French General Staff skillfully adapting its plans to the German commander-in-chief's characterological shortcomings. It is also stated that American publicists prepared a report for President Wilson, analyzing the character of Germany's representatives at the Versailles peace conference.

89. How is a nation's will-to-war psychologically appraised?

Indices for such appraisals are a nation's spiritual and economic currents. Pintschovius and Clauss* report that in the analysis of the French and British people's "will-to-war" the following factors were analyzed:

    a. The share of puritanism in the development of
       the British empire-idea.

---

* Clauss, L. F. "Gloire" und "Sureté." "Rassenpsychologische Betrachtungen zum Abbau der Erbfeindschaft," *Soldatentum,* 1936, 176-180. The author is director of the Archives of Psychological Anthropology at Buckow, near Berlin.

b. Cromwell's influence on British military philosophy.

c. Religious influences: The Unitarian character of
the Church of England. The role played by the
Catholic Church and Jesuits in France.

d. The role of trade-unionism in Britain's and
France's national life.

e. The influence of "gloire," "sureté" and "esprit de
rentier" on the French national outlook.

In America, they studied the influence of moral, intellectual
and economic pacifism on this nation's "will-to-war." Schoenemann found that the "innate pacifism of the American people
often assumes the attitude of messianism . . . War is identical with
militarism which Americans abhor, but a war for peace, a war to
end war, is not only permissible but even necessary . . . The democratic ideology is the core of that crusading mood which led
to American intervention under President Wilson. Under President Roosevelt, it again represents a danger of the first magnitude, threatening our security and our future." (*Die Demokratie
und die Aussenpolitik der U.S.A.* Berlin: Junker & Duennhaupt,
1939.)

90. What are the sources of comparative national psychology?

Previously, the main guide to the study of foreign nations were
travel books. The Germans reject this source as utterly inadequate
and inaccurate. Blau says: "It cannot be reconciled with the fateful
seriousness of our times to abandon a task of such crucial significance to the accidental meetings and subjective individual observations of *ad hoc* travelers. The all-important task must be pursued

consciously in a planned and organized effort, utilizing all the means which objective research can place at our disposal."

He suggests that the task of research and study of foreign nations be assigned to special observers. The psychological observer must follow the cavalcade of daily events, trifling though they may be, in the countries to which he is assigned. He must be capable of detecting and evaluating all political, social and economic currents and under-currents, as well as general trends of political developments.

Conversations with natives and personal inquiries on the spot are held to be the primary sources of this research. Newspapers and periodicals, plays and motion pictures, artistic and sports competitions also provide excellent source-material. The observer must be specially trained to read between the lines of foreign newspapers and to draw important conclusions from seemingly innocuous articles (387, 388). A systematic exploitation of these sources supplies what Blau calls a "symptomatic substitute mass-picture" (*stellvertretendes Massenbild*).

Psychological observers (indeed, psychological spies) "must be virtual artists of their profession blessed with a prodigious sense of devotion to their job, complete adaptability to their foreign environment, and imbued with a fanatical will to achieve their tasks" (421).

Franke (341) says that "geopoliticians, agents, and neutral informers are best qualified to supply the material required for such investigations," adding, "No sensible government should neglect the employment of such observers. The better the service is organized in peacetime, the better it functions prior to the war, the more valuable contributions it will make to the cause after the outbreak of war."

The overwhelming importance of comparative national psychology for the efficient prosecution of psychological offensives is again stressed by Blau (343) when he says that its findings must "determine the weapons and how to deploy and use them in influencing and destroying all opposing morale forces."

X
WEAPONS OF PSYCHOLOGICAL WARFARE

According to Bertkau and Franke (341), propaganda—backed up by "total espionage" (521, 523)*—is the most important weapon of psychological warfare, with the press (both domestic and foreign), radio, film, and leaflets as its chief instruments.

91. What is the German conception of propaganda?

The German conception of propaganda is radical and revolutionary; they see in propaganda a "political instrument which guarantees absolute control over the spiritual forces of a nation" (434).

Unlike the American conception of propaganda, the German notion is closer to the idea which induced Pope Gregory XV in 1622 to found a *Congregatio de propaganda fide*, a congregation of cardinals to propagate the Catholic faith. This, indeed, was the first appearance of organized propaganda as a political instrument.

By 1627, in the *Collegium Urbanum*, the first full-fledged propaganda college of the modern world came into being. Situated on the Piazza di Spagna in Rome, it had its own printing presses,

* For a comprehensive account of espionage in total war, see *Total Espionage,* by Curt Riess, a skillfully dramatized and basically accurate description of the various intelligence services at war. Also *The Story of Secret Service,* by R. W. Rowan, even though somewhat outdated.

library and archives, and a museum. "Propagandists" to be sent abroad were attending numerous foreign-language courses. It is known that a study of the original *Collegium Urbanum* (dissolved in 1884 by the Italian government) helped Dr. Goebbels in setting up the organizational structure of his Propaganda Ministry.

Thus, in an article in the *Voelkischer Beobachter* (February, 1939), he pointed out that, compared with the Church, the Nazi party's and Germany's propaganda machine was a small institution. According to his quoting of Pater Baumgarten, the Church had spent 16,606,370,000 marks on propaganda in the nineteenth century. In 1870, the *propaganda fide* was leaving the Piazza di Spagna in no less than 250 foreign languages. "It was an inspiration to read about this immense organization," he wrote. "Its propaganda helped the Catholic Church to remain in power for almost two thousand years. Our propaganda will accomplish a similar miracle and assure us of a thousand-year reign."

Despite this boast, the foundation to his approach to propaganda was laid, not by the Nazis, but by an anti-Nazi, Edgar Stern-Rubarth (452); and amplified by another non-Nazi, Plenge (442).

Stern-Rubarth wrote in 1921: "We have to travel along new and unbroken paths [opened up by the intellectual weapons of propaganda], since this implement of war is assigned to the task of supplanting rather than implementing the military machine."

This book of twenty-one years ago, written by a German liberal patriot, became the bible of Nazi propagandists. It was greedily read and fully expropriated by them. Thus Hitler as a propagandist can have no claim to inventiveness and originality. His whole propaganda system is but a flagrant case of plagiarism.

According to Stern-Rubarth, propaganda as a political instrument must utilize eight media, playing *with* some or playing *on* others, to be fully effective.

These media are: 1. slogans, including the spoken word; 2. symbols; 3. printed matter, including the press (controlled); 4. music; 5. faith and superstition; 6. martyrs; 7. film; and 8. the radio.

Six (449) and Stark (450) admit that the Nazis have made the widest possible use of every one of these media. To mention but two of their most effective propaganda weapons: their use of the Swastika represents an exploitation of the second medium suggested by Stern-Rubarth. The glorification of Horst Wessel and the sixteen petty revolutionaries who were killed in front of the Feldherrnhalle on November 9, 1923, follows another one of Stern-Rubarth's proposals, his sixth medium, the creation of martyrs. (Also see answer to Question 60.)

92. What is the "scheme of political propaganda"?

More important than this all-inclusive catalogue of media was Stern-Rubarth's *Scheme of Political Propaganda,* published in the last chapter of his book. This scheme, with but slight alterations, became what we today know as, and erroneously call, the Nazi propaganda system.

The *Scheme of Political Propaganda* as drawn up by Stern-Rubarth, foresaw the following five stages:

1. Fixing the target of political propaganda. First we have to decide whom we want to attack, and then we have to determine in advance the space, the race, and the classes which should be reached.

2. Pretesting possible reactions and repercussions. This test must extend to the examination of possible reactions of one's own people, neutrals not involved in the campaign, and that of the attacked. A precondition of successful propaganda "is an almost telepathical understanding of foreign emotions."

3. Selection of means for (a) positive propaganda, (b) prophylactic propaganda (now called preventive

propaganda by Goebbels, who maintains a special section exclusively assigned to propaganda pro-phylaxis), and (c) negative propaganda.

4. Duration of individual propaganda campaigns must also be established in advance, to exploit repetition when and where it is advantageous, or to prevent repetition when and where it is disad-vantageous.

5. Exploitation of the mistakes and faults of the enemy or opponent.

All propaganda campaigns must revolve, not around issues, but around personalities, another important element of Nazi pro-paganda as outlined by Six and Stark, as well as in the famous hate-book *Das Buch Isidor,* by Goebbels and Mjoelnir.

The execution of this scheme must be left to a flexible, if pos-sible privately organized, financed and run organization, since, in the words of Stern-Rubarth, "no bureaucratic machine of state or government can successfully accomplish such a task."

93. What is the Nazi conception of propaganda?

The Nazi conception of propaganda is represented by Hitler (435) who was the Nazi party's first propaganda chief and still is, in his own words, its "chief drummer."

"Propaganda," Hitler wrote, "is a truly frightful weapon in the hands of the expert." It is the basis for creating an *organization* to destroy the existing, and to establish a new, order.

Propaganda must be directed at the emotions, rather than the intellect, of the masses, chiefly because the crowd is feminine in character and susceptible to emotional rather than rational ap-peals. "Propaganda campaigns must adapt their intellectual level to the receptive ability of the stupidest member of the crowd. If aimed at a whole nation, as in the case of war propaganda, intellectual elements must be altogether avoided" (20).

Propaganda must be simple, harping on the same ideas over and over again. Its emotional elements must be based on

love —— and —— hatred

justice —— and —— injustice

truth —— and —— lies.

Political propaganda, boiled down to slogans repeated over and over again, must have a reckless pugnacity. Hadamovsky (334) stresses the lashing, brutal quality of propaganda. "Propaganda and terror are not opposites," he writes. "Violence, in fact, can be an integral part of propaganda." This is what Hitler meant when he said that propaganda is a combination of "political determination and activistic brutality." The role of violence in propaganda is the "lightning effect of excitation to attention."

Thus elaborating the ideas which were first drawn up by Stern-Rubarth, Hitler proclaimed his own "propaganda credo" in Chapter VI of the first, and Chapter XI of the second volume of *Mein Kampf*.

94. What are the basic principles of Nazi propaganda?

The basic principles of Nazi propaganda have been elaborated by Blau (425, 426), Gutterer (433), Hadamovsky (434), Schoenemann (446), Six (449), Stark (450), and Wanderscheck in his preface to 456.

According to these writers, the first principle is to aim this aggressive propaganda at personalities rather than at issues (cf. Question 92).

Second, German propaganda must be painstakingly camouflaged; it must never appear as German and as propaganda.

Third, it must be based on the accurate knowledge of intellectual, emotional, and economic trends in the countries it intends to attack. "It is obvious that the precondition of successful work is the profound knowledge of the nation against which the propaganda is directed" (451, also Blau, 388).

Fourth, it must never create new issues and then proceed to convert a foreign nation to them. It must detect existing issues and concentrate on twisting and then exploiting them.

Fifth, it must not have a fixed, stationary policy, but must be extremely fluid and flexible, adapted to day-by-day developments and trends. Because of this fluidity and flexibility, it was possible to turn the whole German propaganda machine against the Russians when the outbreak of hostilities in 1941 terminated the short-lived Russo-German friendship.

Sixth, it cannot be conducted by remote control. While general instructions may come from abroad,* their execution must be left exclusively to resident agents.

Seventh, it must utilize to their capacity the good offices of existing Fascist or pro-totalitarian organizations on the spot (organizations of natives are preferred), with whom a working alliance must be established.

As far as propaganda aimed at the United States is concerned, here the aim is to win over public opinion as a whole rather than to convert individual personalities, since American personalities depend on public opinion and not vice versa (cf. Schoenemann's paper quoted on page 156). Otherwise Germany's America-

---

* Cf. "General Instructions Concerning German Propaganda-Action in the Two Americas," a document that, in the fall of 1933, was sent to Nazi agents in the United States and the Argentine. A copy addressed to an agent in the Argentine was intercepted and published in France. Its authenticity is beyond the shadow of a doubt. It was first published by *Le Petit Parisien* in November and December, 1933, and then reprinted in *Germany Unmasked*, by the late Robert Dell (London: Hopkinson, 1934).

propaganda is patterned after the principles mentioned above. (For a comprehensive study of this propaganda see 446; also 499, 501, 528, 533, 542, and scores of articles in 502.)

95. What are the Nazi "methods" of propaganda?

The Nazis, in evolving their own domestic propaganda techniques, analyzed the nature of public opinion and the characteristics of the mass mind. Later these methods were made part of psychological campaigns conducted against foreign nations. Nazi propaganda is not something static, rigid or tied to established methods. Goebbels (431) was emphatic in stating that Nazi propaganda has no basic methods. "It only has a goal: the conquest of the masses. Every means which can help to achieve this goal—is good. Anything which does not hit the target—is bad. Success is its only criterion."

Thus recklessness, brutality and pugnaciousness are applied in the *Propagandamarsch,* the display of strength and power; in fact, more strength and power than they actually possess (449). During the German Republic, Nazi battalions were ordered to march into hostile Marxist districts to provoke street fights, to spill blood, to attract aggressive rowdies among Germany's political underworld to the Nazi movement. Their own casualties in the endless street fights were described as "propagandists of action, witnesses of the strength of the idea and the movement."

Their propaganda organs were given aggressive fighting names (*Angriff, Stuermer*) or sinister titles (*Schwarze Korps*) which were propaganda slogans in themselves. While the bourgeois press was conservative and conventional in its make-up, the Nazis introduced into Germany "yellow-sheet" methods, with terse editorials imitating the language of soap-box agitators, venomous cartoons on page one, banner headlines underlined in red ink. Six (449) says that "the front page of the Party press must look like a political poster."

The spoken word is considered more important than printed matter (428). Hitler's own speeches, carefully composed by a huge staff of skilled propagandists with a conscious accent on every paragraph and delivered at strategic intervals, are the heaviest caliber guns of Nazi propaganda. In their printed material, the Nazis prefer stickers to handbills, with pungent slogans like "Germany Awake!" or "The Jews are our Misfortune!" (422). Their leaflets never present new ideas but pick up old ones already anchored in the public mind, explaining or giving them a new twist. In their posters they introduced gigantic placards which became known in Germany as the "Munich Poster."

For propaganda in subjugated and to-be-conquered countries today, the Nazis have taken from their domestic propaganda the technique of displaying power to invoke fear and respect. Their first act after occupation is to change the make-up and format of the native press so that it will have a punchlike impact on the intimidated and humiliated population. Posters are considered even more important than the press because they cannot be evaded and are omnipresent symbols of authority.

96. What is the role of propaganda in war?

The Nazis themselves regard propaganda as an implement of war in its own right. An anonymous writer of the *Militaer-Wochenblatt* wrote in 1935: "Propaganda is one of the great new inventions of modern war. Today, the war of arms and the war of ideas are the two pillars on which our fate rests" (421, also 451).

Blau (426) wrote: "Propaganda is already today an implement of war of very perceptible reality which is fully capable of providing Germany with entirely new tasks in the event of a war."

Fellgiebel (429) remarked: "The execution of a war-propaganda on the largest possible scale requires . . . a grandiose technical and organizational preparation, as well as time and money. I think, however, that the experience of the last years (demonstrating the success of the Nazis' peacetime propaganda) will induce us to develop this latest implement of war to its fullest capacity."

And Banse (386), whose own ideas are but reflections of the concealed plans of the High Command, wrote way back in 1932: "Propaganda must begin in peacetime and be so effective that the country which undertakes it should be able to harvest its fruit immediately upon outbreak of armed hostilities. War propaganda must then be the systematic and intensified continuation of peace propaganda."

Hitler himself (20) devoted a whole chapter to the analysis of war propaganda, outlining the pattern to be followed in what in 1926 was still the "next" war.

Realizing the importance of war propaganda, the High Command of the Armed Forces maintains a special section for the "military conduct of propaganda campaigns." The Propaganda Ministry, on the other hand, is responsible for the defense against enemy propaganda. Even there, an officer, Colonel Wrochem, is in charge.

97. What are the techniques of Germany's war propaganda?

Bertkau and Franke (341, 430) describe propaganda methods in war as follows:

> The most effective propaganda in intellectual war is the show of power and success. A victory of weapons is worth more than persuasion and is also ideal for the influencing of neutral opinion. Propaganda alone is not capable of deciding the war, but it is designed to prepare the struggle for success, to support and expand it by making use of clever tricks and ruses. The use of ruse is permissible by international law and the attempt to gain advantages over the enemy by the use of such means cannot be considered objectionable.

German diplomats are designated as the chief propaganda agents in neutral lands. "They must possess a deeply-seated knowledge of the psychological fabric of the country to which they are accredited" and "must utilize the experience of private personalities who have lived abroad for long periods."

The effectiveness of German propaganda offensives depends upon the observance of three basic rules:

a. When the aim is to terrorize, terror propaganda is backed up by doing terrible things, like the bombing of Rotterdam and Belgrade. When a peace offensive is launched to weaken enemy morale, it is made plausible by putting forward some concrete plan, like the division of Europe into "German and British spheres of interest."

b. Nazi propagandists fit their propaganda to the mentality of the particular group they want to reach and to the peculiar conditions of the moment. They seldom try to make direct converts to their doctrine. They merely try to vanquish resistance by using whatever argument is most likely to influence those to whom it is addressed.

c. Propaganda is not used for the sake of propaganda. It is used in conjunction with a military, diplomatic or economic objective. It obtains its best results in neutral countries, or before the actual outbreak of war, or in stirring up disunity in nonbelligerent nations. Nazi propaganda must win its major victories before the "shooting war" begins. In wartime it is chiefly an auxiliary weapon. It cannot win wars, nor can it prevent defeat, but its psychological techniques, if applied persistently and timed accurately, can be a deciding factor in battles, particularly in total war.*

---

* For the best outline of the German techniques of war propaganda, see *The Strategy of Terror,* by Edmond Taylor. In another little book, *Smash Hitler's International,* Mr. Taylor outlined a brilliant plan for our own propaganda offensive. Unfortunately, however, his original plan has either been disregarded or totally diluted when attempts at its translation into realities were made.

The basic fault of our own propaganda offensive is in our fundamentally wrong approach to propaganda. Unlike the Germans who believe in the "propaganda of action," the origin of which goes back to the Catholic Church (cf. Question 91, today carried by the world-wide organization of the Catholic Action), we still cling to the outdated method of "propaganda by propaganda," the highest expression of which is calling a spade—a spade. Propaganda cannot be conducted in a detached, impassive and independent manner, or in a political and military vacuum, just as it is utterly wrong to make propaganda for the sake of propaganda. Every military move, political speech, economic action and production figure must be, by itself, "propaganda of action" with propaganda inherent in it instead of, as it is now being done, attributed to it. As long as we fail to adopt a strategy of propaganda infiltration, we cannot hope for the success of our own psychological offensives. In this as in every other field of modern war, the Germans are far ahead of us. We have to work hard in an intelligently planned effort if we are to come up to and even overtake them. What is primarily wanted is a carefully prepared propaganda strategy whose execution must not be hampered by contradictory policies, departmental and personal jealousies, and the haphazard assignment of important tasks to utterly incompetent officials. Our so-called propaganda organizations were, up to the appointment of Elmer Davis as director of the Office of War Information, overstaffed and underplanned. Their propaganda was conducted in a test-tube manner with an ivory tower for a radio transmitter. As things stand today, with our political offensive still in its very early stages, our propaganda methods must be improved and new, as well as better techniques added, if American political warfare will ever be able to make a decisive contribution toward victory.

APPENDIX*

Examination of Applicants for Commissioned Rank

The examination of officer applicants is conducted from a synthetic, rather than from an analytical, approach. The work of an officer calls not merely for the summation of a number of isolated qualities, but upon the whole man, and it is essential to select those who possess highly developed character traits of a certain kind. Consequently, tests of personality and temperament occupy an important place beside the necessary intelligence and technical aptitude tests. For this purpose a series of interesting and ever-increasing forms of technique has been devised. Realizing that the morale of the troops depends largely upon the spirit of the officers, it was hoped that certain faults revealed in the old officer corps, during the last war, would be avoided by this means of selection. Further, when building up the officer corps of the

---

* This comprehensive survey of the various test methods actually used in German army psychology has been prepared by Dr. A. H. Martin of Sydney, Australia. In preparing this extraordinary document, Dr. Martin was assisted by a refugee scholar who had at one time served as a psychologist in the German Army. Dr. Martin, too, emphasizes the "free use of qualitative judgments, characteristic of German methods, as opposed to the more strictly quantitative methods of American and British psychologists."

original *Reichswehr*, it was always kept in mind that this troop would sooner or later form the core of a new conscripted army of *Volkscheer*. Hence it was recognized that a high degree of leadership, personal initiative, and sense of responsibility were required.

A psychological examination of applicants for commissioned rank lasts two days with an intervening free day. These tests administered are chiefly individual tests, but paper tests, mainly intelligence and some of the measures of technical aptitudes, are given to groups. These latter occupy the beginning of the first day and comprise the commonly accepted types of intelligence tests and others as well as one presented by medium of a film. In the three-word test the examinee is requested to compose a story using three given words. The degree of imagination expressed, the type of story and its logical and coherent structure are some of the aspects assessed. In the film test, a technical procedure shown on the screen must later be described by the applicant, using a diagram of the objects and mechanisms previously portrayed in operation. The resultant score is assessed on the extent to which the interconnected partial processes have been correctly recognized and described. In addition to completeness and correct description of the essentials, stress is placed upon clear and concise verbal expression and a practical method of description, such as indicating single parts and points on the diagram by letters or numbers.

At the same sitting are administered tests which indicate certain characteristics of mental and emotional maturity and other temperamental trends. Paraphrasing a poem and choosing the most favored reproductions of various pictures of the "Medici Print" type are included. The poems require some powers of literary apprehension and judgment, and a sensitivity of feeling tone capable of appreciating resignation, irony, symbolic or metaphorical significance, et cetera. The aim here is to select officers not only endowed with knowledge, but also those possessing culture, humanity, and breadth of outlook. The pictures chosen reveal general temperamental predilections, for the idyllic, the heroic, the humanistic, and the technical.

The next battery comprises performance tests of intelligence combined with technical aptitude, and some manual dexterity tests. The following cover specific examples:

In the water supply test, different problems are to be solved by making use of a diagram of a complicated system of pipes and conduits. The places where the pipes intersect are left blank in the diagram. The examinee is required to affix appropriate disks on which are represented various types of joints, namely, straight, T-shaped and elbow joints, so that the supply of water be directed to specified points in the plan.

In the bolt-board test, a notched lath is inserted in a grooved board, on both sides of which are bolts which slip into the notches. The pairs of bolts on either side are connected so that the inept pushing of the bolt on one side causes the bolt on the other to slip into a notch. The problem is solved when, in a set time, the lath can be easily withdrawn from the groove.

For the windmill test, the examinee is given a disassembled set of drilled metal strips and plates, bolts and rods. From these he is required to construct the wheel of a windmill to be set up on a vertical plate.

Another test is one of map-reading. It attempts to assess the capacity to visualize concrete objects represented on a map. Previous training in map-reading is not required. Indeed, such special knowledge and experience is taken into account against the candidate in assessing his score.

For the assessment of practical intelligence, that is of a type not involving verbal expression, a performance test requiring the continuation of a given series of objects is used. These objects differ according to size, large and small; weight, light and heavy; surface, rough and smooth; shape, straight and curved; and color of the edges, red and blue. Sufficient of the series is first set out to enable the examinee to discover the underlying principle of classification of that particular group, and he is required to continue it as in a number series test. This material provides possibilities for many different arrangements of varying difficulty. It is apparent that the test requires an aptitude for abstraction without penalizing those who are inept in verbal formulation.

The chief military work sample tests are as follows:

There are two "command" tests, for which purpose some soldiers are always available for use in the laboratory. In one, the examinee is required to give some of the standard commands, "Attention!" "Eyes left!" et cetera. This reveals quality and control of voice and the general attitude of the examinee, whether of shyness, embarrassment and uncertainty, of calm, commanding superiority or blustering domination.

In the other section, the examinee is required to give a soldier certain instructions, such as taking a despatch to a given place by a specified route, avoiding certain indicated danger spots. The written instruction has been given to the examinee in the usual military official language. He is now required to translate it into a form suitable for the ordinary private soldier. The test assesses powers of simple exposition essential for a commissioned officer.

In the next section, the characterological or personality tests, the stress situations are continued for over an hour. Instructions require the candidate to carry out a long series of disconnected tasks which must be remembered in their correct order. The test calls not only upon comprehension and memory, but also upon the agility of the man. Thus he is required to balance on a narrow pole in full military kit.

But the capacity for improvising solutions for technical problems arising in an emergency is also involved. One of these tasks will have been carried out previously under normal conditions. It is now repeated with the suggestion that there is actually existing a stress situation. For instance, it is suggested that a regiment is waiting to cross over the emergency bridge which the examinee is improvising from materials at hand. A superior enemy force is approaching, and its artillery bombardment is causing heavy losses every minute. This situation is supported by noises and other mimicry. The reduction of time in this second performance is taken not only as an effect of practice but also as an indication of the examinee's reliability to act quickly and calmly in such a situation. It also reveals, if present, the degree of nervousness and irritability under strain. Besides the time required and the quality of the completed work, systematic and steady methods of work without halts and haste are favorably scored. Conclusions about temperament can also be drawn from the observation of involuntary nervous gestures, styled technically, "motoric" signs.

Willingness and persistence, in addition to physical strength and agility, are measured by means of a wall of smooth planks which the examinee must climb in full equipment as often as he can. The number of times the wall is scaled is not so important as the readiness to use the last resource of strength. One who climbs six times without tiring and then gives up is not rated so highly as one who has climbed twice with effort and yet tries with all his might a third time.

These tests of personality rating have been increased in recent years by systematic experimentation. One of the most interesting tests involves the following procedure: The examinee sits on a chair with his feet against a rail, and pulls with both hands a spring exercise expander affixed to the wall in front of him. Through the handles of the expander is sent a steadily increasing electrical current. The set task is to hold out as long as possible under this double burden of stress, which sets up considerable strain. The test is not, as it would seem at first sight, merely a measure of will power or muscular strength of the candidate. Behind the wall is set up a film camera unseen by the examinee. This records through a slot his facial expressions, thus affording the material for the judgment of personality by methods expounded in Lersch's *Gesicht und Charakter*.

To this section belong also personality questionnaires. One of the psychologists working in the laboratories is specially experienced in the administration of the Rorschach test, and there is also one experienced in graphology. The results of these test samplings are included in the final estimate.

The examination concludes with a general discussion by the examinees of an allotted topic. The examiners are present but do not participate. The discussion is primarily of clinical significance, revealing such qualities as vivacity, alertness, confidence, aggressiveness, obduracy, range of interests and sympathies, direction and breadth of outlook, and nimbleness in meeting and countering arguments.

Previously examiners tended more frequently to select topics which have been found by experience to educe information on the attitude of examinees to general ethical questions; for example, "What do you think of the bombing of open towns?" Before the Nazi party had won any great influence in the army, candidates who had successfully passed the earlier part of the examination were rejected when they revealed in these discussions points of view incompatible with the principles of military honor and the ethical conduct of warfare. In the course of the two days' examination, tests of persistence and fatigue were also given.

A "follow-up" of each candidate is carefully made. After three, six, and twelve months' training, the training-staff personnel record their opinions about each individual officer applicant who has passed through their hands. It has been found that, on the average, these opinions diverged from those given earlier in the laboratory in only about 2 per cent of the cases. These results show that the preliminary examination is really capable of selecting suitable available human material for officer training to the extent of 98 per cent.

Examination for Specialists

As more numerous and specialized weapons have been introduced into the army, so more numerous and specialized tests had to be developed to select technical personnel. Some of these tests, for instance, those for transport drivers, et cetera, could be absorbed ready-made for extant industrial tests. Others, for instance, those for U-boat listeners, had been already developed in the last war and have been further improved and extended for use in the anti-aircraft section.

One piece of apparatus which is widely used in addition to the general tests is as follows:

It consists of the recognized discrimination reaction time apparatus. All pilots, drivers, and other specialists, who must be able to react quickly and with precision, are rigorously tested by this means. The examinee must react by pressing one of four keys in response to light signals of different color and shape thrown on a screen. Some signals are responded to by the same key, while others are to be ignored. At the same time a pedal on the right must be depressed when a buzz sounds on the right, but when one sounds on the left, it must be responded to by the left foot. To increase the disturbing effect, a lower buzz indicates to the candidate any mistakes made by him. All his responses are registered automatically. Easy preliminary trials are first worked through to acquaint the examinee with the apparatus and to indicate practice effects. The speed of administration is gradually increased during the series of trials.

The rotating chair is used only for pilots. The examinee is blindfolded and the rotations made in two planes, horizontal and vertical. The test indicates the effect of various positions and motions upon the certainty of the examinee's reactions. Imperfections in the semicircular canals, the sense organs of position and motion, passed over in the ordinary medical examination have been discovered by this test. In this way unsuitable candidates have been discovered and rejected at once, thus avoiding disaster both for themselves and others, and material losses of valuable aircraft.

The motor driver's test consists of a further development of the apparatus originated by Munsterberg and improved by Moede. The candidate, seated in the cab of a motor vehicle, has exposed on a screen before him the motion film of his road. He is required to pass other vehicles, cross bridges, climb hills, make turns, get out of traffic jams, et cetera, as in a real driving test. In this case, the position of his own vehicle is indicated by a small rod. All his reactions of braking, accelerating or swerving are automatically recorded, with the nature of and times for each act, as well as the total driving time.

A co-ordination test indicates the capacity for systematic co-ordination of both hands. This is important for artillery men and searchlight and range-finder operators. It follows the principle of the well-known test in which a pencil must be guided by the simultaneous operation of two handles.

This enumeration gives a sampling rather than an exhaustive survey of the test materials and methods of the army laboratory, because new improvements are constantly being made to meet fresh demands.

A follow-up of those successful in the psychological aptitude tests is also made as in the case of the examination for officers. Once a test has passed beyond the experimental stage, failures are as infrequent in the specialist corps as in the officer corps. Psychological tests were of especial importance in the building up of the air force. The fact that Germany, next to Russia, could bring into action the largest air force in the world after only a few years from the reintroduction of its military aviation, was made possible only through an intensive and exceptionally hard training. But this possibility in turn was realized only because the psychological laboratories had sent forward only the best human material for special instruction.

PART FOUR

BIBLIOGRAPHY OF
GERMAN PSYCHOLOGICAL WARFARE

INTRODUCTION TO THE BIBLIOGRAPHY:
CHECK LIST FOR QUICK REFERENCE

This *Bibliography of German Psychological Warfare* contains 561 titles. Although the material was critically selected and items of inferior quality or contributions with no immediate bearing on our problem were omitted, it is still difficult to pick the most important titles in such a mass of bibliographical data.

To facilitate the study of German "psychological warfare" in all its phases, aspects and implications, the Editors compiled and now suggest the following twenty-six books as basic reading. They are listed in numerical order as they can be found in the Bibliography where English translation of the titles and their abstracts are also available. Asterisks denote books of particular importance the reading of which is essential for the understanding of the German theory and practice of "psychological warfare." While most of the originals are available in various American libraries (the New York Public Library has most of them), only three of the books, Nos. 20, 339 and 348, have been translated into English.

   * 16. Haushofer, K. *Grenzen in ihrer geographischen und politischen Bedeutung.*
      17. Hentig, H. v. *Psychologische Strategic des grossen Krieges.*
   * 18. Hesse, K. *Der Feldherr Psychologos.*
   * 20. Hitler, A. *Mein Kampf.*
      27. Ludendorff, E. *Kriegfuehrung und Politik.*

* 35. Rosenberg, A. *Der Mythus des 20. Jahrhunderts.*

* 63. Simoneit, M. *Wehrpsychologie.*

* 192. Hesse, K. *Wandlung des Soldaten.*

255. Freytag-Loringhoven, H. v. *Die Psyche der Heere.*

287. Soldan, G. *Der Mensch und die Schlacht der Zukunft.*

295. Altrichter, F. *Die seelischen Kraefte des deutschen Heeres,* etc.

* 329. Pintschovius, K. *Die seelische Widerstandskraft in modernen Krieg.*

339. Banse, E. *Raum und Volk im Weltkrieg.*

* 343. Blau, A. *Geistige Kriegfuehrung.*

348. Foertsch, H. *Kriegskunst von heute und morgen.*

* 356. Nicolai, W. *Nachrichtendienst, Presse und Volksstimmung.*

* 364. Schumacher, R. v. & Hummel, H. *Vom Kriege zwischen den Kriegen.*

369. Baschwitz, K. *Der Massenwahn,* etc.

428. Dovifat, E. *Rede und Redner.*

* 434. Hadamovsky, E. *Propaganda und nationale Macht.*

* 446. Schoenemann, F. *Die Kunst der Massenbeeinflussung in den Vereinigten Staaten von Amerika.*

* 449. Six, F. A. *Die politische Propaganda der NSDAP,* etc.

* 452. Stern-Rubarth, E. *Propaganda als politisches Instrument.*

454. Thimme, H. *Weltkrieg ohne Waffen.*

463. Eltzbacher, P. *Die Presse als Werkzeug der auswaertigen Politik.*

528. Ehrich, E. *Die Auslandsorganisation der NSDAP.*

(For additional material in the English language the Editors suggest "The German Army," by Herbert Rosinski, "History of Militarism," by Alfred Vagts, "The Guilt of the German Army," by Hans Ernest Fried, "The History of National Socialism" and "Hitler," by Konrad Heidden, "German Philosophy and Politics," by John Dewey, "The Self-Betrayed," by Curt Reiss, and many more.)

I. EXAMINATION AND CRITIQUE OF PAST WARS

1. Anon. "Neugestaltung der Kriegfuehrung," *Militaer-Wochenblatt*, 1935, 18, 747-750; 19, 787-792.

Reorganization of Warfare: An article in the High Command's semi-official weekly treating the complex problems presented by modern warfare (total war), in a philosophical rather than practical vein.

2. Banse, E. "Umrisse einer nationalen Wehrlehre," *Deutsche Wehr*, 1932, 33.

Outlines of a National Military Science: Banse, widely publicized in America for his sensational advocacy of bacterial warfare, is Germany's foremost "strategist of terror" who received official recognition when Hitler made him a professor of military science at the Brunswick Institute of Technology. In this article Banse maintains that military ideology must be imbued in the entire population and envisages a popularization of military science for this purpose.

3. —. "Kriegfuehrung und Politik." *Voelkischer Beobachter*, 6-19-1932.

Conduct of War and Politics: An article stressing the necessity of unified command in total war under a popular but authoritarian leader.

4. Binder, J. *Recht und Macht als Grundlagen der Staatswirksamkeit.* Erfurt, 1921.

Right and Might as Bases of the State's Effective Functions:
see below.

5. —. *Die sittliche Berechtigung des Krieges und die Idee des ewigen Friedens.* Berlin: Junker & Duennhaupt, 1930.

Moral Justification of War and the Idea of Permanent Peace: The author, one of Germany's foremost professors of law and philosophy of law, justifies war as a necessary phenomenon in the nationalist tradition. He agrees with Moltke that permanent peace is a "dream—and not a pretty one at that." Only a nation that has preserved its will to wage war deserves to continue its existence. Hegelian in conception and thought, Binder's book argues that the first World War was morally and politically right, just as future wars will always find their moral justification before a '"superhuman tribunal" which alone is qualified to judge it.

6. Breysig, K. *Psychologie der Geschichte.* Breslau: Marcus, 1935.

Psychology of History. Dr. Breysig died just one year ago.

7. Clausewitz, K. v. *Vom Kriege.* Berlin: Behr's, 1916.

War: A Prussian general of the early nineteenth century and founder of the unique German "war philosophy," Clausewitz believed that war is part and parcel of the state and society. His famous dictum, "War is the continuation of politics by other means," has been resuscitated by the Nazis as the kernel of their whole political philosophy and has become the theoretical basis of their "political warfare." Clausewitz was the first of modern military writers whose conception of the "strategy of inner defense" has been realized in total war. By "strategy of inner defense," his Nazi commentators now assert, he meant psychological preparedness and a proper estimation of morale as decisive factors in war.

8. Deutelmoser, E. *Zwischen gestern und morgen. Politische Anregungen.* Berlin, 1919.

Between Yesterday and Tomorrow. Political Suggestions: A revengeful call to arms, issued practically on the morning after the Armistice. Typical of the postwar German literary flood which refused to accept defeat as final.

9. Dolberg, R. *Die Theorie der Macht.* Wien: Oester. Wirtschafts-verl., 1934.

Theory of Might: A pedantic review of the relationship of power to social forces. The author justifies power and violence as means to political ends, politics being simply a lesson in power-tactics. He pleads for the state's control of internal economy and a barter system abroad, with the instruments of might as deciding factors. Politicians must grasp the significance of authority, tradition, habit and emotions as bases for manipulating power to their ends. The book is dedicated to Benito Mussolini.

10. Feeser, F. "Der totale Krieg," *Zeitschrift fuer Politik*, 1935, 551-569.

The Total War: A review and critique of Ludendorffs "Total War," refuting the "mad General's" ideas on the war of the future. Ludendorff held that Jews, Roman Catholics, and Free Masons were forces hostile to totalitarian militarism. He clamored for a new religion to replace and combat all three. Feeser, on the other hand, believes the time is too pressing for the introduction of a new religion and calls for the total exploitation of all existing spiritual forces within the state, altering rather than eradicating them. A very important article which reveals the conflict between Ludendorff's fanatical irrealism and the Nazis' realism.

11. Foertsch, H. *Die Wehrmacht im nationalsozialistischen Staat.* Hamburg: Broschek, 1935.

The Armed Forces in the National-Socialist State: The official theorist of the German High Command and colonel on the staff of the High Command points out the place of the army in a fully militarized nation imbued with a positive will-to-war and thus predestined to dominate the world by force.

12. Forsthoff, E. *Der totale Staat*. Hamburg: Hanseatische Verlagsanst., 1933.

The Total State: An apologist of the totalitarian state maintains that the German Republic eventually had to give way to the philosophy and organization of a totalitarian regime which is held to be more suited to economic progress, social tendencies, and military necessities of the twentieth century. The philosophy of the totalitarian state is described as being total responsibility in which the freedom of the individual can only be considered as a gift of the state.

13. Grassegger, W. *Der zweite Weltkrieg. Deutschland die Waffenschmiede*. Naumburg: Tancre, 1922.

The Second World War: A militant presentation of Germany as the "arsenal of the second World War" which will finally settle all the problems which the first World War proved incapable of solving. One of the hundreds of books published in Germany after the last war to preserve and heighten militaristic spirit for Der Tag.

14. Guenther, G. "Die Baendigung des Krieges durch den Staat." In *Krieg und Krieger*. Berlin: Junker & Duennhaupt, 1930.

The State as Master of War.

15. Haushofer, K. *Wehrgeopolitik*. Berlin: Junker & Duennhaupt, 1932.

Military Geopolitics: Haushofer is the head of the German Academy of Munich (fount of contemporary Germanic imperialism), a retired Bavarian general, and now professor of political geography at the Munich University. He was Hitler's greatest influence in the writing of Mein Kampf and is primarily known as the inventor of the Nazi slogan—"living space." Writing in a flowery and metaphysical style, Haushofer approaches military science from the geographical-political angle. "Living space" is defined as not only a "place in the sun," but as the conquest of an area which can be made self-sufficient in agriculture, raw materials, and industrial goods. The proposed living space is claimed on the basis of German cultural nuclei existing in Continental and overseas areas. Haushofer distinguishes between active and passive areas, the former being battlefields; the latter, centers of agricultural and industrial supply. Geopoliticians are given the preliminary task of establishing tide living-space area, while the military have the task of acquiring and maintaining it. The co-ordination of this dual task is called by Haushofer and his school "military geopolitics."

16. —. *Grenzen in ihrer geographischen und politischen Bedeutung.* (Second edition.) Heidelberg: Vowinkel, 1939.

The Geographical and Political Importance of Frontiers: The bible of German expansionism. Frontiers are not determined by geography, but by the forces which impose their demands for living space and their culture on certain areas. Frontiers are living organisms which grow and die in the fluidity of historical processes, often accelerated by great leaders, like Caesar and Alexander, whom Haushofer calls "frontier-makers." To understand the principles underlying the Nazi philosophy of expansion, a thorough examination of Haushofer's works is indispensable.

17. Hentig, H. v. *Psychologische Strategic des grossen Krieges.* Heidelberg: Winter, 1927.

Psychological Strategy of the Great War: Major in the World War, member of an old patrician German family, and outstanding criminologist of the German Republic, von Hentig was the author of the most remarkable single work on the role of psychology in military operations during the last war. An uncompromising liberal, von Hentig left Germany of his own free will and is now living in Boulder, Colorado, working on his memoirs. He is an active member of the Committee for National Morale.

18. Hesse, K. *Der Feldherr Psychologos. Ein Suchen nach dem Fueh-rer der deutschen Zukunft.* Berlin: Mittler, 1922.

War Lord Psychologos; A Search for the Leader of the German Future: A first lieutenant in the last war, Hesse joined the dis-gruntled Fascist-minded officers' clique after the Versailles Treaty limited Germany's army to 100,000 men. Disturbed by an out-break of panic in his own regiment, Hesse spent several postwar years minutely examining its psychological factors. His findings revolved around the problem of leadership, "men with unfailing nerves" being considered the basic need and prime asset of mil-itary organization. Of greatest practical value is Hesse's detailed analysis of the impact of military events on civilian morale. Hesse later became a war-economist, and at the outbreak of war joined the Nazi propaganda regiment as an official newspaper correspon-dent with the rank of colonel.

19. Hierl, K. *Grundlagen einer deutschen Wehrpolitik.* Muenchen: Eher, 1929.

Foundations of a German Military Policy: The writer is the leader of the German Labor Service and one of Hitler's chief military advisers. He helped formulate Nazi military philosophy —militarization of the whole German nation to carry out its "his-toric mission" of world revolution, by which is meant the German domination of the world.

20. Hitler, A. *Mein Kampf.* (Two volumes.) Muenchen: Eher, 1926, 1928.

My Struggle: The best translation of this work is that pub-lished by Reynal and Hitchcock, New York, 1940. Of its total of twenty-seven tedious chapters, especially important are: Volume I, Chapters I-III, for the psychological background of the phenome-non Hitler; Chapter VI, on propaganda during the last war and a blueprint of Germany's present war propaganda; Chapter XI, for his obsession of anti-Semitism; Chapter XII, for the early history of the Nazi party. Volume II, Chapter II, organizational structure of the Nazi state; Chapter XI, the dual Nazi weapon of propaganda and organization; Chapters XIII-XV, his foreign policy.

21. Horneffer, E. *Nietzsche als Vorbote der Gegenwart.* Duesseldorf: Bagel, 1935.

Nietzsche as the Forerunner of Contemporary Germany: Follows the familiar Nazi pattern of distortion and exploitation of Nietzsche's superman-philosophy.

22. —. *Pazifismus. Eine philosophische Untersuchung.* Erfurt, 1929.

Pacifism: An emotional German argument describing pacifism as a destructive force and contrary to the nature of heroic human beings.

23. Juenger, E. "Die totale Mobilmachung." In *Krieg und Krieger.* Berlin: Junker & Duennhaupt, 1930.

Total Mobilization: The writer is the leader of a small but influential group of German military intellectuals who were stunned by the defeat in 1918, and joined together to salvage the "heroic spirit" of the first World War. Juenger urges the necessity of the voluntary participation of a heroic nation united in what he calls "German Socialism," conditioned and morally mobilized for the accomplishment of the only possible goal: permanent struggle, i.e., war.

24. Juenger, F. G. *Der Krieg.* Berlin: Widerstands Verlag, 1936.

The War: Another member of Ernst Juenger's militant intellectuals writes more about war (rather than peace) as a basic national aim.

25. Juncker, W. "Militarismus," *Soldatentum,* 1936, 180-183.

Militarism: A scientist employed by the Psychological Laboratory of the German High Command discusses the psychological and philosophical impact of Germany's "spiritual militarism" on the principles guiding the world outlook of the armed forces.

26. Ludendorff, E. v. *Meine Kriegserinnerungen, 1914-1918*. Berlin: Mittler, 1920.

My War Memoirs: Written as an embittered answer to critics who accused him of needlessly prolonging the war by refusing to agree to a negotiated peace in 1917-18. In an attempt to vindicate himself, Ludendorff charged that Germany's political leadership failed to co-operate with the High Command and did nothing to counter the enemy propaganda which, according to him, destroyed morale on the home front and finally brought about the "stab in the back" legend.

27. —. *Kriegsfuehrung und Politik*. Berlin: Mittler, 1922.

Conduct of War and Politics: More on Ludendorff's general thesis with special emphasis on a unified political and military command as an essential precondition of success in modern war. It was over these ideas that Ludendorff and Hitler united for the overthrow of the Weimar Republic.

28. —. *Urkunden der Ohersten Heeresleitung ueber ihre Taetigkeit in 1916-18*. Berlin: Mittler, 1920.

Documents of the Supreme Command About Its Activities in 1916-18: Important among these documents are Ludendorffs memoranda on propaganda and counter propaganda, his plan for the patriotic education of troops, morale on the military and home fronts, and the protocol of one of the last meetings of Germany's Imperial War Cabinet in which Ludendorff showed distinct signs of vacillation between an immediate peace as suggested by Wilson and continuing the war until a spring offensive in 1919 could bring about German victory. The documents were arbitrarily published by Ludendorff in another attempt to prove that the war was lost because the political leadership refused to accept the advice of the High Command.

29. Metzsch, H. v. *Krieg als Saat*. Breslau: Hirt, 1934.

War as Seed: The author sees war as the natural and necessary crop sown by the political leadership of the National State.

Metzsch's ideas about the supreme importance of militant propaganda were challenged by a soberheaded colleague of his, General Wilhelm Marx, writing from the disadvantageous position of retirement while Metzsch had full authority as Inspector General of the German Army's entire educational system. Marx's article, one of the most conservative and humane ever written by a high German officer, appeared in the 1934 volume of *Militaer-Wochenblatt*.

30. —. "Zeitgemaesse Gedanken ueber Clausewitz," *Hochschule fuer Politik, Schriften,* Abt. 1, Heft 30. Berlin: Junker & Duennhaupt, 1937.
Topical Ideas About Clausewitz.

31. Moser, O. v. *Die obersten Gewalten im Weltkrieg.* Stuttgart: Belser, 1931.
The Supreme Powers in the World War: The author, a retired general and monarchist, maintains that England's superiority was due to political insight and that the reason for British victory was the trust of the armed forces and the whole British population in the political leadership and personality of Lloyd George. France was victorious more through bravery, self-sacrifice and chance. Principal contributory factors to German defeat were the weakness of the Kaiser and his statesmen, insufficient co-ordination of political and military leadership, ineffectiveness of the press, political confusion of the Reichstag, and deficiency of elementary morale factors. Although rich in material and examples, the study lacks a basic historical sense of values.

32. Niemann, A. *Kaiser und Heer. Das Wesen der Kommandogewalt und ihre Ausuebung durch Kaiser Wilhelm II.* Berlin: Verlag fuer Kulturpolitik, 1929.
The Kaiser and the Army; the Nature of the Power of Command and Its Practice by Emperor William II.

33. Oertzen, K. L. v. *Grundzuege der Wehrpolitik.* Hamburg: Hans. Verlagsan., 1933.

Principles of Military Policy: A very important essay by the late great military theorist of the Reichswehr.

34. Oncken, H. "Politik und Kriegfuehrung," *Muenchener Universitaetsreden,* 1929, 12, 1-32.

Politics and Conduct of War: In a lecture at Munich University, one of Germany's foremost contemporary historians asserts that Germany—despite apparent defeat—won the war in the military sense, but lost it in the political field. Through weak and vacillating political leadership, the population became confused and indifferent to war aims, giving rise to psychological conflicts which proved irreparable when the crisis came in September, 1918.

35. Rosenberg, A. *Der Mythus des 20. Jahrhunderts.* Muenchen: Hoheneichen, 1932.

Mythos of the 20th Century: Rosenberg is the chief pamphleteer and pseudo-philosopher of the Nazi movement. His ambition is to become the "philosophical educator" (*weltanschaulicher Erzieher*) of the German people. In this much discussed, widely sold, but most unread of all Nazi books, Rosenberg lays the foundation of all the fantastic theories on which Nazi "philosophers" thrive today. In the center of Rosenberg's "mythos" is the Aryan Superman (arischer Lichtmensch), living in a spiritually and racially determined community welded together by common blood and a common consciousness of national honor. It is his right and duty to safeguard his blood and national honor. For that reason, he must separate himself from "alien races" (*andersartige Menschen*), to prevent the contamination of his blood and encroachment upon his superior national honor. Blood and honor are the sole sources of his might and claim to supremacy. Neighborly love and Catholicism, sources of Christian might, are summarily rejected, since they are likely to weaken the Aryan Superman's determination to protect his blood and uphold his honor.

36. Scheler, M. *Der Genius des Krieges und der deutsche Krieg*. Leipzig: Verlag der Weissen Buecher, 1917.

The Genius of War and the German War: Writing in the midst of the last war, Scheler conceived Germany's historic mission to be the break-up of the liberal philosophy of life. He saw two possible outcomes of the war. (1) Division of the world into three great commonwealths: A Mongolian Empire under Japanese domination, a Russian state completely covering Western Europe, and a mechanized America. England would be politically independent, albeit serving a Russianized Europe, with Germany, Italy and France culturally paralyzed. (2) A victorious Austro-Germany solidifying all of Europe under German military leadership, purging Europe of English-American capitalism and Calvinist-Puritan Christianity as "foreign poisons." The movement of expansion would then be transferred from the west to the east. Scheler's remarkable historic sense has had considerable influence on the shaping of Nazi expansionism. The book also contains an appendix entitled: "Psychology of the English *Ethos*."

37. Schering, W. M. *Die Kriegsphilosophie von Clausewitz*. Hamburg: Hanseatische Verlagsanstalt, 1936.

Clausewitz's War Philosophy: A biography of the Prussian general by a major of the German Army and a lecturer of war philosophy at the Berlin University. Schering maintains that Clausewitz helped direct German thought into a philosophical system that could prevent the ideals of the French revolution from penetrating too deeply into German life. He describes the Nazi system as the renascence of a positive war philosophy based on Clausewitz's ideas and Nazi military strategy as an adaptation of the general's tenet: "Defense is the strongest military policy with negative results, attack is the weakest military policy with positive results."

38. Schmitthenner, P. *Politik und Kriegfuehrung in der neueren Geschichte*. Hamburg: Hanseatische Verlagsanstalt, 1938.

Politics and Conduct of War in Recent History.

39. Schramm, W. v. "Schoepferische Kritik des Krieges." In *Krieg und Krieger*. Berlin: Junker & Duennhaupt, 1930.

A Creative Critique of the War: Another member of Juenger's group of militant intellectuals explores the psychological aftermath of the first World War and finds that defeat left a mental burden of oppression in the German mass mind. The psychologist and honest critic are given the task of liberating the German people from the war's disastrous effects by scientifically examining every aspect of the conflict and giving it its place in history and its meaning for the present. Conclusion: "We can only find a way to national unity by building a new type of German whose motivations will be inspired, as at the front, by human comradeship."

40. Schwertfeger, B. *Die politischen und militaerischen Verantwortlichkeiten im Verlaufe der Offensive im Jahre 1918*. Berlin: Mittler, 1927.

The Political and Military Responsibilities in the Course of the 1918 Offensive: A scholarly work written by a retired major of the intelligence service, basing his analysis on official documents in the Reichs Archives. Another attempt to prove the guiltlessness of the military command in the failure of the March offensive.

41. Simoneit, M. *Wehrethik*. Berlin: Bernard & Graefe, 1936.

Military Ethics: Simoneit, scientific head of the High Command's psychological laboratory, modifies the principle that "the end justifies the means" to read: "The socially meaningful, nobly genuine ethical sentiment justifies and sanctions the means." Translated into plain English, Simoneit is trying to say that the Nazi social spirit of comradeship and missionary fervor deserves the use of any means to achieve world power.

42. ——. "Bericht ueber die Taetigkeit der Abteflung fuer Wehrpsychologie," *Jahrbuch der Deutschen Gesellschaft fuer Wehrpolitik und Wehrwissenschaften*, 1936-38, 231-232.

Report on the Activities of the Department of Military Psychology of the German Society of Military Politics and Military Sciences.

43. Spengler, O. *Preussentum und Sozialismus.* Muenchen: Beck, 1920.

Prussianism and Socialism: Spengler, a philosopher turned political prophet, "discovered" during the war years the close identity of Prussianism to Socialism. Prussianism and "genuine Socialism"—not of Marx, but of Friedrich Wilhelm I, which was authoritarian, antidemocratic and antirevolutionary—are consolidated in the old Prussian spirit and are equal to each other because both mean power. This thesis was taken up by the Nazis in what was called "Socialism of action," Socialism meaning comradeship, service, and duty, not class struggle.

44. —. *Untergang des Abendlandes.* (Two volumes.) Muenchen: Beck, 1926.

Decline of the Western World: The familiar Spenglerian pessimism that western culture is dying and the future belongs to a new civilization in the east.

45. —. *Jahre der Entscheidung.* Muenchen: Beck, 1933.

Years of Decision: The aging, gloomy, disappointed Spengler sharply criticizes the application of his theories by the Nazis whom he disparagingly regarded as "boy scouts" cheapening and perverting his ideas on Prussianism. Published in 1933, this was one of the last works of independent thinking to appear in Nazi Germany.

46. Steinmetz, R. *Soziologie des Krieges.* Leipzig, 1929.

Sociology of War: The author, a prominent Dutch sociologist and a genuine opponent of force, argues that war is neither an irrational force nor a psychosis of civilization but must be viewed as a manifestation and cultural motivation of the human species of all races in all periods of man's development. Religion, culture, morality, revolution, and technology have not changed the picture. Neither could a "world state" with its much-vaunted "community of power," since war would be then termed "civil" rather than international.

47. Szczepanskt, M. v. *Politik als Kriegfuehrung*. Berlin: Schlieffen, 1926.
    Politics as a Part of the Conduct of War.

48. Volkmann, E. O. *Marxismus und das deutsche Heer*. Berlin: Mittler, 1925.
    Marxism and the German Army in the World War; Volkmann, a former intelligence officer and a high official of the Reichs Archives, publishes documents from official sources in an attempt to prove that Marxism was a major contribution to the demoralization of Germany's armed forces. While his conclusions are biased, the documents are highly illuminating.

49. Wolff, W. v. *Vom Sinne des Krieges*. Berlin, 1926.
    The Meaning of War.

II. PSYCHOLOGY IN TOTAL WAR
1. Mobilization of German Psychology

50. Anon. "Die behoerdlichen psychotechnischen Einrichtungen in Deutschland,," *Ind. Psychotechn.*, 1930, 339-352.
    Official Psychotechnical Establishments in Germany.

51. Anon. "Laufbahnbestimmungen fuer Wehrmachtspsychologen," *Z. angew. Psychol.*, 1937. 53, 3/4, 261-264.
    Instructions Regulating the Career of Army Psychologists: Official regulations concerning rank and specific duty of army

psychologists, required qualifications, preparatory training, and special psychological tests. An exhaustive translation of important excerpts is included in the Survey under No. 8.

52. Anon. "Psychologie und Offizier," *Militaer-Wochenblatt,* 1935, 46.
   Psychology and Officer: An obviously inspired article in the High Command's official weekly, outlining the specific psychological duties to be assigned to army psychologists on the one side, and field and staff officers on the other.

53. Goldschmidt, R. H. *Kurzer Bericht ueber Eignungspruejungen.* Muenster: Wehrkreiskommando VI, Abt. Ia., 1920.
   A Short Report on Aptitude Testing published by the Central Psychological Testing Station of the Muenster district command.

54. Grunwaldt, H. H. "General von Voss. Zehn Jahre deutscher Wehrmachtpsychologie," *Arch. ges. Psychol.,* 1939, 103, 3, 273-275.
   General von Voss; Ten Years of German Army Psychology: The author, director of the Psychological Testing Station of the 3rd Army Corps of Berlin, commemorates ten years of General Hans von Voss's command of the army's Psychological Laboratory. Contains considerable information on the organization and history of German military psychology.

55. Jaensch, E. R. *Die Lage und die Aufgabe der Psychology.* Leipzig: Barth, 1933.
   The Present Position and Task of Psychology: Jaensch, famed professor of psychology at Marburg University, visualizes himself as the "psychological brain" of the Nazi revolution. In this politically supercharged, highly emotional book, he proclaims "German Psychology" as the molder of a new mankind. To achieve this end, he calls for a general mobilization of psychologists to the service of the Nazi state—to make this age "the Century of German Psychology." Dr. Wladimir Eliasberg writes on Jaensch: "He is a definitely diagnosed paranoiac, with persecution ideas, full to the brim of

resentment, because of his failure to get a professorship in Berlin. At the same time, however, he is one of the cleverest self-propagandists."*

56. —. "Deutsche Wehrmachtspsychologie und deutsche Hochschulpsychologie," *Z. Psychol.*, 1936, 239-248.

German Army Psychology and German Academic Psychology: In a speech delivered at the opening of the palatial building erected to house the High Command's Psychological Laboratory, Jaensch urges academic psychologists to contribute to the research of the army's psychological general staff, and advocates a steady interchange of material between army and academic psychologists.

57. Krueger, F. "Die Lage der Seelenwissenschaft in der deutschen Gegenwart," *Ber. Kongr. dtsch. Ges. Psychol.*, 1934, XIV, 9-36.

The Role of Psychology in Contemporary Germany: The late president of the German Psychological Association, a renegade liberal who hurried to the Nazi flag immediately after the Machtübernahme, outlines the induction of psychologists into the service of the state, Nazi Party, and the German Army. Another bugle call for the general participation of German psychologists in attacking and solving problems raised by the changed political and philosophical scene.

58. Linnebach, K. "Kriegsphilosophie und Wehrpsychologie." In *Die Wehrwissenschaften der Gegenwart*. Berlin: Junker & Duennhaupt, 1934.

War Philosophy and Military Psychology: A short review of selected German literature by an official of the Reichs Archives.

---

* The Editors acknowledge their gratitude to Dr. Eliasberg for this and additional data which have been incorporated in the Bibliography.

59. Piorkovski, C. "Die Entwicklung der Psychotechnik in Deutschland waehrend des Krieges," *Deutsche Politik,* 1918, 3.
Development of Psychotechnics in Germany During the War.

60. Rieffert, J. B. "Psychotechnik im Heere," *Ber. Kongr. dtsch. Ges. Psychol.,* 1921, VII, 79-96.
Psychotechnics in the Army: A very important historical article by Berlin University's professor of psychology who later became the behind-the-scene organizer and chief scientific adviser of Germany's army psychology. The author, in a truly sensation-packed article, describes the test methods used during the last war for the selection of drivers and aviators.

61. Schack. "Psychologie und Offizier," *Militaer-Wochenblatt,* 1935, 15, 628-632.
Psychology and Officer: A polemic on the introduction of psychological research into the army curriculum written by a first lieutenant on the eve of general army conscription in Germany.

62. Seeckt, H. v. "Das Wesentliche." In *Gedanken eines Soldaten.* Berlin: Verlag fuer Kulturpolitik, 1929.
Thoughts of a Soldier: An article in this book entitled *The Essentials* criticizes the sudden flurry of sentiment demanding the independent establishment of psychological services manned by professional "outsiders."

63. Simoneit, M. *Wehrpsychologie.* Berlin: Bernard & Graefe, 1935.
Military Psychology: The basic German textbook of military psychology written by the scientific director of the High Command's Central Psychological Laboratory, a student of Ach of Goettingen. Dr. Simoneit's writings lose much of their appeal through the cumbersome and flowery style of their author. This book, however, is "must-reading" for all the students of German military psychology.

64. —. "Der psychologische Faktor in der wehrwissenschaftlichen Forschung," *Wissen und Wehr,* 1934, 10.

The Psychological Factor in Military Scientific Research: Popular article on the place and role of military psychology within the framework of Germany's immense new military sciences.

65. —. "Wehrpsychologie." In *Handbuch der neuzeitlichen Wehrwissenschaften,* I, 712. Berlin: Gruyter, 1936.

Military Psychology: A handy but fragmentary condensation of the author's exhaustive *Military Psychology,* published in the official *Manual of Modern Military Sciences.* For the busy reader it gives an illuminating insight into the aims, functions and organization of German military psychology. The author, with Kreipe and Zilian, was a pupil of Ach in Goettingen. Nevertheless, at the XVth Psychological Congress, Ach was attacked by Kreipe as well as Simoneit. This, indeed, is a characteristic phenomenon among the younger German psychologists: raised in the awe of their master, they turn against him as soon as opportunity favors such a "revolt."

66. Voss, H. v., and Simoneit, M. (editors). *Soldatentum.* Berlin: Bernard & Graefe, Vol. I, No. 1. Bi-monthly.

Soldierdom: Prior to this war, this was the official periodical of the German High Command's psychological laboratory with articles on military psychology in general, psychological pedagogy and selection in particular. Since early in 1940, the paper has been published by the firm independently, seemingly having no official status any longer. Wartime censorship is extremely strict, and recent articles are, therefore, of gradually diminishing interest. The same goes for the *Militaer-Wochenblatt,* the High Command's semi-official weekly, whose articles are now largely confined to anti-British propaganda material or indulge in mere generalizations.

67. Voss, H. v., and Simoneit, M. "Abhandlungen zur Wehrpsychologie," *Beih. Z. angew. Psychol.,* 1936, 72, iii.

Contributions to Military Psychology: In the foreword, General von Voss presents information about the organization of army psychologists.

2. Psychological Problems of Leadership

68. Ach, N. "Ueber die Determinationspsychologie und ihre Bedeutung fuer das Fuehrerproblem," *Ber. Kongr. dtsch. Ges. Psychol.,* 1933, XIII, 111-112.

Determination-Psychology and Its Significance for the Problem of Leadership: Condensation of a paper read by Professor Ach of Goettingen at the XIIIth Congress of the German Psychological Association.

69. ——. "Zur neueren Willenslehre," *Ber. Kongr. dtsch. Ges. Psychol.,* 1936, XV, 125-155.

Toward a More Modern Study of Will: An extremely interesting report on the revaluation of the will-theory. Ach's approach to the freedom of will replaces Kant's categoric imperative with the tenet: "Always act according to your responsibility." Ach's examples of will-prognostication are especially useful.

70. Altrichter, F. *Der soldatische Fuehrer.* Oldenburg: Stalling, 1938.

The Soldierly Leader: The author is a colonel in the armed forces, now acting as commanding officer of an infantry school in Dresden.

71. Anon. "Fuehrertum. Diskussion." *Ber. Kongr. dtsch. Ges. Psychol.,* 1935, XV, 208-211.

Leadership: A discussion at the XVth Congress of the German Psychological Association with Simoneit in the chair, Jaensch, Schmeing, Pintschovius, and others participating. Principal topic discussed was methods of leadership, and its dependence on time, environment, and specific tasks. Interesting is the rift that developed between the typologists represented by Jaensch and the opposing school of characterologists.

72. Augustin, R. *Der arische Fuehrertypus als Baumeister des Lebens.* Furth: Deutscher Hort, 1939.

The Aryan Leader Type as the Master-Builder of Life: Purports to be a "psychological explanation of the contemporary leader type." In reality it is a pseudo-scientific eulogy of Germanic leadership, interesting as an example of sophistic Nazi reasoning which skillfully conceals utter vulgarism behind a facade of high-sounding scientific terms.

73. Binder, J. "Fuehrerauslese in der Demokratie," *Paedagogisches Magazin.* Heft 1247, 1-67. Langensalza: Beyer, 1929.

Selection of Leaders in Democracy.

74. Dirks, H. Josef Pilsudski. "Ein Beitrag zum Problem des Fuehrertums," *Soldatentum,* 1938, 227-235.

Joseph Pilsudski; A Contribution to the Problem of Leadership: While Pilsudski may have made a considerable contribution to the practice of leadership, his biographer, an army psychologist, fails to make a contribution to its scientific study. Nevertheless, the paper is interesting as an exposé of the Nazi method of analyzing leader-personalities by studying memoirs and biographies.

75. Dohlhoff, G. H. *Handbuch der Gemeinschaftspflege.* Muenchen: Eher, 1938.

Manual of Community-Development: Written in co-operation with the Propaganda Ministry and other Nazi organizations, it contains instructions for subleaders on how to make the best use of their position and how to be "educators as well as leaders."

76. Justrow, K. *Feldherr und Kriegstechnik.* Oldenburg: Stalling, 1935.

Field Marshal and War Techniques: A study of Count Schlieffen's famed plan and lessons derived therefrom for leadership, the establishment of an army, and national defense.

77. Lehmann, R. "Die Herausbildung des Fuehrertums bei primitiven Voelkem," *Ber. Kongr. dtsch. Ges. Psychol.*, 1934, XIV, 148-150.

Development of Leadership in Primitive Society: An interesting and perhaps unwittingly anti-Nazi comparison between leadership in primitive society and in highly developed cultures. The author maintains that in small communities, such as tribes, leaders obtain and preserve their power through outstanding personal qualifications, thus ruling out hereditary leadership. In larger communities, like the modern state, leadership either rests on a psychological interrelationship between leader and followers or becomes an instalment of despotism.

78. Lippert, E. "Zur Psychologie des Fuehrers in der alten und neuen Jugendbewegung," *Zeitschrift fuer paedagogische Psychologie und Jugendkunde,* 1935, 35, 7-8.

Psychology of the Leader in Past and Present Youth Movements: An excellent analysis of youth ideology within youth organizations in the democracies and in the Nazi state.

79. Lufft, H. "Das Ermuedungsproblem beim Feldherrn," *Arch. ges. Psychol.*, 1939, 103, 276-298.

The Problem of Fatigue of the Supreme Commander: The author, an economist and expert on America, makes a cautious excursion into the psychology of the high-placed political and military leader. His considerations, reviewed in the Survey, are seriously accepted by the German psychological laboratory for whom the paper was written.

80. Mueller-Roemer, —. "Der Einfluss der Fuehrerpersoenlichkeiten und ihrer Fuehrungsmittel bei ploetzlich eintretenden Gefahren," *Soldatentum,* 1938, 56-58.

The Influence of Leader Personalities and Their Means of Leadership in Suddenly Encountered Dangers: A major previously attached to the Stettin Army Corps cites three specific examples of leadership in crisis.

81. Nuber, H. "Die psychische Elastizitaet des militaerischen Fuehrers," *Ber. Kongr. dtsch. Ges. Psychol.,* 1934, XIV, 206-207.

Mental Elasticity of the Military Leader: An excellent article on the leader's ability to meet unexpected situations and adapt himself to the rapidly changing methods and requirements of modern warfare.

82. Rendulic, L. "Die Fuehrung und ihre Mittel," *Militaerwissenschaftliche Mitteilungen,* 1937, 12, 963-968.

Leadership and Its Means: An article of generalities written by a major of the defunct Austrian Army who was given a commission by the Germans after the Anschluss.

83. Ritter, R. "Der Anteil des mathematischen Denkens am formalen Denken des militaerischen Fuehrers," *Soldatentum,* 1935, 162-166, 230-233.

The Role of Mathematical Reasoning on the Formal Thinking of the Military Leader.

84. Simoneit, M. "Grundsaetzhches aus der Praxis der Psychologie vom Fuehrertum," *Ber. Kongr. dtsch. Ges. Psychol.,* 1935, XV, 202-205.

Basic Ideas from the Practice of Psychology in Leadership.

85. Vershofen, W. "Fuehrung im Arbeitsleben," *Ber. Kongr. dtsch. Ges. Psychol.,* 1935, XV, 212-216.

Leadership in Industry and Labor: Moral and mental qualities are considered more indispensable for factory management than technical skill. The author deals with his subject from the Nazi leader-principle angle. An extreme interpretation of this principle, as presented in this paper, leads Vershofen to describe the producer as a leader and the consumer as a follower. All conflicts of leadership in industry and labor must be settled by the state.

86. Wetzell, G. "Das Bild des modernen Feldherrn," *Militaer-Wochenblatt,* 1939, 5, 268-271.

The Portrait of the Modern Field Marshal: Wetzell, general of infantry and editor of the High Command's weekly, opposes the general idea of unified political and military leadership in war. In Part III of this series of articles, in which he discusses the problem of the war lord in future wars, the author maintains that, even though the politicians must have military, and the generals must have political, knowledge, they must be responsible only for their specific branch of service with the head of the state retaining final responsibility for both. See also next abstract.

86a. —. "Heer und Kampffuehrung." In *Die Deutsche Wehrmacht.* Berlin: Mittler, 1939.

The Army and Leadership in Battle: The author is emphatic in his contention that the strategical leadership must in all circumstances remain in the hands of the military during the battle. This article has been interpreted as the General Staff's rebuff to Hitler's assumption of complete military and political command. This attitude, purposely put on record, is considered as a convenient way out for the generals if and when operations go astray. Ironically, the generals would be repeating substantially the same accusations they used against the politicians in the last war.

87. Wilhelm, W. "Psychologische Betrachtungen ueber das operative Denken," *Soldatentum,* 1938, 201-209.

Psychological Observations of Operative Thinking.

88. Zilian, E. "Fuehrertum und Kameradschaft," *Soldatentum,* 1934.

Leadership and Comradeship.

89. Zillig, M. "Gemeinschaftsleben, Gruppenbildung, Fuehrertum, und Gefolgschaft in der Schulklasse," *Ind. Psychotechn.,* 1936, 202-212.

Community Life, Group Education, Leadership, and Followers in the Schoolroom: An interesting attempt to use the classroom as a yardstick for determining leadership. Applying the Nazi leader-principle to a typical "grade-school community," the author divides pupils into five types: 1. the "natural leader" influences his classmates by his superiority in creative and organizing ability; 2. The "dominating type" is effective principally through his use of violence; 3. The "despot" operates under the protection of the classroom's highest authority, the teacher; 4. The "stimulating personality" brings new ideas into the classroom; 5. The "organizer" accepts these ideas and translates them into action. The author asserts that children are brought up intensely conscious of "leader" and "follower" as a result of class lessons, play, and order of rank. Various types are those who show anxiety when given responsibility, those who adhere to ideals of the leader, those who revolt mentally and physically against leaders, those who have no faith in their own ability, and those who let others do their work. Rivalry results in the classroom when several leader-personalities are present. This either leads to open conflict or to a compromise among the leaders.

3. Selection and Testing of Personnel
a) Principles and Techniques of Selection

90. Ammon, O. *Die natuerliche Auslese beim Menschen.* Jena: Fischer, 1893.

The Natural Selection of Men: Largely outdated but interesting historically. Written by a medical officer attached to the Ducal Army of Baden, the book is among the first published in Germany advocating selection on the basis of anthropological examination of conscripts.

91. Anon. "Charakterologische Eignungspruefungen bei der Wehr-macht," *Soldatentum,* 1936, 184-187.

Characterological Aptitude Tests in the Army: Excerpts from the official regulations describing characterological aptitude tests in general terms and the actual procedures followed.

92. Becker, F. "Die Intelligenzpruefung unter voelkischem und typologischem Gesichtspunkt. Ein Beitrag zum Problem der Aus-lese," *Z. angew. Psychol.,* 1938, 55, 1, 15-111.

Intelligence Testing from the Racial and Typological Point of View: A disciple of Jaensch criticizes intelligence test meth-ods devised by American and German-Jewish psychologists. The American system is held to be too rigid and standardized, while pre-Hitler German psychologists overestimated the value of "pure intellect" The author denies the existence of a homogeneous form of intelligence and maintains that intelligence is dependent on "types" and racial character. In the strident language of a pam-phleteer, he demands the adaptation of typology and racism to intelligence testing.

93. Borstell, W. v. "Psychologie und Fuehrerauslese," *Jahrbuch des deutschen Heeres,* 1936, 43-48.

Psychology and Selection of Leaders: Popular article in the German Army Yearbook by an army major attached to a psycho-logical testing station. Written to acquaint rank-and-file soldiers with the psychological services in the armed forces.

94. Brecht, —. "Was verstehen wir Soldaten unter Charakter und warum wiegen im Kriege die Eigenschaften des Charakters schwer-er als die des Verstandes," *Soldatentum,* 1939, 198-204; 260-267.

What We Soldiers Understand by Character and Why Charac-ter Is More Important in War Than Intelligence: A captain teach-ing at the Berlin War Academy cites historical examples to prove his case.

95. Brosius, O. "Methode und Auswertung kurzer zum Zwecke des Menschenerkennens durchgefuehrte Aussprachen," *Soldatentum*, 1937, 130-134.

Methods and Evaluation of Brief Interviews Conducted for the Purpose of Judging People: An army psychologist, attached to the Berlin testing station, describes the technique of interviewing officer-candidates. Usually conducted at the end of the army characterological test, interviews are considered important for determining the whole personality.

96. Dach, J. S. "Die wesentlichen Aeusserungen der Persoenlichkeit im Sprechen und in der Sprache," *Soldatentum*, 1937, 124-129.

Essentials of Personality as Expressed in Voice and Speech: Dr. Dach, an army psychologist at the Wiesbaden testing station, outlines the ways of discovering personality traits by the analysis of voice and speech. Three examples are given of actual tests.

97. Eckstein, L. *Psychologie des ersten Eindrucks.* Leipzig: Barth, 1937.

Psychology of the First Impression: "Is the first impression of a person a valid key to his character?" Eckstein, an army psychologist now in Hannover, believes the first impression is a valuable short cut to personality analysis if the interviewer is a skilled psychologist. The book contains many examples to validate its author's contention. A comparison of the conclusions reached by various interviewers of the same person showed 66 percent agreement in the analysis based on first impression. Later, an exhaustive examination of the interviewees showed that 70 percent of them displayed traits identical to the results of the first impression.

98. —. "Der Begriff des Stiles als charakterologische Kategorie," *Beih. Z. angew. Psychol.*, 1938, 79, 72-91.

Writing Style as a Characterological Category: A lecture delivered to army psychologists at the 1938 post-graduate course of the High Command's Central Psychological Laboratory.

99. Engel, W. "Berechtigung der charakterpsychologischen Eignungspruefungen," *Ind. Psychotech.,* 1938, 4-6, 180-188.

Justification of Characterological Aptitude Tests: A cautious article by a Viennese psychologist in which characterological aptitude tests are seen to have certain limits, chiefly because they depend so heavily on the tester's own personality. Predictions based on such tests cannot be considered completely trustworthy. To increase the trustworthiness of these tests, the tester must be trained in the vocation he is testing, and must beware of false objectivity, strained interpretation of symptoms, standardization of analysis, obscure descriptions, too rapid judgment and overdependence on typology. Although extremely careful, the author has managed to put over a sharply critical appraisal of present German test methods.

100. Fischer, G. H. *Ausdruck und Persoenlichkeit.* Leipzig: Barth, 1934.

Expression and Personality: An army psychologist working in the Muenster testing station.

101. —. Die Beziehungen zwischen der Rassenforschung und der Typenlehre von E. R. Jaensch zugleich im Hinblick auf die Charakterkunde," *Soldatentum,* 1938, 21-27.

Relations Between Race Research and Jaensch's Typology with Reference to Characterology: The article, in line with the "united front" policy of Nazi psychology, investigates biological and typological group formations, racial influence on physical structure and psychological types, and how far these theories can fit into characterology.

102. Fischer, G. H. and Ohnesorge, K. "Ueber den Einfluss koerperlicher Veranlagungen auf das Persoenlichkeitsbild," *Beih. Z. angew. Psychol.,* 1938, 79, 51-72.

Influence of Physical Disposition on Personality.

103. Guenther, H. R. G. "Gesichtspunkte kurzer Persoenlichkeits-beschreibungen fuer militaerische Zwecke," *Soldatentum,* 1937, 134-138.

Principles of Brief Personality-Descriptions for Military Purposes.

104. Hansen, —. "Betrachtungen ueber Fuehrerauslese," *Soldatentum,* 1936, 285-289.

Observations on the Selection of Leaders: Pertinent observations of a retired admiral. Foreseeing a war in the near future, Hansen pins his hopes for victory on the selection of Germany's mental elite for leadership in high and low places, particularly since young men whose leader-capacities have not yet reached full maturity will be given responsibility and authority. Hansen believes the selection of Germany's leadership is the primary task of rearmament.

105. Hartnacke, —. "Laesst sich die Kriegsbewaehrung der Berufs-gruppen und Staende statistisch erfassen." *Soldatentum,* 1938, 50-55.

Can the Fitness for War of Occupational Groups and Social Classes Be Statistically Determined: An army psychologist's comments on Gauer's *Peasantry, Bourgeoisie and Working Classes.* Cf. Psychological Aspects of Military Life.

106. Hesse, K. "Die Heereseignungspruefungen," *Ind. Psychotechn.,* 1930, 7, 372-378.

Aptitude Testing in the Army: An excellent summary of the reasons why psychological tests were introduced into the army, and a still valid description of the army test methods.

107. Klages, L. Die Grundlagen der Charakterkunde. Leipzig: Barth, 1926.

Principles of Characterology: German military psychology has been tremendously influenced by this basic and well-known work.

108. Kreipe, K. "Der erste Eindruck und die wirkliche Persoen-lichkeit bei neu eintretenden Rekruten," *Soldatentum,* 1937, 18-23; 72-76.

The First Impression and the Genuine Personality of New Con-scripts: An excellent guide on how to judge and handle incoming recruits in reception and training centers. Kreipe is a prolific army psychologist who is held in high repute by the psychological gen-eral staff. Also see No. 65.

109. —. "Zur Methodik der Exploration," *Beih. Z. angew. Psy-chol.,* 1936, 72, 103-114.

Methods of Exploration.

110. —. "Stellungnahme zu einzelnen Willenstheorien von der wehrmachtpsychologischen Praxis aus," *Ber. Kongr. dtsch. Ges. Psy-chol.,* 1936, XV, 158.

Critique of Individual Will Theories from the Point of View of Military-Psychological Practice: The complete paper was pub-lished by Beyer of Langensalza.

111. —. "Die funktionelle und strukturelle Bedingtheit des Charakters," *Ber. Kongr. dtsch. Ges. Psychol.,* 1938, 16, 60-66.

Functional and Structural Conditions of Character.

112. Kuenkele, Ph. "Eignungsauslese unter psychologischen Ge-sichtspunkten," *Soldatentum,* 1936, 289-297.

Psychological Principles of Aptitude Testing: An article outlin-ing the methods used by army psychologists in conducting charac-terological aptitude tests. Especially interesting are the checks and balances to control and eradicate error, chance, and opinionated judgment in making out test reports.

113. Lersch, P. *Gesicht und Seele. Grundlinien einer mimischen Diagnostik.* Dresden, Reinhardt, 1932.

Face and Mind: A well-known volume on which German army psychologists base their analyses of mimetic expression.

114. Lucke, —. "Koerperbau und Charakter," *Soldatentum*, 1937, 203-208.

Physique and Character: The director of the Dresden psychological testing station discusses the relationship of bodily types and character.

115. Marx, W. "Die Auswahl der Fuehrer im Heere," *Militaer-Wochenblatt*, 1939, 49, 3306-3310.

Selection of Leaders in the Army: A retired general and close friend of the late President Hindenburg, Marx approaches the problem of selection from a practical military point of view. He ignores the selection of leaders on psychological principles and recommends that leaders be chosen by their performance during maneuvers, superior officers being the best judge of the army's needs.

116. Masuhr, H. "Zur Untersuchung militaerischer Menschenauslese durch soziologische Statistiken," *Soldatentum*, 1934, 145.

Military Selection by Use of Sociological Statistics: A staff member of the Central Psychological Laboratory, Masuhr presents an analysis of environmental influence on character as revealed by statistical data. This includes the investigation of those cultural and population divisions in a given regiment which he considers particularly good and bad. The statistical break-up of the regiment's regional, religious, occupational, urban or rural background, provide indices of army adaptability.

117. —. "Ueber den Wert psychologisch-soziologischer Statistiken fuer die Anlageforschung," *Z. Psychol.*, 1938, 143, 14-18.

The Value of Psycho-Sociological Statistics for the Study of Attitudes.

118. Nubeh, H. "Berufswahl und Berufsethos," *Ber. Kongr. dtsch. Ges. Psychol.*, 1935, XV, 157-158.

Choice and Ethics of Profession: Psychological tests must take into consideration the person's general ethical attitude toward the army as a profession. The analysis of the temperament is particularly important since it conditions the ethical attitude.

119. Renthe-Fink, L. v. "Gedanken ueber die Rolle der Graphologie in der Wehrmachtpsychologie," *Soldatentum*, 1937, 77-87.

The Role of Graphology in Army Psychology: The army's foremost authority on graphology, using methods developed by Klages, believes that graphology provides valuable additional information on character and temperament. To prove his own usefulness and worth, Renthe-Fink asserts that 74 percent of the graphological examinations were in complete agreement, and 95 percent were in partial agreement with the results of the entire oral and written examinations.

120. —. "Die Bedeutung der Graphologie fuer die psychologische Entwicklungsaussage," *Z. f. Menschenkunde*, 1939, 15, 2, 76-81.

The Significance of Graphology in Assessing Psychological Development.

121. —. "Die Bedeutung der Graphologie fuer die psychologische Begutachtung Jugendlicher," *Soldatentum*, 1939, 97-102.

The Significance of Graphology in the Psychological Examination of Youth.

122. Rieffert, J. B. "Methoden und Grundbegriffe der Charakterologie," *Ber. Kongr. dtsch. Ges. Psychol.*, 1933, 13, 98-108.

Methods and Principles of Characterology.

123. Bobertag, O. *Schuelerauslese. Als Manuskript gedruckt*. Berlin, 1934.

Selection of Students. (The Editors apologize for the wrong alphabetical listing of this item.)

124. Roth, H. "Zur Formulierung psychologischer Gutachten bei wehrpsychologischen Eignungsuntersuchungen," *Soldatentum,* 1938, 175-185.

The Composition of Psychological Reports of Army Aptitude Tests: A critical article discussing techniques of making out reports of psychological army tests.

125. Ruehl, H. "Kennzeichen-Auslese der Fuehrerpersoenlichkeit," *Ind. Psychotechn.,* 1937, 1, 11-19.

Indices of Leader-Personalities: An article verifying the findings of Professor O'Connor of the Human Engineering Laboratory, Stevens Institute of Technology, Hoboken, N. J. Ruehl believes that O'Connor's "executive" prototype could be well adapted to the needs of Germany's military, political and industrial organization.

126. —. "Das Profilbild der Persoenlichkeit und seine Messung," *Ind. Psychotechn.,* 1937, 7-8, 240-245.

Personality Profiles and How to Measure Them: The article is based on a lecture by Professor E. M. Ligon of Union College, Schenectady, N. Y.

127. Schaenzle, J. *Der mimische Ausdruck des Denkens.* Berlin: Bernard & Graefe, 1939.

Mimetic Expressions of Thinking.

128. —. "Mimische Aeusserungen als Hilfsmittel der Menschenkenntnis," *Soldatentum,* 1937, 249-255.

Mimetic Expressions as a Means of Judging People: A rather superficial presentation of expressive movements and their analysis for determining the personality of officer-candidates.

129. Schimrick, D. "Die psychologische Beurteilung von Jugendlichen in Hinsicht auf die militaerische Erziehung," *Soldatentum,* 1934, 137.

Psychological Appraisal of Youth with Reference to Military Education.

130. —. "Die psychologische Beurteilung Dienstpflichtiger bei Musterung und Aushebung," *Soldatentum,* 1939, 24-27
Psychological Appraisal of Conscripts at Their Medical Examination and Induction: A highly suggestive article describing the possibility of psychological preselection during the limited time when conscripts are physically examined and inducted.

131. Schleip, W. "Mitarbeit der Hitler-Jugend am Arbeitseinsatz der Jugendlichen," *Ind. Psychotechn.,* 1939, 1-3, 9-41.
Co-operation of the Hitler Youth in the Labor Mobilization of Youth.

132. Simoneit, M. "Zur charakterologischen Auswertung von Reaktionspruefungen," *Arch. ges. psychol.,* 1932, 83, 357-384.
Characterological Evaluation of Reaction Tests.

133. —. "Ueber Menschenauslese-Methoden," *Soldatentum,* 1934, 55-57.
Methods of Selecting Men: Leaders in Germany today must be "invented" and not "discovered," since "natural" selection, although best, takes too long for present needs. Thus the role of psychology in the Third Reich is viewed as the acceleration of the leader-selection process.

134. —. "Moeglichkeiten und Grenzen der Erfassung der Willensveranlagung bei wehrpsychologischen Eignungsuntersuchungen," *Soldatentum,* 1935, 254-260.
Possibilities and Limits of Analyzing Will-Capacity in Army Psychological Aptitude Tests.

135. —. "Zur Willensuntersuchung in wehrmachtpsychologischen Eignungspruefungen," *Ber. Kongr. dtsch. Ges Psychol.,* 1935, XV, 157.

The Examination of Will in Army Psychological Aptitude Tests.

136. —. *Wehrpsychologische Willenuntersuchungen*. Langensalza: Beyer, 1937.
Examination of Will in Military Psychology.

137. —. "Das diagnostische Problem in der praktischen Psychologie," *Z. Psychol.*, 1938, 143, 1-3.
The Problem of Diagnosis in Practical Psychology.

138. Strehle, H. "Die unwillkuerlichen menschlichen Ausdruckserscheinungen als Kunden der Seele," *Soldatentum*, 1937, 119-124.
Involuntary Human Expression as a Reflection of the Mind.

139. —. *Die Analyse des Gebarens*. Berlin: Bernard & Graefe, 1938.
Analysis of Behavior.

140. Valentiner, Th. "Ueber die Begutachtung des Charakters fuer die Auslese. Mitteilungen aus der praktisch-psychologischen Arbeit des Instituts fuer Jugendkunde," *Ind. Psychotechn.*, 1935, 10, 308-315.
Appraisal of Character for the Purpose of Selection: A report on the practical psychological work of the Bremen Institute of Youth Study.

141. Volkenborn, —. "Die Sprechweise im Rahmen einer Persoenlichkeitsanalyse," *Soldatentum*, 1936, 187-189.
The Role of Speech in Personality Analysis: The author, a psychologist attached to the Wilhelmshaven naval testing station, analyzes personality by studying modulation, volume, articulation, timbre, tempo, and rhythm of speech.

142. Walther, R. H. "Die Praxis der Formulierung charakterologischer Befunde," *Beih. Z. angew. Psychol.*, 1936, 72, 115-139.

The Formulation of Characterological Reports.

143. Wohlfahrt, E. "Die Interessenforschung als Hilfsmittel der Persoenlichkeitsdiagnose," *Beih. Z. angew. Psychol.*, 1938, 79, 118-131.

The Study of Interest as an Aid to Diagnosing Personality: A lecture at the 1938 post-graduate course of the High Command's Central Psychological Laboratory. Also see "Gruppenstatistische Ergebnisse zur Frage: Wesenart und Interessenrichtung," by the same author in *Z. angew. Psychol.*, 1938, 55, 124-153. The writer polemizes with the interest test developed by E. K. Strong and reveals that an altered form of his questionnaire was used in the German Army.

144. Zeise, L. "Zur praktischen Bedeutung der Sprachanalyse," *Ber. Kongr. dtsch. Ges. Psychol.*, 1934, XIV, 293-294.

Practical Importance of Speech Analysis.

145. —. "Wesen und Uebung des bildhaften Erkennens," *Beih. Z. angew. Psychol.*, 1936, 72, 89-102.

Nature and Practice of Imagination: The connection between imagination and thinking is discussed along lines developed by Klages.

146. Zielasko, G. "Psychologische Auswahlmethoden in den Heeren fremder Laender," *Soldatentum*, 1938, 74-80.

Psychological Methods of Selection in Foreign Armies.

147. Zilian, E. "Zur Pruefung der Intelligenz innerhalb einer militaerischen Menschenauslese," *Ber. Kongr. dtsch. Ges. Psychol.*, 1934, XIV, 287-291.

Intelligence Testing in Military Selection: To obtain qualitative analysis of a candidate's intelligence in contrast to quantitative results. See No. 65.

148. Zilian, E. "Gesichtspunkte der Rassenseelenforschung im Bereich der Wehrmachtpsychologie," *Beih. Z. angew. Psychol.*, 1936, 72, 86-89.

The Study of Race Psychology in the Sphere of Military Psychology: This article marks the somewhat cautious entry of Nazi ideology into German military psychology.

149. —. "Rasse und seelenkundliche Persoenlichkeitsauslese in der Wehrmacht," *Rasse*, 1938, 5, 321-333.

Race and the Psychological Selection of Personality in the Army: It must be said that Zilian, an army psychologist stationed in Berlin, enjoys a reputation of obscurity even among German military psychologists, but obscurity is expedient in this article.

b) Selection of Officers

150. Baeyer, W. v. "Kinder- und jugendpsychiatrische Gesichtspunkte in der Aussprache mit Offizierbewerbern," *Z. angew. Psychol.*, 1938, 55, 2-4, 238-256.

Interviews with Officer-Applicants from the Point of View of Child and Youth Psychiatry.

151. Keilhacker, M. "Auffallende anthropologische Abweichungen vom normalen Stammestypus der eingesessenen Bevoelkerung ihrer Herkunftbezirkes bei Offizierlaufbahnbewerbern," *Soldatentum*, 1938, 36-40.

Unusual Anthropological Deviations Among Officer-Applicants from the Normal Type of the Population Native to Certain Regions.

152. Masuhr, H. "Zur Offizieranwaerter-Bewaehrungskontrolle," *Beih. Z. angew. Psychol.*, 1936, 72, 139.

Validation of Tests Given to Officer-Candidates. Contains only hints but no actual validations.

153. —. *Psychologische Gesichtspunkte fuer die Beurteilung von Offiziersanwaertern.* Berlin: Bernard & Graefe, 1937.

Principles of a Psychological Appraisal of Officer-Candidates: The author, an army psychologist, intended this book to be a basis for the co-operation of commanding officer and army psychologist in the selection of future officers.

154. Nuber, H. *Die Wahl des Offizierberufes.* Berlin: Bernard & Graefe, 1935.

The Choice of the Officer Profession: Nuber, a colonel now stationed in Vienna, finds that the motives leading young men to seek commissions in the army are of an economic, social or purely personal nature. Categorizing officers according to their ethical and characterological dispositions proves extremely useful for finding officers suited to the special needs of a specific war situation. For instance, officers with aggressive temperaments are needed in the attack, while sober-headed officers are better suited to defense. If not properly chosen for the task which best suits their characters, the consequences may be serious in both a personal and military sense.

155. Schoene, G. "Befoerderung und Vorgesetztenauslese," *Ind. Psychotechn.*, 1935, 6, 175-182.

Promotion and Selection of Superiors.

156. Simoneit, M. "Psychologische Offiziersanwaerter-Eignungspruefung," *Umschau,* 1937, 41, 13.

Psychological Aptitude Testing for Officer-Candidates: An article written in one of Germany's best popular-scientific magazines describes the system of selecting officers for the army.

157. —. *Leitgedanken ueber die psychologische Untersuchung des Offiziernachwuchses in der Wehrmacht.* Berlin: Bernard & Graefe, 1938.

GERMAN PSYCHOLOGICAL WARFARE

The Psychological Examination of the New Generation of Officers in the Armed Forces: The basic work on principles and techniques of selecting officers for army, navy and air force.

c) Selection of Noncommissioned Officers

158. Ruppert, H. "Gesichtspunkte fuer die Auslese von Unteroffizieren," *Soldatentum,* 1936, 239-244.

Principles of Selecting Noncommissioned Officers: The author, an army psychologist of the Stuttgart-Cannstatt testing station, describes the particular requirements of the "subleader situation."

d) Selection of Specialists

159. Benary, W. "Untersuchungen ueber die psychische Eignung zum Flugdienst," *Schriften zur Psychologie der Berufseignung und des Wirtschaftslebens,* Heft 8. Leipzig: Barth, 1920.

Psychological Aptitude for Aviation: The author belongs to the pre-Hitler school of German psychologists who, rather belatedly, became interested in specific problems of military psychology. Here, in co-operation with Kronfeld, E. Stern and Selz, he describes a number of performance tests, some of which are still used by the new psychologists of the German air force. The investigations of Otto Kronfeld and Otto Selz, carried out along similar lines and published at the same time, must also be mentioned. Also Otto Lipmann's "Eignungspruefungen fuer Funker" in *Handbuch der biologischen Arbeitsmethoden* (edited by Abderhalden), 4, Cl, 7, 1928; Otto Klemm's "Eignungspruefungen an messtechnischem Personal," *ibid.* As to the unemployment and the psychology of soldiers inducted into the army after a long period of idleness, see "Die Arbeitslosen" by Marienthal, and Eliasberg's "Richtungen und Entwicklungstendenzen" in der Arbeitswissenschaft, *Archiv fuer Sozialwissenschaft und Sozialpolitik,* 56, 3.

160. —. "Eignungspruefungen fuer Fliegerbeobachter," *Schriften zur Psychologie der Berufseignung und des Wirtschaftslebens*, Heft 12. Leipzig: Barth, 1921.

Aptitude Tests for Reconnaissance Pilots: Contains purely functional tests, since the book was written in a period when no emphasis was placed on the characterological approach to aptitude testing.

161. Dietsch, W. "Ueber Funkveranlagung," *Beih. Z. angew. Psychol.*, 1936, 72, 140-148.

Qualifications of Radio Operators: An army psychologist at the Berlin testing station offers a useful insight into the principles which regulate the selection of naval, aerial and signal-corps radio operators.

162. Donat, A. "Das Meldepersonal der Flak-Artillerie und seine psychotechnischen Auswahlmethoden," *Ind. Psychotechn.*, 1936, 259-274.

Personnel of the AA-Artillery and Methods of Selection. This is the German translation of the following French article on methods used in the French army: "Selection des guetteurs de D. C. A.," *Rev. Artill.*, 1936, 117, 448-473.

163. Flik, G. "Der Einfluss der verschiedenen Tiefensehfaktoren auf das Entfernungsmessen." *Soldatentum*, 1939, 157-161; 211-220.

The Influence of Various Factors of Visual Perception of Depth on Range-Finding.

164. Goessinger, K. "Versuche ueber Dechiffrieren," *Z. angew. Psychol.*, 1936, 1-2, 71-111.

Experiments in Decoding.

165. Kreipe, K. "Ueber Funkveranlagung," *Beih. Z. angew. Psychol.*, 1936, 72, 148-153.

Qualifications of Radio Operators: A supplement to the paper read by Dr. Dietsch at a post-graduate course of the Central Psychological Laboratory.

166. Lipmann, O. "Die psychische Eignung der Funktelegraphisten," *Schriften zur Psychologie der Berufseignung und des Wirtschaftslebens.* Heft 9. Leipzig: Barth, 1921.

Psychological Qualifications of Radio Operators: Dr. Lipmann is another member of the pre-Hitler school of psychologists whose methods are still in use although their author's names are no longer mentioned in connection with them.

167. Lubbich, W. "Die wesentlichen psychologischen Gesichtspunkte der Spezialistenauslese," *Soldatentum,* 1937, 138-142.

The Main Principles of Selecting Specialists: The author is an army psychologist in Berlin.

168. Masuhr, H. "Zur Frage der regionalen oder zentralen Auslese fuer den Spezialistendienst in der Wehrmacht," *Soldatentum,* 1936, 63-69.

The Question of Regional or Central Selection of Specialists in the Armed Forces.

169. Metz, P. "Funktionelle und charakterologische Fragen der Fliegereignung," *Beih. Z. angew. Psychol.,* 1936, 72, 153-172.

Functional and Characterological Problems of the Qualifications of Aviators: The author is director of the German air force's Berlin testing station.

170. Mierke, K. "Versageranalyse bei Funkern," *Arch. ges. Psychol.,* 1937, 98, 1-2, 297-310.

Analysis of Failures of Radio Operators: The author is a naval psychologist stationed in Kiel. (See Appendix I.)

171. —. "Ueber die praktische Veranlagung," *Z. angew. Psychol.,* 1938, 55, 154-192.

The Practical Disposition.

172. Moede, W. "Kraftfahrer. Eignungspruefungen beim deutschen Heer," *Ind. Psychotechn.,* 1926, 3, 23-28.

Automobile Drivers; Aptitude Tests in the German Army: The author describes the methods used in the German army in 1917-18, which are still in use.

173. Mueller, O. "Ueber stammespsychologische und geophysische Einfluesse auf die Eignung zum Entfernungsmesser," *Soldatentum,* 1937, 87-89.

Psychological, Racial and Geophysical Influences on the Qualifications for Range-Finding: The author, a naval psychologist stationed in Wilhelmshaven, lists a series of statistical tables which have no particular interest outside of Germany.

174. Nass, G. "Regionale Begabungsunterschiede bei Entfernungsmesserpruefungen," *Soldatentum,* 1936, 168-172.

Regional Variations of Ability in Tests for Range-Finders: In addition to regional influences, the author, a naval psychologist in Kiel, describes educational and professional differences.

175. —. Persoenlichkeit des Kampfwagenfuehrers," *Beih. Z. angew. Psychol.,* 1938, 79.

The Personality of the Tank Driver: This is the best available characterological paper on the requirements of German tank drivers.

176. Neumann, E. "Psychotechnische Eignungspruefung und Anlemung im Flugmotorenbau," *Ind. Psychotechn.,* 1938, 4-6, 111-162.

Psychotechnical Aptitude Testing and Training for the Building of Airplane Engines: This article is listed here because armament workers are considered "military specialists" in Germany, and because Neumann's paper deserves mention for its excellent examples and test methods.

177. Schmidt, H. "Gesamtpersoenlichkeitsanalyse des Hoehen-fliegers nach Leistung und Verhalten," Ind. Psychotechn., 1938, 7-8, 212-238.

Analysis of the Whole Personality of High-Altitude Flyers on the Basis of Performance and Behavior: A comprehensive article describing techniques of testing the whole personality of high-altitude flyers and telling how such tests are validated. The author describes an interesting flight with one of the testees and the tests conducted in the stratosphere. A partial description of the methods are included in this survey but the whole article deserves close attention.

178. Schmidt, O. "Auswahl und Anlernung von Erwerbslosen fuer die Luftfahrt-Ruestungsindustrie," *Ind. Psychotechn.,* 1939, 1-3, 44-81.

Selection and Training of Unemployed for the Aircraft Industry: Lack of skilled labor in metal industries resulted in the training of unemployed for this branch of German armament production. The author outlines actual tests used for the selection of the best human material among unemployed and disabled ex-servicemen.

4. PSYCHOLOGY OF MILITARY LIFE
a) Psychology of Military Training and Indoctrination

179. Altrichter, F. *Das Wesen der soldatischen Erziehung.* Oldenburg: Stalling, 1935.

The Nature of Soldierly Education.

180. Anon. *Richtlinien fuer die Ausbildung im Heere.* Teil II: "Leitfaden fuer Erziehung und Unterricht." Berlin: Reichswehrministerium, 1931.

Directions for Training in the Army: Part Two of this official manual of the German War Ministry is intended as a guide to the education and teaching of soldiers in peace and for war. It describes the psychological program of the pre-Hitler army as the inculcation of professional pride and "honor, trust, loyalty, obedience, and courage as a national way of life."

181. Bonin, R. v. "Wehrvorbereitung." In *Handbuch der neuzeitlichen Wehrwissenschaften,* Vol. I, 730-732. Berlin: Gruyter, 1936.

Military Preparation: The author is a naval officer attached to the intelligence staff of the German Admiralty.

182. Braun, —. "Kann man Helden erziehen?" *Militaer-Wochenblatt,* 1938, 23, 1491.

Can Heroes Be Trained? A lieutenant colonel of the army answers the question in the negative and says that soldiers must be imbued with the more apparent qualities of heroism—duty, readiness to sacrifice, determination.

183. Dirks, —. "Psychologische Faktoren der soldatischen Erziehung," *Soldatentum,* 1937, 10-18.

Psychological Factors of Military Education: An army psychologist examines the tensions inherent in the transition from civilian education to army education. The army conscript is consciously stripped of his individualism and personal values; military education, therefore, must develop in the conscript an understanding of his place in the people's army and win him over gradually to wholehearted enthusiasm.

184. Eickemeyer, —. "Der Wert der Betaetigung des Offiziersanwaerters als HJ-Unterfuehrer," *Militaer-Wochenblatt,* 1939, 40, 2694.

The Value of Subleaders in the Hitler Youth as Officer-Candidates: Hitler Youth leaders are considered good officer material, since their previous training has already prepared them for "army requirements."

185. Fecht, O. *Wehrkundliche Stoffe fuer den deutschen Geschichtsunterricht.* Frankfurt a.M.: Diesterweg, 1935.

Military Material for the Teaching of German History: A guide for teachers on how to handle military events and personalities in the teaching of history.

186. Franke, H. "Wehrerziehung." In *Handbuch der neuzeitlichen Wehrwissenschaften,* Vol. I, 671-672. Berlin: Gruyter, 1936.

Military Indoctrination: The author is a retired general, one of the army's foremost theorists and editor of the official Handbook of Modern Military Sciences.

187. Groetenherdt, —. "Wie denkt der gesunde, natuerliche, einfache Mann?" *Soldatentum,* 1937, 209-212.

How Does the Healthy, Natural, Simple Man Think? Largely psychological "fiction."

188. Grunwaldt, H. H. "Psychologisch-paedagogische Probleme in den Heeresdienstvorschriften," *Beih. Z. angew. Psychol.,* 1936, 72, 173-196.

Psycho-Pedagogic Problems in Army Service Regulations: Dr. Grunwaldt is deputy director of the Psychological Laboratory and chief psychologist of the Berlin testing station.

189. Hansen, W. "Zur Frage einer paedagogisch-psychologischen Schulung des Unteroffizierkorps," *Soldatentum,* 1936, 233-239.

The Problem of the Pedagogical and Psychological Education of Noncommissioned Officers: The author is an army psychologist assigned to the Muenster testing station.

190. —. "Die Stellung der Psychologie in der Lehre von der militaerischen Erziehung," *Beih. Z. angew. Psychol.,* 1938, 79, 208-219.

The Role of Psychology in the Science of Military Education: Aside from the selection of personnel, the psychologist can make important contributions to military indoctrination and education.

Although the ideological basis of the army and state is leveled to a specific doctrine, various branches of the armed services require different approaches of indoctrination. A combat pilot must be conditioned psychologically to aggressive action, while listening posts and radio operators must be educated to calm, deliberate thinking. The psychologist has a particularly important role in advising the officer how to handle "problem soldiers."

191. Heeren, ——. "Erziehung des Soldaten zu Volkstum und Heimat," *Militaer-Wochenblatt*, 1938, 34, 2162-2164.
    Indoctrination of the Soldier in Folkdom and Fatherland.

192. Hesse, K. *Wandlung des Soldaten*. Berlin: Mittler, 1930.
    Transformation of the Soldier: Hesse considers the officer a pedagogue as well as a leader. His relation with his subordinates should be that of a teacher to his students. He must set himself up as a model soldier and awaken military virtues, spirit of comradeship, and a consciousness of "military socialism" in his charges. The training of the professional "leader-soldier" should include motor mechanics, electricity, photography, architecture, gliding, stenography, military geography, a knowledge of foreign languages (French, English, Polish, and Russian), theatrical arts, and singing.

193. ——. "Militaerisches Erziehungs- und Bildungswesen in Deutschland." In *Die deutsche Wehrmacht*. Berlin: Mittler, 1939.
    The System of Military Education in Germany: The period of military training should be the crowning point in the education of German youth. The article describes special military schools for the formation of a military and political elite.

194. ——. "Der Weg zum Offizier," *Jahrbuch des deutschen Heeres*, 1938, 37-48. Leipzig: Breitkopf & Haertel, 1939.
    The Path Toward Becoming an Officer: An important blueprint of the educational phases of the officer. (Fully dealt with in the Survey.)

GERMAN PSYCHOLOGICAL WARFARE

195. Hoelter, —. "Die Wehrerziehung der deutschen Jugend,"
Militaerwissenschaftliche Rundschau, 1936, 4, 463-472.

Military Education of German Youth: An army captain demands that the state must fully indoctrinate and prepare the youth
of Germany for military needs and ultimate war. One of the most
important articles, published in the General Staffs monthly, form-
ing the basis of pedagogical co-operation of state and army.

196. Kauffmann, —. Der Offizier der Wehrmacht und die Aus-
gestaltung seiner eigenen Persoenlichkeit," *Soldatentum,* 1934, 95.

The Army Officer and the Formation of His Personality.

197. Kayser, —. "Truppe und weltanschauliche Schulung," *Jahrbuch des deutschen Heeres,* 1936, 162-164.

The Ideological Schooling of the Troops.

198. Krogh, O. "Erziehung im Heere. Ein Beitrag zur Nationalerziehung der Erwachsenen," *Paedagogisches Magazin,* No. 1091.
Langensalza: Beyer, 1920.

Education in the Army: A contribution to adult education on
a nationalistic basis.

199. —. "Paedagogische Psychologie im Dienste voelkischer Erziehung," *Z. f. Paedag. Psychol. und Jugendkunde,* 1937, 38, 1-13.

Pedagogical Psychology in the Service of Racial Education:
Another turncoat liberal who joined the Nazis while the joining
was good and then proceeded to outdo them in zeal and industry.

200. Kuhl, H. v. *Friedenserziehung und Kriegserfahrung.* Berlin:
Reichswehrministerium, 1923.

Peacetime Education and Wartime Experience: This book, an
official publication of the War Ministry, has more than historical
value. It contains an outline of those educational principles which
the pre-Hitler Reichswehr introduced to preserve a "soldierly spirit"
for the second World War.

201. Lucke, V. "Probleme der soldatischen Erziehung," *Soldatentum,* 1934, 41.

Problems of Military Education.

202. —. "Zur Psychologie der militaerischen Erziehung, *Ber. Kongr. dtsch. Ges. Psychol.,* 1934, XIV, 285-286.

Psychology of Military Indoctrination: The ultimate aim of military indoctrination must be "the will and determination to fight to the last." Lucke's slogan for the German soldier: "While you live, you should further our cause. When you die, your death should be honorable so that you will continue to live in our spirit."

203. Muehle, O. "Die wehrgeistige Arbeit der hoeheren Schulen," *Soldatentum,* 1939, 79-91.

Inculcation of Military Spirit in Secondary Schools: The author is the principal of a Dresden Gymnasium.

204. Schmidt-Logan, —. "Wehrgeist, Wehrwille, Wehrkraft und die Aufgabe der SA," *Militaer-Wochenblatt,* 1938, 7, 398; 8, 466.

Military Spirit, Will, Strength, and the Task of the Storm Troops: The Brown Shirts are considered by General Schmidt-Logan to be the preservers and carriers of military virtues among the 22.5 million men in Germany who are not eligible for army conscription.

205. Schmuck, L. "Wehrerziehung, Wehrmannschaft, Erbe der Front," *Soldatentum,* 1939, 247-251.

Military Education, the Troops, the Heritage of the Front: The author is a high officer in the Storm Troops.

206. Schwertfeger, B. "Soldatenerziehung und Disziplin." In *Die deutsche Soldaterikunde,* 331-351. Leipzig, Bibl. Institut, 1937.

Discipline and the Education of Soldiers: A short history of the educational principles of the German Army.

207. Sorge, —. *Der Marine-Offizier als Fuehrer und Erzieher*. Berlin: Mittler, 1934.

The Naval Officer as Leader and Educator.

208. Weisser, E. *Die deutsche Bildungsidee*. Frankfurt a.M.: Diesterweg, 1934.

The German Idea of Education: Especially interesting is Part 2, discussing problems of "heroic education."

209. Weniger, E. *Wehrmachtserziehung und Kriegserfahrung*. Berlin: Mittler, 1938.

Education of the Army and Conduct of War: The author professor at the Berlin University, is an exponent of the classic Prussian military training which objects to the overestimation of psychological and pedagogical theories and advances the "German principle" in its basic sense—that every German can be raised as a soldier and that the German army proved this principle by its accomplishments in the first World War.

210. Wieneke, F. *Charaktererziehung im Nationalsozialismus*. Soldin, 1936.

The Building of Character and National Socialism: The greatest problem of pedagogy in the Third Reich is the education and upbringing of German youth. Nazism has changed the whole conception and ideals of education. Instead of egoism and individualism which Wieneke claims led to a complete decline of German culture and morality, a new "organic" system is emerging which will be closely related to the national consciousness of responsibility. The author believes that all education, whether physical or mental, should be dedicated entirely to the formation of character, because national stability in the present and future can be maintained only through the decisive, firm, and strong-willed character of a nation's individuals.

211. Wilfert, M. "Die seelische Eigenart des Unteroffiziers und ihre erziehliche Beeinflussung," *Soldatentum,* 1936, 214-223.

The influence of education on the noncom's mental make-up.

212. Ziegler, H. W. *Wehrerziehung im neuen Geist.* Erfurt: Stenger, 1935.

Military Education in the New Spirit: The author attributes the "decadence of the German youth spirit" to Republican political education. He allots to the Nazi Reich the task of raising German youth with a deeply imbedded sense of "loyalty, comradeship, brotherhood, and *esprit de corps.*" This will be accomplished by training Germans in "inner-able-bodiedness."

b) Psychological Aspects of Military Life

213. Anon. "Die wichtigsten Alltagsinteressen des einfachen Soldaten," *Soldatentum,* 1934, 77.

The Most Important Every-Day Interests of the Common Soldier: Valuable observations jointly prepared by officers of the 5th Infantry Regiment.

214. Anon. "Psychologische Alltagssorgen einer Kompagnie," *Soldatentum,* 1934, 77.

Psychological Every-Day Problems of a Company: Prepared by the same officers.

215. Baumbach, K. "Zur Frage der Bestrafung von Selbstmordversuchen," *Soldatentum,* 1936, 91-93.

The Problem of Punishing Attempted Suicides.

216. Bock, A. "Das Heimweh im Soldatenleben," *Soldatentum,* 1936, 73-83.

Homesickness in the Life of the Soldier: The author, a prominent Nuremberg physician, analyzes homesickness in various aspects of military life and suggests the urgent introduction of a homesickness therapy.

217. Deegeneb, —. "Sonderlinge unter tauglichen Rekruten," *Soldatentum,* 1936, 69-72.

Eccentrics Among Physically Fit Conscripts: The author is an army psychologist attached to one of the two Berlin garrisons.

218. Eichenberg, A. "Der toelpische Mensch als Rekrut," *Soldatentum,* 1937, 243-248.

The Clumsy Man as Recruit

219. Eichberg, A. "Der Intellektuelle als Rekrut," *Soldatentum,* 1938, 65-68.

The Intellectual as Recruit.

220. Gauer, H. *Vom Bauerntum, Buergertum und Arbeitertum in der Armee.* Heidelberg: Winter, 1938.

Peasantry, Bourgeoisie and the Working Class in the Army: A study of social classes and their adaptability to army requirements. Interesting only from the German point of view, but supplies a valuable contribution to the understanding of the German army's sociological problems.

221. Gerathewohl, —. "Eigenart und Behandlung des Einzelgaengers," *Soldatentum,* 1938, 163-168.

Peculiarity and Treatment of the Individualist: The author is director of the psychological testing station of the Breslau garrison.

222. Grunwaldt, H. H. "Das erotische Moment im Rekrutenleben," *Soldatentum,* 1937, 31-36.

Sex in the Life of the Recruit.

223. Heberle, R. "Bau und Gefuege der Truppe," *Soldatentum,* 1936, 112-120.

Organization of Army Troops: A professor of sociology at the Kiel University describes the army as a social unit with organization, leadership, and structure as its sociological elements. The tasks of military sociology is to investigate the individual problems of these elements.

224. Jordan, —. "Der geborene Soldat," *Soldatentum,* 1937, 114-119.

The Born Soldier: A captain formerly with the 57th Regiment of the 1st Army Corps adapts Jaensch's typology to the psychological problems of military life. The article was accepted for publication in the official organ of the Psychological Laboratory, not as a valuable contribution, but as an example of the outsider's approach to military psychology and to stimulate the interest of army officers in psychology.

225. Kreipe, K. "Die Bedeutung der Sinneswahrnehmung (insbesondere des Sehens und Hoerens) fuer den soldatischen Dienst," *Soldatentum,* 1934, 9.

The Significance of Sensory Perception (Especially Seeing and Hearing) in Military Service.

220. —. "Der Rekrut der allgemeinen Wehrpflicht," *Soldatentum,* 1936, 94-98; 136-141.

The Recruit of the Compulsory Military Service: The introduction of compulsory military service in 1935, expanding the "professional leader army" into a "people's army," confronted the army psychologist with important problems of training and indoctrination. This article is of special significance from the American point of view, since our own transition from a standing professional army to a selective service army raises problems similar to those which the Germans faced and solved.

227. Legius, M. "Seltsame Vorgaenge im Soldatenleben," *Soldatentum,* 1938, 115-122.

Strange Occurrences in the Life of the Soldier: An interesting analysis of superstition as it affects the efficiency of the soldier.

228. Lonicer, —. "Die religioese Situation des Rekruten," *Soldatentum*, 1937, 37-42.

The Religious Situation of the Conscript: The author is chief chaplain of the Breslau garrison, obviously a representative of the Nazi faction of German Protestantism.

229. Luederitz, R. R. "Selbstwertglaube und Unterordnung," *Soldatentum*, 1937, 67-72.

Self-Appreciation and Subordination: The author, an army psychologist in Koenigsberg, surveys his subject in the general sense and from the specific military point of view.

230. Marbe, K. "Ueber Psychologie des Befehlens," *Ind. Psychotechn.*, 1930, 7, 103-198.

The Psychology of Command.

231. Meier-Welcker, —. "Gedanken ueber Gehorsam," *Soldatentum*, 1938, 68-73.

Thoughts on Obedience: The author is a captain in the Berlin garrison.

232. Mierke, K. "Gefaehrdete Kameradschaft," *Soldatentum*, 1939, 130-141; 188-197.

Endangered Comradeship: Among the crises of comradeship, Dr. Mierke investigates psychological problems arising from disgust with the service and others caused by selfish, vain, and unruly soldiers among the troops.

233. Oelrich, W. "Soldatentum und buergerliche Welt," *Soldatentum*, 1935, 106-115; 179-181.

Soldierdom and the Bourgeois World: An army psychologist discusses the important problems of transition from the civilian to the military way of life. The premilitary service of practically every German youth now eliminates most of the tensions which formerly arose from this transition.

234. Pallokat, —. "Was foerdert oder hemmt den Aufbau der Gemeinschaft junger Soldaten?" *Soldatentum,* 1937, 24-31.
   What Furthers or Impedes the Building of a Young Soldier's Community: An article by a Berlin army psychologist.

235. Roth, H. "Soldatentum und Natur," *Soldatentum,* 1934, 122-126.
   Soldierdom and Nature: The author, an army psychologist attached to the Muenchen testing station, investigates the influence of natural environment on the soldier.

236. Roth, H. "Psychologische Schwierigkeiten bei der militaerischen Ausbildung der aelteren Freiwilligen-Jahrgaenge," *Soldatentum,* 1936, 110-112.
   Psychological Difficulties in the Training of Older Volunteer Classes: An interesting contribution to the problem of age conflicts in the army.

237. Ruppert, H. "Soldatentum als Religion," *Soldatentum,* 1934, 69-76.
   Soldierdom as a Religion: This article, written by a prominent army psychologist attached to the Breslau testing station, tries to alleviate the tension between the anti-religious attitude of the Nazi party and the army's decision to continue religious education. Solution: elevate "soldierdom" into a religion since "Germans are eternal soldiers" who are able to develop "a religious realization of soldierly sentiment." The author comes to the conclusion that some sort of religion is inevitably indispensable for army morale.

238. Scherbening, —. "Der Kompagniechef und seine Soldaten," *Soldatentum,* 1938, 168-171.

The Company Commander and His Soldiers: An excellent article by a colonel of a Muenster regiment, containing valuable advice on how to cultivate an inner relationship between officers and men.

239. —. "Einfluss der soldatischen Persoenlichkeit," *Soldatentum*, 1939, 142-149.

Influence of the Soldierly Personality: The commanding officer must be an impressive personality, since the best means of influencing his troops is his exemplary conduct in peace and war.

240. Schmidt-Logan, —. "Offizier und SA-Fuehrer," *Militaer-Wochenblatt*, 1939, 29, 1917-1921.

Officer and Storm-Troop Leader.

241. Schulz, —. "Losloesung und Einfuegung im Soldatenleben," *Soldatentum*, 1937, 2-10.

Separation and Assimilation in Army Life.

242. Simoneit, M. "Ehre und Ehrhaftigkeit in der soldatischen Lebensform," *Soldatentum*, 1934, 118.

Honor and Honorableness in the Soldierly Way of Life: Simoneit offers another contribution to the "new" German way of life as an ethical conception which receives its greatest impulse in militarism.

243. —. "Soldatentum als Lebensform," *Soldatentum*, 1934, 65-68.

Soldierdom as a Way of Life: The article elaborates on the thesis that military service is the highest expression of the "Germanic way of life."

244. —. "Die allgemeine Wehrpflicht als psychologisches Problem," *Soldatentum*, 1936, 58-62.

Compulsory Military Service as a Psychological Problem: This article is of considerable topical interest from the American point of view, since it deals with those specific problems which were raised by the introduction of compulsory military service.

245. Thofern, —. "Standes- und Berufspflichten des Unteroffi-ziers," *Soldatentum,* 1936, 228-232.

Class and Professional Duties of the Noncommissioned Offi-cer: A colonel's advice to noncoms on how to conduct themselves in the face of their "social" place in the army and their conscious-ness of duty.

246. Wuth, O. "Ueber den Selbstmord bei den Soldaten," *Sol-datentum,* 1936, 84-90.

Soldier Suicides: Professor Wuth, a high medical officer of the army, treats the problem of military suicides from the physician's point of view.

247. Ziegleb, H. W. "Zur Psychologie des Soldatentums," *Ber. Kongr. dtsch. Ges. Psychol.,* 1934, XIV, 128-130.

Psychology of Soldierdom.

5. PSYCHOLOGY OF COMBAT
a) War Psychology

248. Binder-Krieglstein, C. v. *Ein Krieg ohne Chancen.* Wien, 1893.

A War Without Chances: Written by a general of the Imperial Army who saw action in the wars of 1860-71. The second part of this book, "Psychology of the Great War," is perhaps the first con-scious psychological approach to the problems of modern warfare in German military literature.

249. Bircher, E. "Militaerpsychologie," *Schweiz. Milit. Blaetter,* 1919, 193-200; 225-230; 257-261-289-297.

Military Psychology: Dr. Bircher is a prominent Swiss physi-cian, now serving as a division commander in Switzerland's citizen army. As a doctor interested in psychology and an observer of the last war from the neutral vantage point in Switzerland, he began studying the psychological problems of modern warfare long before German military writers became interested in the psychological amplification of strategy and tactics. On his series of articles is based a great deal of present German psychological warfare. He maintains that, regardless of new weapons in the technological sense, the balance between genuine victory and defeat depends on the solution of individual and mass morale problems.

250. Dessoir, M. "Kriegspsychologische Betrachtungen," *Zwischen Krieg und Frieden,* No. 37, Leipzig: Hirzel, 1916.

Psychological Observations of War: The author was invited by the Supreme Command to visit the Russian front and report his observations. In this book, he describes what he saw in the trenches, the spirit of the troops, and the psychological aspects of trench warfare: fear, courage, discipline, and the relationship between officers and men.

251. Dix, K. W. *Psychologische Betrachtungen ueber die Eindruecke des Krieges auf Einzelne wie auf die Masse.* Langensalza: Beyer, 1915.

Psychological Observations on the War's Impact on the Individual and on the Mass: Dr. Dix was among the few German psychologists who investigated the psychological problems of warfare during the first World War.

252. Duewell, W. *Vom inneren Gesicht des Krieges.* Jena: Diederichs, 1917.

The Inner Nature of War: Psychological and sociological study of individual soldiers in the World War in relation to the demands of army organization and its totalitarian spirit. A complete, although journalistic, picture of the psychological reactions of soldier, officer, and civilian in various periods of war. Valuable first-hand observations.

253. Everth, E. *Von der Seele des deutschen Soldaten im Felde*. Jena: Diederichs, 1915.

The Mental Life of the German Soldier at the Front: The author, member of the Pan-German Tat (Action) group, asserts that a soldier on the battlefield actually feels freer and safer than at home, since war dissolves his petty problems and cares and sublimates his religious emotion. Obedience is praised as a blessing since it removes the great burden of responsibility from the soldier. The author claims that European culture, which was supposed to have weakened the human fiber, actually strengthened it and revealed hidden powers of resistance in crises. Most interesting is the comparative analysis of German, French, and Senegalese soldiers. See also *Das innere Deutschland nach dem Kriege*, by the same author (Jena, 1916), with illuminating chapters on the "people's army."

254. Freud, S. *Zeitgemaesses ueber Krieg und Tod*. Wien: Internatl. Psychoanalyt. Verlag, 1924.

Contemporary Thoughts on War and Death: Freud's book is still widely read and anonymously quoted among German army psychologists.

255. Freytag-Loringhoven, H. v. *Die Psyche der Heere*. Berlin: Mittler, 1923.

The Psyche of Armies: An authoritative psychological appraisal of various armies in history, by the late general and professor of military sciences at Berlin University. The author regards the last war as the supreme test of modern warfare. The time-honored principle, according to which "war is the business of the armed forces," gave way to the principle of "total war" in which entire populations were set against one another. Mass armies have outlived their usefulness, and today the soldier's morale must be fortified on his conviction that he is "not a mere number on an identification tag" and that "the barrier between him and his superior is dissolved through common aim and will and mutual trust."

Especially interesting is the author's appraisal of the American soldier of the last war. He finds him an "outstanding warrior" who succeeded despite the inefficiency and ultra-conservatism of his inferior officers.

256. Fuchtbar, v. "Der Vemichtungsgedanke—entscheidend auch in der neuzeitlichen Kriegfuehrung," *Militaer-Wochenblatt,* 1932, 10.

The Principle of Destruction—Decisive Even in Modern War.

257. Hesse, K. "Die psychologische Lehren des Weltkrieges fuer den Soldaten," *Allg. Schweiz. Militaerztg.,* 1932, 6-7.

Psychological Lessons of the World War for the Soldier: A recapitulation of Colonel Hesse's ideas, somewhat doctored for Swiss consumption.

258. —. *Persoenlichkeit und Masse im Zukunftskrieg.* Berlin: Mittler, 1933.

Personality and the Mass in the War of the Future: In the form of a somewhat esoteric discussion among young officers, Hesse presents the psychological problems of conditioning troops prior to and during battle, the influence of the military leader on the actual execution of military operations, the various phases of military action from a psychological point of view, the basic differences between fighting with a professional army and a conscripted army, and, above all, the psychological relations, both human and material, of the individual to the mass.

259. Hirschfeld, M. *Kriegspsychologisches.* Bonn: Marcus, 1916.

War Psychology: Germany's famed sexologist considers patriotism, desire for martyrdom, adventure, heroism, conquering spirit, the trinity of freedom-brotherhood-comradeship, blood lust, and desire for superiority as the motivations and stimuli of all wars.

260. Hoche, A. *Krieg und Seelenleben.* Freiburg: Speyer, 1915.

War and Mental Life: An academic and sketchy lecture dealing with war psychoses and the various mental illnesses arising from warfare among both soldiers and civilians.

261. Plaut, P. "Psychographie des Kriegers," *Beih. Z. angew. Psychol.*, 1920, 21, 1-123.

Psychography of the Warrior: Perhaps the best German monograph on the psychological problems of the last war, obtained through an inquiry into the observations of German psychologists after the war. An interesting questionnaire from this book, embracing all problems raised by modern warfare, is printed in the appendix.

262. —. "Prinzipien und Methoden der Kriegspsychologie." In *Handbuch der biologischen Arbeitsmethoden,* Abt. VI. Berlin-Wien, 1921.

Principles and Methods of War Psychology: The author was a prominent psychologist in the Vienna of pre-Hitler days.

263. Scholz, L. *Seelenleben der Soldaten an der Front.* Tuebingen: Mohr, 1920.

The Mental Life of Soldiers at the Front: This document, one of the most outstanding on war psychology produced by the last war, was found on the body of Dr. Scholz, a neurologist in civilian life, who was killed in action while fighting on the Russian front. He describes relations between officers and men, and impressions during advances into enemy territory. Analyzing fear and the soldier's state of mind in the trenches, on furlough, and in attack, the author concludes that it is easier to accomplish mass morale than individual morale. In actual fighting, the soldier soon overcomes squeamishness, his prime impulse being self-preservation as a result of fear. The noble feelings of patriotism may or may not return after the danger has passed.

264. Stekel, W. *Unser Seelenleben im Kriege*. Berlin, 1921.
    Our Mental Life in War.

265. Vischer, A. L. "Ueber Kriegspsychologie," *Allg. Schweiz. Militaerztg.*, 1921.

War Psychology: The author is a prominent Swiss physician who wrote many articles on the various problems of military psychology and had a considerable influence on German military literature. This paper, however, is confined to generalities.

266. Wunderle, G. *Das Seelenleben unter dem Einfluss des Krieges. Eine psychologische Skizze*. Eichstaett: Broenner, 1914.

Mental Life Under the Influence of War: Stating that Germans are born soldiers, Wunderle cites reports of psychiatrists that many cases of melancholy were encountered in clinics as a result of grief and deeply hurt feelings over military unfitness and rejection. This author describes shock resulting from bombardment as a "spiritual feeling of elation." More powerful than fear is the "gruesome desire" to remain amidst shellfire. Rage and frenzy drive soldiers forward even in the face of death and destruction. These are held to be the components of the will-to-fight. These qualities are innate in a people of whom the historians say: "The Germans must dominate the world or humanity will go under." '

b) Combat Experiences and Effects of Military Action

267. Bathe, R. *Der Feldzug der 18 Tage. Die Chronik des polnischen Dramas*. Oldenburg: Stalling, 1941.

The Campaign of the 18 Days: An outstanding book written by a radio commentator with the Nazi troops during the Polish campaign of 1939. The author describes the tremendous morale force which drove the Germans to victory in their first Blitzkrieg. Technological weapons would have meant little without that morale force. Most interesting is his revelation of the Nazi's most important slogan: "One drop of sweat saves ten drops of blood." This slogan was intended to spur tired soldiers on to further action, and it was found to work to perfection.

268. Delbanco, G. A. *Von der Seele des Kriegsfreiwilligen*. Magdeburg: Stahlhelm Verlag, 1925.
The Mind of the War Volunteer.

269. Franz, W. *Deutsches Empfinden im Kampf mit angelsaechsischen Kriegswillen*. Dresden: Leipzig, 1918.
German Sentiment in the Struggle with the Anglo-Saxon Will-to-War.

270. Fritzsching, L. "Der seelische Zustand von Soldaten vor der Gefangennahme," *Soldatentum*, 1938, 221-236.
The Soldiers' Mental State Before Being Taken Prisoner: An interesting study of the psychological causes of the slackening of resistance which leads to surrender. The author is an army psychologist of Munich.

271. Glaessner, G. "Die Willensbetaetigung beim Gewaehrschiessen," *Arch. ges. Psychol.*, 1937, 98, 1-2, 311-320.
The Function of Will in Rifle-Shooting: A highly technical study introducing an apparatus to measure will functions.

272. Guenther, A. E. "Die Intelligenz und der Krieg." In *Krieg und Krieger*. Berlin: Junker & Duennhaupt, 1930.
Intelligence and War.

273. Hanslian, R. *Der chemische Krieg*. Berlin: Mittler, 1937.
The Chemical War: An exhaustive scientific volume on the military aspects of gas warfare, and the use of artificial smoke. The second volume is of particular importance, since it presents strategy and tactics of chemical warfare, outlines the future of "gas war," and describes the effect of poison gas on men and animals.

274. Hesse, K. "Die Feuertaufe," *Militaerwissenschaftliche Mitteilungen*, 1933, 3.

Baptism of Fire: The prolific Colonel Hesse here describes the mental state of soldiers going into action for the first time.

275. Hesselmann, —. "Ueber die seelischen Einwirkungen des Trommelfeuers," *Soldatentum*, 1937, 277-290.

The Mental Impact of Protracted Bombardment (Drumfire): The author was a major with the Berlin army corps.

276. Juenger, E. *In Stahlgewittern*. (5th edition.) Berlin: Mittler, 1925.

In a Blizzard of Steel: War experiences of a shock battalion commander, who became the idol of German youth, inspired by this emotionally supercharged volume. Interesting is the esoteric description of the morale force, arising from the ultra-patriotism of Germanic education, which drove German shock battalions over the top and which is today still the main driving force of German attacks.

277. —. *Der Kampf als inneres Erlebnis*. Berlin: Mittler, 1926.

The War as a Spiritual Experience: War is described as the "religion of combat" in which Germans fight for the sake of fighting. The most important book for understanding the motivating power of German youth in battle.

278. Juenger, F. G. *Krieg und Krieger*. Berlin: Junker & Duennhaupt, 1930.

War and the Warrior.

279. Mierke, K. "Die wesenswandelnde und wesensformende Kraft des Kriegserlebnisses," *Beih. Z. angew. Psychol.*, 1938, 79, 1-27.

The Changing and Formative Influence of War Experience.

280. Muenzer, A. "Die Psyche der Verwundeten," *Berliner Klin. Wochenschrift*, 1915, 52, 10, 234-235.

The Mind of Wounded Soldiers.

281. Ruppert, —. "Vom Sinn und Wert des Kampfes," *Soldatentum*, 1936, 281-284.

Meaning and Value of War: A controversial article by an army psychologist of Stuttgart-Cannstatt which caused the editor to caution his readers against "overestimating struggle as the culmination of existence."

282. Schauwecker, F. *Im Todesrachen. Die deutsche Seele im Weltkrieg*. Halle: Diekman, 1921.

In the Jaws of Death—the German Soul in the World War.

283. Schmidt, H. "Die Hoehenkrankheit und ihre Bekaempfung," *Ind. Psychotechn.*, 1938, 4-6, 162-180.

Altitude Sickness and How to Overcome It: A survey of causes, origins, and effects of high-altitude sickness. Especially interesting is the presentation of the functions and possible injuries of the substratosphere pilots with quantitative results of examinations. The latest precautionary measures are fully described.

284. —. "Die Hoehenfestigkeit im Flugdienst," *Ind. Psychotechn.*, 1935, 12, 366-373.

Altitude Adaptability in Flying.

285. Schroetter, H. v. "Zur Psychologie und Pathologie des Feldfliegers," *Wiener mediz. Wochenschrift*, 1919, 12, 13, 14.

Psychology and Pathology of the Combat Pilot.

286. Simoneit, M. "Wehrpsychologische Gedanken ueber den Angriffsgeist der Infanterie," *Militaerwissenschaftliche Rundschau*, 1938, 4, 547.

The Offensive Spirit of the Infantry—Military Psychological Observations.

287. Soldan, G. *Der Mensch und die Schlacht der Zukunft.* Oldenburg: Stalling, 1932.

Man and the Battle of the Future: An excellent critique of world war strategy and its implications for the future. The author contends that against modern weapons of war the best human material proves useless. German victories of 1914 were a tragic, meaningless sacrifice of the best part of the army and, above all, they cost the Reich its active officer corps. In the battle of modern weapons, infantry is outmoded and the accent must be on the superiority of steel rather than of men. Gas is ruled out since it demoralizes attacking troops, slows down both men and machines, and makes the use of war material extremely difficult. Soldan maintains that the "war of the future" will be fought by comparatively small front armies, extremely swift and adaptable, equipped with the most modern technical arms and composed of the best human material. The modern struggle for the existence of nations can recognize no morality, nor the spirit of international co-operation. "Only a strong, deeply rooted nationalist spirit, combined with the exploitation of all national energies and skills, can stand the burden of modern war." The author's ideas, first published in 1925, have been realized in the present war's Blitzkrieg strategy.

288. Spitta, H. *Heldentod. Studien zur vergleichenden Psychologie.* Tuebinger Kriegsschriften, 1915, 10, 32.

Heroic Death—Studies of Comparative Psychology.

289. Stoerring, G. E. "Gedaechtnisverlust durch Gasvergiftung." (Ein Mensch ohne Zeitgedaechtnis.) *Ber. Kongr. dtsch. Ges. Psychol.,* 1936, XV, 208-211.

Amnesia Caused by Gas Poisoning. Description of a case.

290. Strauss, H. "Ueber die seelischen Einwirkungen bei Minens-prengungen," *Soldatentum,* 1937, 60-64.
Mental Effects of Mine Explosions.

291. Tausk, V. "Zur Psychologie des Deserteurs," *Internatl. Z. f. aerztliche Psychoanalyse,* 1916-17, 4-5.
Psychology of Desertion.

292. Vischer, A. L. *Die Stacheldrahtkrankheit. Beitraege zur Psychologie des Kriegsgefangenen.* Zurich: Rascher, 1918.
Barbed-Wire Sickness: A Swiss medical officer and outstanding war psychologist discusses the psychology of the prisoner-of-war.

293. Walther, R. H. "Ansaetze einer Psychologie des Kraftfahrens und Fliegens," *Soldatentum,* 1934, 14.
Psychology of Driving and Flying.

c) Positive and Negative Factors in Stimulating Military Morale

294. Ach, N. "Ueber Verantwortung und Charakter," *Ind. Psychotechn.,* 1938, 9-10, 306-308.
Character and Responsibility: Individual interests and responsibility to one's self must be subordinated to responsibility to the community and national interests. Professor Ach claims that only the introverted Nordic is capable of such subordination.

295. Altrichter, F. *Die seelischen Kraefte des deutschen Heeres im Frieden und im Weltkriege.* Berlin: Mittler, 1933.
The Spiritual Forces of the German Army in Peace and in the World War: An excellent analysis of the psychological factors, trials and errors, in the German army during the last war and in the peace interval leading up to the Nazi regime. The author's approach to his subject is primarily concerned with the relative position

of the individual soldier in mass psychology. As basic stimuli for individual inspiration in wartime, Altrichter lists tradition, *esprit de corps,* feeling of superiority, the feeling of belonging to a specific branch of service, and the consciousness of mass strength. Psychological discipline is held to be the fulcrum of military morale. The author outlines methods of educating military leaders and analyzes psychological developments of the last war. The book ends with a summary of the psychological problems within the army, particularly the psychological effects of changes in organization, the leadership, personality, character, and temperament of the supreme field commander, disciplinary methods, patriotic education, and the psychological training of officers.

296. —. "Die Seele." In *Handbuch der neuzeitlichen Wehrwissenschaften,* I, 621-624. Berlin: Gruyter, 1936.
    The Mind: A handy condensation of Altrichter's book described above, containing all the important features and conclusions.

297. Anon. "Ueberraschung," *Militaer-Wochenblatt,* 1936, 39, 1743.
    Surprise: One of a series of articles on psychological aspects of war. Others are listed below.

298. Anon. "Dienstfreudigkeit," *Militaer-Wochenblatt,* 1939, 40, 2683.
    Pleasure in Military Service.

299. Anon. "Vertrauen," *Militaer-Wochenblatt,* 1939, 51, 3454-3459.
    Trust.

300. Banse, E. "Psychologie des Zusammenbruchs," *Voelkischer Beobachter,* June 19, 1932.
    Psychology of Collapse.

301. Beck, W. "Zum Panik Problem," *Soldatentum,* 1937, 296-306.
    The Problem of Panic: The author is an army psychologist now attached to the Breslau garrison, formerly a guest professor at

Boston University. His article is a contribution to a series of studies on the problem of panic which *Soldatentum* published in several issues.

302. Dirks, —. "Zuverlaessigkeit, eine Grundvoraussetzung fuer den technischen Dienst des Soldaten," *Soldatentum,* 1936, 190-193.
Reliability—a Prerequisite for the Soldier's Technical Service.

303. —. "Ueber den Kampfgeist der Panzerabwehrgruppe," *Soldatentum,* 1939, 11-17.
The Fighting Spirit of Antitank Gunners: An army psychologist suggests ways and means to condition the fighting spirit of antitank gunners, perhaps the most vulnerable section of the army, since they are directly exposed to the attack of superior forces and are dependent on an unequal means of defense, the small antitank gun. His suggestions were subsequently criticized by an officer of the Panzer divisions whose article is listed below. This controversy shows that the psychologist's advice is not accepted without criticism and is often summarily rejected as inadequate and incompetent in the face of actual combat experience. See No. 305.

304. Endres, F. C. *Reichswehr und Demokratie.* Muenchen, Leipzig: Duncker & Humblot, 1919.
The Reichswehr and Democracy: A Bavarian sociologist surveys the incompatibility of a strictly co-ordinated military organization in a democracy. The article is important, since it shows the liberal approach of a democratic observer baffled by the incompatibility of maintaining an army organization within a democratic society, such as the German Weimar Republic tried to realize.

305. Engels, —. "Ueber den Kampfgeist der Panzerabwehrgruppe," *Soldatentum,* 1939, 75-78.
The Fighting Spirit of Antitank Gunners: An aide de campe of General Guderian, commander-in-chief and creator of the Panzer-divisions, argues against methods suggested by army psychologists

to bolster and maintain the fighting spirit of antitank gunners. See No. 303.

306. Epp, K. "Paniken und ihre Vermeidung," *Militaerwissenschaftliche Mitteilungen,* 1937, 10, 783-799; 11, 876.

Panic and Its Avoidance: An officer of the defunct Austrian army examines panics, their causes and elimination, with conclusions that are generally accepted by German army theorists. An interesting and valuable presentation of the problem.

307. Erfurth, W. *Ueberraschung im Kriege.* Berlin: Mittler, 1938.

Surprise in War: A historical review by an army general of the effect and importance of the element of surprise in warfare, with much valuable information directly linked to present events.

308. Freytag-Loringhoven, H. v. *Die Macht der Persoenlichkeit im Kriege.* Berlin: Mittler, 1905.

The Power of Personality in War: A forerunner of the innumerable books subsequently written on this important subject. General Freytag-Loringhoven's ideas have had great influence on contemporary German theorists who have never deviated from the ideas first outlined in this book.

309. Grassel, E. "Die Willensschwaeche. Gleichzeitig eine Theorie des Willens," *Beih. Z. angew. Psychol.,* 1937, 77.

Weakness of Will.

310. Grunwaldt, H. H. "Wehrpsychologische Gedanken zur militaerischen Ausruestung und Symbolik," *Soldatentum,* 1934, 22-37.

Military Equipment and Symbols—Military and Psychological Observations.

311. —. "Ueberlegungen zum Problem der Orientierungsfaehigkeit," *Soldatentum,* 1934, 128.

The Capacity for Orientation.

312. Hesse, K. "Disziplin und Volksheer," *Deutsche Wehr,* 1933, 21.
Discipline and the People's Army.

313. Holzheimer, —. "Kaempferischer Einsatz aus dem Erlebnis der Pflicht," *Soldatentum,* 1939, 289-293.
Readiness to Fight as Evolved from the Experience of Duty.

314. Jungblut, —. "Kriegsverluste," *Militaerische Rundschau,* 1938, 2, 237.
War Casualties: A medical officer of the German Army discusses the psychological effect of human losses in modern warfare.*

315. Kuebler, —. "Vom 'Todesprinzip' des Angriffs und seiner Ueberwindung," *Militaer-Wochenblatt,* 1938, 3, 130-134.
The "Death Principle" in Attack and How to Overcome It: The author of this interesting article is a major of the General Staff and a professor at the War Academy.

316. Lau, A. "Die Bedeutung der Einstellung fuer Befehlen und Gehorchen," *Psychotechn. Z.* 1934, 93-114.
Obedience and the Importance of Adaptation.

317. Lucke, V. "Der 'Mannestrotz' als seelische Grundlage des Kampfes," *Soldatentum,* 1939, 294-298.
"Masculine Defiance" as the Mental Basis of Fighting.

318. Ludwig, W. "Beitraege zur Psychologie der Furcht im Krieg," *Beih. Z. angew. Psychol.,* 1920, 21, 125-172.
Psychology of Fear in War: An excellent study by a member of the group of psychologists who gathered around W. Stern and

---

* For another interesting study on the medical aspects of military psychology see: Bircher, E. "Was muss der Truppenfuehrer vom sanitaetsoffizier verlangen?" *Allg. Schweizerische Militaerzeitung,* 1940, 86, 7, 321-338.

O. Lipmann, the men who investigated psychological problems of the last war after the armistice.

319. Luederitz, H. "Das Gemeinschaftserlebnis in der vordersten Linie," *Beih. Z. angew. Psychol.*, 1938, 79, 28-42.
Community Life in the Most Advanced Outposts.

320. Maday, S. v. "Lustsoldat und Pflichtsoldat," *Umschau*, 1915, 19, 37.
The Soldier by Choice and the Soldier Inspired by Duty.

321. Meiebfrankenfeld, —. "Soldatentum und Religion im Weltkrieg," *Soldatentum*, 1935, 69-74.
Soldiering and Religion in the World War.

322. Mierke, K. "Die soldatische Haltung zur Angst," *Beih. Z. angew. Psychol.*, 1936, 72, 1-25.
The Soldierly Attitude to Fear: Mierke's ideas, fully reviewed in the Survey, are neither systematic nor exhaustive. Nevertheless, they are stimulating reading and invite a more thorough study of the problem along the lines which are presented only briefly by Mierke. The article contains a sketchy study of the biology of fear, the psychological approach to fear, symptoms and occurrences of fear, the factors that promote and impede fear, the disposition toward fear, and the meaning and conquest of fear.

323. Muennich, K. "Der Mensch als Unfallursache bei Flugzeugungluecken," *Ind. Psychotechn.*, 1939, 1-3, 1-8.
Human Beings as Causes of Plane Accidents: The author maintains that more than half of all crashes are caused by certain deficiencies of flying personnel on the ground and in the air. He concludes that more adequate training of human material is necessary to avoid accidents.

324. Nass, G. "Das Gefuehl des Magischen," *Soldatentum*, 1938, 102-105.

The Feeling of the Supernatural: The article attempts to present the psychological solution for problems raised by the influence of supernatural influences.

325. —. "Landschaftsform und soldatische Leistung," *Soldatentum*, 1938, 29-35.

The Influence of Landscape on Soldierly Efficiency.

326. Oelrich, W. "Ueber den Einsatz aus idealistischer Begeisterung," *Soldatentum*, 1939, 285-289.

Voluntary Participation as a Function of Idealistic Enthusiasm.

327. Otto, —. "Frontsoldatentum und Religion im Weltkrieg," *Soldatentum*, 1935, 59-69.

Religion and Soldiers at the Front in the World War.

328. Pfuelf, E. Die Panik im Krieg. Muenchen: Gmelin, 1908.

Panic in War: Colonel Pfuelf's little booklet together with Stark's monograph are considered the "last word" in Germany's panic-literature even though both books were written more than thirty years ago.

329. Pintschovius, K. *Die seelische Widerstandskraft im modernen Krieg*. Oldenburg: Stalling, 1936.

The Power of Mental Resistance in Modern War: The author, an army psychologist of great reputation, an economist and a poet in his own right, states that mechanized wars present new and dangerous psychological problems which "superficial remedies like propaganda" are unable to solve. His book, a courageous and original critique of the mass-psychological approach to these problems, demands the recognition of the "rational qualities of modern man whom life in the city and technological skill have accustomed to asking questions before making up his mind." The book is a veritable mine of interesting conclusions especially valuable for a democracy where a rational approach to problems raised by mechanized war is still permissible.

330. Reinicke, —. "Stimmung und Stimmungsberichte," *Militaer-Wochenblatt,* 1935, 3, 101-102.
    Reports on the Soldier's Frame of Mind.

331. Schiche, E. "Ueber Todesahnungen im Felde und ihre Wirkungen," *Beih. Z. angew. Psychol.,* 1920, 21, 173-178.
    Forebodings of Death at the Front and their Effects: This is the third and last of the monographs by a group of pre-Hitler psychologists on the psychological problems of the last war. Although prepared twenty years ago, it is still an interesting and stimulating report.

332. Schurch, E. "Armeefeindliche Kraefte," *Neue Schweizer Rundschau,* 1935, 1.
    Forces Hostile to the Army: This article written by a Swiss newspaper editor is particularly interesting for American readers, since it brings up problems pertinent to U. S. conscription. The author investigates the conflict between independent democratic will and the authoritarian obedience necessary for a disciplined army.

333. Simoneit, M. *Zufall und Schicksal im soldatischen Handeln.* Berlin: Bernard & Graefe, 1937.
    Chance and Fate in Military Action: Philosophical and psychological training and indoctrination are held to provide checks and balances which lessen the effects of chance in military actions.

334. Stark, F. "Paniken," *Beih. Militaer-Wochenblatt,* 1904.
    Panics: The basic study underlying all the later German investigations.

335. Teisinger, H. *Zum Studium psychischer und anderer Friktionen im Kriege.* Wien, 1905.

The Study of Psychological and Other Frictions in War.

336. Wetzell, G. "Ueberraschung im Kriege," *Militaer-Wochenblatt,* 1939, 50, 3378.

Surprise in War: A review of General Erfurth's book with some of the author's own ideas.

337. Winkler, —, and Oelrich, W. "Zum Panik Problem," *Soldatentum,* 1937, 291-296.

The Problem of Panic: Written by a colonel and an army psychologist of the Stettin garrison.

338. Winkler, H. *Die Monotonie der Arbeit.* Ein Beitrag zu dem Problem des psychischen Verhaltens bei gleichfoermiger koerperlicher Arbeit. Schriften zur Psychologie der Berufseignung und des Wirtschaftslebens, Heft 19. Leipzig: Barth, 1922.

The Monotony of Work: Although based on psychological industrial experience, this monograph contains many valuable suggestions on the causes and effects of monotony in military life.

III. PSYCHOLOGICAL WARFARE
1. STRATEGY AND TACTICS

339. Banse, E. *Raum und Volk im Weltkrieg.* Oldenburg: Stalling, 1931.

The Role of Geography and People in the World War: Banse, an independent military and political theorist, created a sensation all over the world with the publication of this book which accurately forecast the present techniques of German psychological warfare on both the military and home fronts. He maintained that geography (space) and psychology (people) are more important in modern warfare than traditional military science. The Nazis considered the publication of this book untimely and withdrew it from sale with the explanation that it was "merely the senseless babblings of an irresponsible armchair strategist." Banse, nevertheless, was appointed to the important position of professor of military sciences at the Brunswick Institute of Technology where many German air-force pilots receive their technical training. Banse may not have direct connections with the German High Command, but his book is a mirror of their guiding ideas, and, therefore, its reading is highly advisable. It has been recently republished by Harcourt, Brace & Company of New York.

340. —. *Wehrwissenschaft.* Braunschweig, 1932.

Military Science: This little book contains Banse's notorious theories on bacterial warfare which have been widely quoted and even more widely misunderstood. He merely suggests that a country should resort to bacterial warfare if disarmament strips it of other weapons.

341. Bertkau, F., and Franke, H. "Geistiger Krieg." In *Handbuch der neuzeitlichen Wehrwissenschaften,* I, 105-109. Berlin: Gruyter, 1936.

Intellectual Warfare: A short but very illuminating exposé of the strategy and weapons of psychological warfare.

342. Bircher, E., and Clam, E. *Krieg ohne Gnade. Von Tannenberg zur Schlacht der Zukunft.* Zurich: Scientia, 1937.

War Without Mercy; From Tannenberg to the Battle of the Future: Bircher in co-operation with a Swiss major outlines the strategy and tactics of "the war of the future"—which have been largely realized in the present war.

343. Blau, A. *Geistige Kriegfuehrung.* Potsdam: Voggenreiter, 1938.

Intellectual Warfare: The basic German textbook of psychological warfare by the colonel who is in charge of its preparation and prosecution. Because of his importance, his background should be mentioned. Son of a Berlin merchant, Blau was born on November 6, 1885. He received his first commission in 1907, and in 1910 was transferred to the Academy of Military Technology where he attended Professor Schmoller's lectures dealing with the history of social classes. He participated in the last war, was discharged in 1921 with the rank of captain, and apparently went into the publishing business. In reality, however, he remained with the Reichswehr as a supernumerary officer, expanding his studies in order to be assigned to the psychological branch of the armed forces. He matriculated in the Berlin Institute of Technology, majoring in economic sciences under Professors Goetz, Briefs and W. Prion. In 1929, he was recalled to active service with the rank of major and joined the psychological testing station of the 3rd Army Corps. He received his doctor's degree in 1932 for a thesis entitled "The Advertising Market in German Newspapers." In 1934, he was assigned to devote all his time and energy to the study of "comparative national psychology," a German phrase which camouflages psychological intelligence and propaganda. He was promoted to a colonelcy in 1938 and may be a major general at the present time. He is high up on the staff of the psychological general staff, specializing in intellectual warfare on a pseudo-scientific basis. His books are extensively reviewed in the Survey.

344. —. "Geistige Kriegfuehrung im Rahmen der Gesamtkrieg-fuehrung," *Jahrbuch fuer Wehrpolitik und Wehrwissenschaften,* 1939, 93-106.

Intellectual Warfare Within the Framework of Total War: A lecture delivered to the German Society of Military Politics and Military Sciences, containing all the interesting features of Blau's longer book on the same subject. (An English translation of this article may be obtained from the Committee for National Morale.)

345. Braun, —. "Soldatische Gedanken zu politischen Ereignissen und Gestalten des Krieges," *Militaer-Wochenblatt,* 1939, 19, 1011.

Soldierly Thoughts on Political Events and Phases of War: The author is a colonel in the German Army.

346. —. "Der strategische Ueberfall ('Blitzkrieg')," *Militaer-Wochenblatt,* 1938, 18, 1134.

The Strategic Attack ("Lightning War"): Theory, strategy and tactics of the Blitzkrieg—presented on a single magazine page in an enlightening and fascinating manner.

347. Endres, F. C. "Vom naechsten Krieg," *Archiv fuer Sozialwissenschaft und Sozialpolitik,* 1928, 59, 48-74.

The Next War: A Bavarian sociologist, himself a former officer, accurately foretells the psychological character of the present war, partly on the basis of an article written by General Sherman Miles (now commanding officer of the First Army Corps Area) in the *North American Review.*

348. Foertsch, H. *Kriegskunst von heute und morgen.* Berlin: Andermann, 1939.

The Art of War Today and Tomorrow: The "brain" of the German General Staff assigns to morale forces an equal, if not greater, role than military forces. The book was published in the United States by Oskar Priest of New York, with an interesting foreword by Major George Fielding Eliot.

349. Keller, C. v. "Das moralische Element in der Taktik," *Jahrbuch fuer die deutsche Armee und Marine,* 1914, 2, 249-265.

The Morale Element in Tactics: A German general writing on the eve of the last war clearly recognizes the importance of morale in modern warfare, and makes suggestions for its exploitation within military strategy and tactics.

350. Krauss, A. *Theorie und Praxis in der Kriegskunst.* Muenchen: Lehmann, 1936.

Theory and Practice in the Art of War: A former Austrian general, long known for his Nazi sympathies, echoes the German ideas on strategy and tactics in modern war, emphasizing fast-moving troops and psychological offensives.

351. Ludendorff, E. *Der totale Krieg*. Muenchen: Ludendorffs Verlag, 1937.

Total War: A much discussed book of exaggerated value, it shows distinct signs of the mental deterioration that plagued Ludendorff in his last years. Ludendorff attempts to present himself as a greater military theorist and war philosopher than Clausewitz. The present war has refuted many of Ludendorff's military ideas, but confirmed everything he had to say on the importance of morale in both an offensive and defensive sense.

352. Ludovici, J. W. *Totale Landesverteidigung*. Oldenburg: Stalling, 1936.

Total Defense: Economic and psychological measures for the defense of the Fatherland must precede and then run parallel to military measures.

353. Metzsch, H. v. "Das Problem des Zukunftkrieges," *Wehr und Waffen*, 1932, 11.

Problems of the Future War: A wordy article by a retired general now busy propagandizing Nazism from the military point of view.

354. —. *Schlummernde Wehrkraefte. Neue soldatische Blickfelder*. Oldenburg: Stalling, 1935.

Latent Military Forces: A collection of articles popularizing the idea of total defense, particularly concerning the civilian population's active participation.

355. Mueller-Loebnitz, —. "Politik und Wehrmacht als Mittel der Kriegsfuehrung," *Militaerwissenschaftliche Rundschau*, 1935, 5-6, 592.

Politics and Armed Forces as Means of Warfare: A colonel of the German General Staff outlines the importance of political warfare supporting the military in operations.

356. Nicolai, W. *Nachrichtendienst, Presse und Volksstimmung.* Berlin: Mittler, 1920.

Intelligence Service, Press and the People's Frame of Mind: This is an important book of immense topical interest despite the fact that it was published twenty-one years ago. Nicolai, a protégé of General Ludendorff, was wartime chief of Section III-B (Intelligence and Politics) of the Imperial General Staff, and was made chiefly responsible for the blunders of the German intelligence. Written in self-vindication, this book is a bitter accusation of Germany's political leadership and an impassioned defense of the Ludendorffian school of military strategy. Nicolai had great influence on the shaping of Hitler's espionage tactics which were candidly revealed to Hermann Rauschning.

357. Poppelreuter, W. "Hitler der politische Psychologe," *Paedagogisches Magazin* 1391. Langensalza: Beyer, 1934.

Hitler, the Political Psychologist: A professor of psychology at Bonn University presents Hitler as a psychologist rather than politician.

358. —. "Probleme der politischen Psychologie," *Ber. Kongr. dtsch. Ges. Psychol.,* 1934, XIII, 59-60.

Problems of Political Psychology.

359. —. "Psychologie des politischen und wirtschaftlichen Geschehens," *Ber. Kongr. dtsch. Ges. Psychol.,* 1934, XIII, 204.

Psychology of Political and Economic Events.

360. Ringel, J. "Der totale Krieg," *Militaerwissenschaftliche Mitteilungen,* 1937, 12.

Total War: The author is an officer of the defunct Austrian army. In this article he stresses the importance of economic and psychological factors in modern warfare.

361. Ross, C. "Die Neuverteilung der Erde," *Z. f. Geopolitik,* 1936, 9, 582-596.

The Redistribution of the Earth: Written by the foremost political agent of the Haushofer group, this is the most convincing evidence that the Nazis actually aim at world domination. This article, representative of the many similar contributions to the problem, was selected for its clear style and concise presentation.

362. Scherke, F., and Vitzthun, U. *Bibliographie der geistigen Kriegsfuerhung.* Berlin: Bernard & Graefe, 1938.

Bibliography of Intellectual Warfare: A publication of the German Society of Military Politics and Military Sciences, obviously prepared to assist German propagandists in finding material from the last war. Incomplete, fragmentary, and propagandistic, it lists those books which present Germany as a power harassed by jealous enemies.

363. Schumacher, R. v. *Der Raum als Waffe.* Berlin: Runge, 1935.

Geography as a Weapon: The secretary of the Haushofer group elaborates on his chief's ideas. (See No. 14 and 15 in Bibliography.)

364. Schumacher, R. v., and Hummel, H. *Vom Kriege zwischen den Kriegen. Die Politik des Voelkerkampfes.* Stuttgart: Union, 1937.

The War Between the Wars: Advances the theory that the highest type of military strategy is victory without resort to armed force. The authors, advocating a political, psychological and commercial offensive, examine minutely the nations, peoples and minorities which lie in the path of Nazi aspirations for world power. Uncannily described is the "future" German psychological and economic offensive in Yugoslavia, Danzig, Poland, Czechoslovakia and Spain, with repeated references to England and the United States as the main adversaries. It is also predicted that it will be imperative to "free" Suez and the Panama Canal. From the psychological point of view, the chapter entitled "Mentality War" is of particular importance, but the whole book deserves careful scrutiny for a real understanding of the German strategy and tactics of psychological warfare.

365. Seifert, A. "Von der politisierten Weltwirtschaft zur politischen Wirtschaft des Staates," *Z. f. Geopolitik,* 1937, 7, 590-594.

From a Political World Economy to the Political Economy of the State.

366. Thomas, G. "Wehrwirtschaft." In *Die deutsche Wehrmacht.* Berlin: Mittler, 1939.

War Economy: The brilliant chief of the German Economic General Staff and a power behind Goering's economic throne points out the place of total economy in total war.

367. Wohltat, H. C. H. "Die staatliche Lenkung der Aussenwirtschaft," *Z. f. Geopolitik,* 1937, 7, 585-589.

The State's Control of Foreign Trade: An undersecretary of the German Ministry of Economics and one of the foremost commercial strategists of the Third Reich (now in Japan) outlines the strategy of economic warfare.

2. Fields of Psychological Campaigns

368. Adler, G. *Die Bedeutung der Illusionen fuer Politik und soziales Leben.* Jena: Fischer, 1904.

The Role of Illusions in Political and Social Life.

369. Baschwitz, K. *Der Massenwahn, Ursache und Heilung des Deutschenhasses.* Muenchen: Beck, 1932.

Mass Delusions: A liberal intellectual of the Weimar Republic investigates the causes and cure of foreign animosity toward Germany, suggesting a return to fair play, restoration of rights and international law. Interesting is the study of superstition and the psychology of atrocity stories, implicitly refuting propaganda's overall importance.

370. —. *Du und die Masse. Studien zu einer exakten Massenpsychologie.* Amsterdam: Feikema, 1938.

You and the Masses: A liberal student of mass psychology, now continuing his work outside Germany, asserts that people do not think differently when emerged in masses, but that they can as a mass be misled by the terror-strategy of a strong-willed ignorant minority. Obviously referring to the Nazis, Baschwitz attributes their effect on the mass to the "power of the paralyzing idea," which arouses a feeling of guilt and fear. To overcome such a regime, it is necessary to overcome this feeling of paralysis. A valuable study to determine methods of a morale offensive against terroristic regimes. The prerequisite of such an offensive is an exact analysis of mass psychology and its practical manipulation.

371. Bauer, W. *Die oeffentliche Meinung und ihre geschichtliche Grundlagen.* Tuebingen: Mohr, 1914.

Public Opinion and Its Historical Bases: An exhaustive historical review of the public mind and its conditioning from the standpoint of power politics. A companion piece to the author's work on "Public Opinion and World History."

372. —. *Die oeffentliche Meinung in der Weltgeschichte.* Potsdam: Athenaion, 1929.

Public Opinion in World History: A monumental history of public opinion and propaganda from ancient China through the Greek-Roman era and medieval times up to 1920. The author asserts that speech, the oldest medium of news dissemination, is the most powerful psychological instrument for swaying the masses, a theory fully accepted by Hitler, Goebbels and the Nazi propaganda machine in general. A rambling, disorganized work for the most part obviously biased, but contains much unexplored material.

373. Endemann, H. *Die Hetze als Gefaehrdungsproblem*. Mannheim, 1924.

Agitation as a Problem of Endangerment.

374. Freud, S. *Massenpsychologie und Ich-Analyse*. Wien: Internationl. Psychoanalyt. Verlag, 1923.

Mass Psychology and the Analysis of the Ego: This fundamental work is the raw material upon which the Nazis base a major part of their psychological offensives.

375. Friedlaender, A. *Die Bedeutung der Suggestion im Voelkerleben*. Berlin: Kohlhammer, 1913.

The Importance of Suggestion in the Life of Nations.

376. Gersdorff, K. v. *Ueber den Begriff und Wesen der oeffentlichen Meinung*. Leipzig, 1846.

Meaning and Nature of Public Opinion: One of the first German works written on public opinion, published two years before German public opinion revolted in Frankfurt.

377. Holtzendorff, F. v. *Wesen und Wert der oeffentlichen Meinung*. Muenchen: Rieger, 1880.

Nature and Significance of Public Opinion: Of historical interest, being representative of the Bismarckian German attitude toward public opinion.

378. Loewenfeld, L. *Die Suggestion in ihrer Bedeutung fuer den Weltkrieg*. Muenchen: Bergmann, 1917.

The Importance of Suggestion in the World War: A psychiatrist's examination of the problem written during the last war.

379. Moede, W. *Experimentelle Massenpsychologie*. Leipzig: Hirzel, 1920.

Experimental Mass Psychology: Professor Moede of the Berlin Institute of Technology is one of the foremost German industrial psychologists.

380. Schoene, W. "Das Geruecht," *Gestalten und Erscheinungen der politischen Publizistik,* Heft 8, Leipzig: Noske, 1936.

The Rumor: The author, unconsciously or not, examines his subject as a phenomenon of the totalitarian state. Reviewed in the Survey.

381. Toennies, F. *Kritik der oeffentlichen Meinung.* Berlin: Springer, 1922.

An Analysis of Public Opinion: A sociological textbook on the theoretical aspects of public opinion. Toennies, an outstanding German sociologist, discusses the fundamental conceptions of meaning, perception, and thought in their interrelationship to religion and science as prerequisites toward determining "public opinion" and "collective will." A very careful analysis is made of public opinion and its various forms in England, France, Germany, and the United States, its relations to "press opinion" and political policy in the World War and afterwards.

382. Wagner, L. *Der Voelkerhass.* Esslingen: Langguth, 1916.
International Hatred.

383. Wolf, H. *Weltgeschichte der Luege.* Leipzig: Weicher, 1922.
World History of the Lie.

384. Zwehl, J. v. *Der Dolchstoss in den Ruecken des siegreichen Heeres.* Berlin: Mittler, 1921.

The Stab in the Back of the Victorious Army: A German general prints the first reference to the "legend" which became the basis of the German army's psychological campaign of self-vindication.

3. NATIONAL PSYCHOLOGY

385. Banse, E. "Psychologie des Gegners," *Voelkischer Beobachter,* June 29, 1932.
Psychology of the Opponent.

386. —. "Voelkerpsychologie als Waffe," *Braunschweigische Landeszeitung*, September 26, 1932.

National Psychology as a Weapon: Banse incorporated these two articles in his book listed under No. 339.

387. Bessenbodt, O. "Charakterkunde der Fremdvoelker. Eine militaerische Wissenschaft," *Deutsche Wehr*, Beilage 2. 1937.

Characterology of Foreign Nations; A Military Science: The author suggests psychological espionage based on the "character" of foreign nations.

388. Blau, A. "Grundgedanken zur vergleichenden Voelkerpsychologie," *Beih. Z. angew. Psychol.*, 1938, 148-162.

Basic Ideas of a Comparative National Psychology: For the biography of this important author see No. 343. The article, reprint of a lecture delivered in a postgraduate course of army psychologists in 1938, is fully reviewed in the Survey. It reveals the aims and methods of German military espionage on a psychological basis.

389. Block, M. "Die voelkerpsychologische Struktur Suedosteuropas als Beispiel einer voelkerpsychologischen Untersuchung," *Beih. Z. angew. Psychol.*, 1938, 79, 162-186.

The National Psychological Structure of Southeastern Europe as an Example of National Psychological Research: The author, an army psychologist attached to Colonel Blau's staff, presents a model of psychological espionage reports.

390. Gauger, H. *Die Psychologie des Schweigens in England*. Anglistische Forschungen 84, Heidelberg: Winter, 1937.

The Psychology of Silence in England: An interesting essay praising the Englishman's talent for silence and understatement. It confirms its success not only in domestic policy, but in England's role as a world power. Quoting Carlyle, "Silence is the most mysterious power of all," the author concurs that the ability to hold one's tongue is the prerequisite of human greatness. Silent discipline, acquired in the hard school of life, has made England great. The British technique of understatement and unofficial propaganda is said to have brought America into the World War, whereas German propaganda was too open and direct, without tact or finesse. The series of books published by Heidelberg's Institute of Anglistic Studies, of which Miss Gauger's volume is one, shows the trend of German interest in Great Britain. Prior to Hitler's advent, the books dealt chiefly with strictly scientific subjects; now they are devoted to what the Nazis call "comparative national psychology," exploring weak or strong spots in the mental structure of their enemies.

391. —. *Persoenlicher Besitz als Grundlage von Fuehrertum und Verantwortungsbewusstsein in England.* Anglistische Forschungen 82, Heidelberg: Winter, 1936.
Private Property as a Basis of Leadership and Consciousness of Responsibility in England: Duty, the aristocratic principle, and preservation of private property are considered the principal elements of the British power-philosophy.

392. Goldenberg, —. "Das Wissen vom Gegner," *Soldatentum,* 1938, 259-263.
Knowledge of the Enemy: The author, an army psychologist, analyzes the importance and methods of psychological espionage during war.

393. Gramm, W. *Die Koerperpflege der Anglosachsen.* Anglistische Forschungen 86. Heidelberg: Winter, 1938.
The Physical Culture of the Anglo-Saxons: Another pseudoscientific contribution to the large-scale Nazi investigation centered on the problem: what makes England tick? The unequivocal answer maintains that Britain's tradition of sports has left its marks on the national character in both peace and war.

394. Hartmann, K. J. "Zur Psychologie der zwischenmenschlichen Kontaktbildung," *Z. f. Psychol.*, 1936, 164-191.

Psychology of Interhuman Contact.

395. Hellpach, W. "Voelkertum als Gegenstand der Voelker-Charakterologie," *Ber. Kongr. dtsch. Ges. Psychol.*, 1938, XVI, 104-110.

Folkdom as the Subject of National Characterology.

396. —. Einfuehrung in die Voelkerpsychologie. Stuttgart: Enke, 1938.

Introduction to National Psychology: Hellpach, one of Nazi Germany's foremost "national characterologists," determines a nation's character by the study of psychology, sociology and cultural history. Of Hellpach, Dr. Eliasberg writes: "A former liberal and Democratic candidate for the German presidency in 1924. Liberal Minister of Education in Baden, a *summa cum laude* graduate of Wundt's laboratory. And now, Hellpach is one of the most servile professors in Naziland, a typical example of the annihilation of spirit and honesty of German science."

397. Jaensch, E. R. "Der Gegentypus der deutschen voelkischen Bewegung," *Ber. Kongr. dtsch. Ges. Psychol.*, 1934, XIII, 56-58.

The Countertype of the German National Movement: Jaensch considers his S-type to be composed of men who are incapable of understanding the dynamism of the Nazi movement. It goes without saying that Jews are placed in this category.

398. Keilhacker, M. "Grundzuege des englischen Volkscharakters aufgezeigt an einer psychologischen Untersuchung der Welt Gladstones," *Beih. Z. angew. Psychol.*, 1938, 79,187-208.

The Basic Principles of the English National Character Established by a Psychological Examination of the Gladstone Era: This is an interesting and highly significant paper prepared by one of Colonel Blau's "psychological intelligence officers." Delivered to army psychologists at a post-graduate course, its conclusion is that Britain is not a decadent nation, since she has not been defeated in any of the wars of the last 150 years. This seems to be indicative of the High Command's attitude toward England which tried to eliminate her as an opponent of Germany; Britain was held to be invincible because of the impossibility of breaking down her morale.

399. Lersch, P. "Grundformen mitmenschlicher Einstellung," *Ber. Kongr. dtsch. Ges. Psychol.*, 1935, XIV, 119-122.
Basic Forms of Human Relations.

400. Loesch, K. C. v. *Das deutsche Volk, sein Boden und seine Verteidigung.* Berlin: Volk und Reich, 1937.
The German People, Their Country and Their Defense.

401. Marx, W. "Tacitus und der Weltkriegsdeutsche," *Soldatentum*, 1938, 59-64.
Tacitus and the German of the World War: An amazingly frank analysis of the German national character, asserting that Tacitus' findings are still valid as to the mental deficiencies and characterological shortcomings of the German people.

402. Muehlmann, W. *Rassen und Voelkerkunde. Lebensprobleme der Rassen, Gesellschaften und Voelker.* Leipzig: Vieweg, 1936.
Race Study and Ethnology; Life Problems of Races, Societies and Peoples.

403. Naegelsbach, —. "Allgemeine Gedanken zur Frage einer Charakterologie der Volksstaemme," *Soldatentum*, 1934, 105.
General Thoughts on the Characterology of Tribes.

404. Preuss, K. T. Lehrbuch der Voelkerkunde. Stuttgart: Enke, 1937.
Textbook of Ethnology.

405. Scheler, M. *Die Ursachen des Deutschenhasses.* Leipzig: Wolff, 1919.

Causes of World Hatred of Germany: A searching analysis of world prejudice and hatred toward Germany. This basic work is an exhaustive and objective treatment on its origin, and continuation on psychological, sociological and economic grounds.

406. Schulze-Gaevernitz, G. v. "Die geistesgeschichtlichen Grundlagen der anglo-amerikanischen Weltsuprematie," *Archiv fuer Sozialwissenschaft und Sozialpolitik,* 1926, 56, 58, 61 (160 pages).

The Spiritual Basis of Anglo-Saxon World Supremacy: The author, decidedly sympathetic toward the aims of Anglo-American democracy, asserts their political power is based on commerce and cultural influence throughout the world. Calvinism and Puritanism are considered the cultural bases of Anglo-American supremacy. Anglo-Saxon Puritanism produced a sexual discipline which eventually found its way into the political and cultural realm by effecting voluntary national discipline and freedom of conscience. America, inheriting the Puritan democracy of Roger Williams and William Penn, has become great through adherence to democratic ideals. Patriotic feeling is a silent and self-evident assumption of daily life. Laissez faire and fair play are evidences of Puritanism in Anglo-American commercial ethics. Nevertheless, the author warns that its basic concepts are endangered by super-capitalism and corrupt administration.

407. Schulze, F. E. O. "Die Struktur des freien Menschen," *Ber. Kongr. dtsch. Ges. Psychol.,* 1934, XIII, 173-175.

The Structure of Free Man: An involved attempt to prove that the Germans under the Nazis are really free, while the citizens of the democracies are slaves of conflicting political, social and economic interests.

408. Seeberg, R. *Unsere Hauptgegner und wir.* Berlin: Siegismund, 1918.

Germany and Her Principal Enemies: The importance of this material in psychological warfare is its use in determining the offensive operations of morale policy. The author analyzes hostility among belligerent powers in the World War from the standpoint of individual and national psychology. According to Seeberg, the four basic psychological types—sanguine, choleric, phlegmatic, melancholic—manifested themselves in the national character of the warring powers. He cites the "sanguinely inclined" Frenchman and the more "phlegmatically inclined" German as a pure contrast and considers this fact as a fundamental basis for relations between individual Frenchmen and Germans. He describes the English as "choleric": hardheaded, practical, of quick decision and maximum exhibition of energy. The Russians are termed sentimental melancholics incapable of sustained will, tenacity or decision. The stormy Frenchmen and vacillating Russians cannot match the competent will and capability of the English. The German, on the other hand, has an inner power, a basic culture and disciplined mind which, according to the author, are the true sources of world antagonism toward Germany, and not their so-called "barbarism."

409. Stransky, E. *Der Deutschenhass*. Wien-Leipzig, 1919.

Animosity Toward the Germans: An investigation of world animosity toward Germany and the German spirit written before the last war. Extremely valuable as a basic reference for German propagandists in their efforts to change and influence public opinion in foreign countries. The author views his subject from the standpoint of German national psychology and the psychological attitudes of other nations toward Germany. Economic, political and social factors are not overlooked. Stransky asserts that the hostile attitude toward the Reich is so impregnated that it can hardly be overcome. He allots to German propaganda the task of counteracting the caricature and distortion of Germans as barbarians and supermen. Of this author, Dr. Eliasberg writes: "Of Jewish origin, was baptized as an adult, and became the typical persecuté persecutor."

410. Weiser-Aal, L. *Volkskunde und Psychologie.* Berlin: Gruyter, 1937.
Ethnology and Psychology.

4. WEAPONS OF PSYCHOLOGICAL WARFARE

411. Anon. "Das Spottbild als politisches Kampfmittel der Gegenwart," *Der Weg zur Freiheit,* 1927, 11.
Caricature as a Contemporary Weapon of Politics.

412. Behne, A. *Das politische Plakat.* Charlottenburg: "Das Plakat," 1919.
The Political Poster.

413. Erdmann, K. "Aussenpolitik und Erziehung," *Z. f. Geopolitik,* 1937, 3, 177-186.
Foreign Policy and Education.

414. Evola, J. "Die Waffen des geheimen Krieges," *Die Tat,* 1939, 2, 745-753.
Weapons of Intellectual Warfare: The author, an Italian, has had great influence on the shaping of Germany's intellectual warfare. He is accepted by the imperialistic Tat-Kreis as one of their own men.

415. Mogens, V. "Politik, Propaganda, Presse, Publikum," *Deutsche Rundschau,* 1927, 54, 3.
Politics, Propaganda, Press, Public.

416. Scurla, H. "Strukturwandel der auswaertigen Kulturpolitik," *Jahrbuch der Hochschule fuer Politik,* 1939, 163-178.
Changes in the Structure of Foreign "Kulturpolitik": The author describes Kulturpolitik as a military weapon, accusing Great

Britain and the United States of making greater use of it than Germany and Italy.

417. Ziegfeld, A. H. "Kartengestaltung—Ein Sport oder eine Waffe," *Z. f. Geopolitik,* 1935, 4, 243-247.

Topography—Sport or Weapon? One of Haushofer's geopoliticians decides that topography is a weapon. Its role is to assist political leadership in singling out geographical localities to be attacked by the military.

a) Propaganda

418. Anon. "Geschichtliche Propagandawirkung," *Deutsche Allgemeine Zeitung,* 1926, 296.

Historical Effects of Propaganda.

419. Anon. *Die Ursachen des deutschen Zusammenbruchs im Jahre 1918.* Berlin: Reichswehrministerium, 1928.

Causes of Germany's Collapse in 1918: An official memorandum of the German Admiralty. Part One describes the methods and effectiveness of enemy propaganda, while Part Two reveals Germany's countermeasures. The book is remarkable for its objectivity.

420. Anon. "Propaganda und nationale Macht," *Deutsche Wehr,* 1933.

Propaganda and National Might.

421. Anon. "Propaganda—eine Kriegswaffe," *Militaer-Wochenblatt,* 1935, 38, 1503-1505.

Propaganda—A Weapon of War: The official weekly of the German War Ministry recognizes propaganda as a military weapon, and points out that German propaganda abroad must soften up foreign populations for the actual military attack.

422. Bauer, W. "Das Schlagwort als sozial-psychologische und geistesgeschichtliche Erscheinung," *Historische Zeitschrift,* Vol. 122 (3. Folge, 26), 1920, 189-240.

The Slogan as a Social-Psychological and Spiritual-Historical Phenomenon.

423. Berndt, A. I. *Ein Jahr Reichsministerium fuer Volksaufklaerung und Propaganda.* Special issue of the Deutsches Nachrichten Bureau, March 10, 1934.

One Year of the Reich Ministry of Public Enlightenment and Propaganda: The author, one of the highest officials of the Propaganda Ministry, reviews the reasons which led to the establishment of a Propaganda Ministry and describes its activities during its first year of existence.

424. Bie, R., and Muehr, A. *Die Kulturwaffen des neuen Reiches.* Jena: Diederichs, 1935.

Kultur Weapons of the New Reich: Addressing themselves directly to the men now responsible for German "Kultur," the authors describe how Nazism is formulating "a new order of mental and spiritual leadership." Slightly valuable for its psychological implications but written with a conspicuous lack of objectivity.

425. Blau, A. *Propaganda als Waffe.* Sonderdruck. Deutsche Gesellschaft fuer Wehrpolitik und Wehrwissenschaften. Third Series, October 1935.

Propaganda as a Weapon: Colonel Blau reprints the lecture which he delivered to a special session of the German Society of Military Politics and Military Sciences.

426. —. *Propaganda als Waffe.* Berlin: Bernard & Graefe, 1937.

Propaganda as a Weapon: Colonel Blau's basic textbook written for the enlightenment of general staff officers and not available to the public. It is by far the most interesting, illuminating and important of all German books on propaganda in modern warfare.

427. Classen, W. *Aussengeltung des Reiches*. Arbeiten zur auswaerti-gen Kulturpolitik. Heidelberger Akten der von Portheim Stiftung. Heidelberg: Winter, 1938.

Foreign Recognition of the Reich: An essay on the use of "cultural weapons" (propaganda) to secure world-wide recognition of German superiority.

428. Dovifat, E. *Rede und Redner*. Ihr Wesen und ihre politische Macht. Meyers Kleine Handbuecher 8. Leipzig: Bibl. Institut, 1937.

Public Speaking and Public Speaker: A director of the Nazi Public Speaking School claims that before National Socialism ushered in a new era of young German oratorical genius, the German bourgeoisie developed few great speakers outside of the first successful mass agitator, Ferdinand Lassalle, a Jew, and Bebel, a Marxist. National Socialism finally produced great speakers who devoted their ability no longer to individuals, parties, or groups, but who spoke to and for the "entire people." According to the author, Hitler and Mussolini are the forerunners of the European renascence in oratory after the tradition of the ancient Greek speechmakers. Valuable information on the organization and training of the Nazi speaker corps and practical advice on the nature of political speeches, effective speaking, climax and build-up. Also, interesting comparisons of famous men as speakers, among them Lloyd George, Clemenceau, Wilson, Kaiser Wilhelm.

429. Fellgiebel, E. "Aufklaerung und Propaganda durch Nachrichtenmittel," *Militaerwissenschaftliche Rundschau,* 1936, 4, 493.

Enlightenment and Propaganda Through Means of News Communications: General Fellgiebel is the chief of the German signal corps and in charge of propaganda by means of radio communications within the German psychological general staff. His ideas are fully presented in our Survey.

430. Franke, H., and Bertkau, F. "Wehrpropaganda." In *Handbuch der neuzeitlichen Wehrwissenschaften,* vol. 1, 710- 712. Berlin: Gruyter, 1936.

Military Propaganda: The authors describe the means and aims of publicizing the armed forces to secure the people's admiration and respect.

431. Goebbels, J. *Revolution der Deutschen*. Oldenburg: Stalling, 1933.

Revolution of the Germans: Speeches by the Nazi propaganda minister after Hitler's "seizure of power." After tirades against Republican statesmen and the "Weimar system," Goebbels says in a classic example of German domestic propaganda: "I declare here solemnly before Germany and the whole world that we desire only peace. The German people do not want war. We do not have the intention to create enemies unnecessarily. We wish those nations well who do not interfere with our honor and who permit us to earn our daily bread. We feel sorry for those nations who have fallen victim to the Jewish atrocity campaign against Germany. We deplore the fact that many people have been given a false picture of Germany. . . . We must therefore use other means to clarify German aims to the world. . . ." Goebbels has written scores of books, but they are far from being illuminating beyond being excellent pen-pictures of his own split-personality.

432. —. "Rassenfrage und Weltpropaganda," *Paedagogisches Magazin* 1390. Langensalza: Beyer, 1934.

The Race Question and World Propaganda: A pamphlet on the Jewish problem and anti-Jewish laws in Germany in which Jewry is stamped as the aggressor boring from within. The familiar thesis is set forth that Jewry dominated German intellectual life, and after the Nazi seizure of power instigated the boycott and atrocity propaganda against the Third Reich. Goebbels asserts the world should be thankful that the Nazis opened the eyes of the world to the "Jewish danger" and predicts that the whole world will be forced in the future to solve their own Jewish problem after the Nazi fashion.

433. Gutterer, L. "Propaganda als Politik," *Z. f. Politik,* 1935, 34-40.
   Propaganda as Politics.

434. Hadamovsky, E. *Propaganda und nationale Macht. Die Organisation der oeffentlichen Meinung fuer die nationale Politik.* Oldenburg: Stalling, 1933.
   Propaganda and National Might; Organization of Public Opinion for National Politics: Hadamovsky, the Nazi party's chief propaganda theorist and Germany's radio dictator, has had inestimable influence on the principles and practice of Nazi propaganda. In this volume, which must be considered as required reading, he describes the specific functions of radio in political education, the co-ordination of the press, how to use news services, churches, schools, universities, cultural societies, the theater, and movies for propaganda purposes. Numerous references are made to historic development of all these propaganda media during the World War and under the German Republic. The successful manipulation of the mass demonstration is held to be the reason for the phenomenal rise of Nazism. Hadamovsky's central thesis is that violence and propaganda go hand in hand, that terror and a display of power supplement verbal and written bombast. The author believes that all propaganda and indoctrination should be directed toward creating a "new type of Germanic man (*Germane*)" conscious of the national goal and a definite enemy. A few characteristic quotations from Hadamovsky may help the reader to form a better idea of this man. For example: "It is not the inherent truth of a word that refutes utterances of others, but only a new word pitted against an old one." Or: "Propaganda is the will-to-power and an instrument whose use alone can secure our sole domination of spirit and intellect."

435. Hitler, A. *Mein Kampf.* Muenchen: Eher, 1933.

Mein Kampf: The sections dealing with propaganda can be found on the following pages: Vol. 1, 193-204; Vol. II, 532, 649, 652, 654, 701, 716-718. See also No. 20.

436. Loesner, A. "Die Propaganda als Waffengattung in der Roten Armee," *Deutsche Wehr*, 1935, IX.

Propaganda as a Branch of Service in the Red Army: The present German system of propaganda in the armed forces conducted by a special section called PK (Propaganda Company), which includes all war correspondents and war photographers who are given military rank and special uniforms, is patterned after the pioneering Russian system which is described in this article.

437. Loibl, R. "Wehrpropaganda in der Wehrmacht," *Militaer-Wochenblatt*, 1936, 42, 1894-1899.

Military Propaganda in the Armed Forces.

438. Martin, O. "Propaganda als Kriegsmittel," *Deutsche Wehr*, 1931, 51.

Propaganda as a Weapon of War: Written by a Reichswehr lieutenant during the Weimar Republic, long before the Nazis appreciated his foresight, which was undoubtedly shared by the masters of the Reichswehr.

439. Morgen, K. *Kriegspropaganda und Kriegsverhuetung*. Leipzig: Noske, 1936.

War Propaganda and Prevention of War: An essay attempting to expose foreign war propaganda and Germany's efforts to preserve peace.

440. Muenzenberg, W. *Propaganda als Waffe*. Paris, 1937.

Propaganda as a Weapon: This is the only book by a German refugee included in the bibliography, but it is sufficiently objective and vitally informative to warrant its listing. Muenzenberg was reported killed after the Germans entered Paris. He was a prominent Communist newspaper editor in Germany who turned against Stalin after the signing of the Russo-German nonaggression pact.

441. Picht, W. *"Das Oberkommando gibt bekannt."* Berlin: Mittler, 1940.

"The High Command Announces": A popular attempt to prove the truthfulness and accuracy of German war-communiques and the inaccuracy and mendacity of the communiques of the enemy. Primarily an effort to increase the Germans' faith in official war news.

442. Plenge, J. *Deutsche Propaganda. Die Lehre von Propaganda als praktische Gesellschaftslehre.* Bremen: Angelsachsen Verlag, 1922.

German Propaganda; The Science of Propaganda as a Practical Social Science: The author, director of the first German Propaganda Research Institute of the University of Muenster, advocates (already in 1922) the establishment of a new national system of upbringing and education. There, he predicts, lies the secret of German power in the future. The book treats propaganda as an imperative medium for influencing public opinion, and contains a short analysis of propaganda and counterpropaganda tactics, some of which were later adopted by the Nazis who have a high regard for this volume.

443. Prosch, W. *Die Propaganda. Ihre Anwendung in der Politik and ihre Bedeutung fuer Deutschlands Aufstieg.* Dissertation. Hamburg, 1924.

Propaganda; Its Application in Politics and Its Importance for Germany's Rise.

444. Scheffer, P. "Forderungen statt Propaganda," *Das Reich,* Oct. 15, 1940.

Demands Instead of Propaganda: The author was New York correspondent of the Propaganda Ministry's own political weekly.

445. Scheleher, W. "Politische Schlagworte," *Deutsche Rundschau,* 1923, 49, 10.

Political Slogans.

446. Schoenemann, F. *Die Kunst der Massenbeeinflussung in den Vereinigten Staaten von Amerika.* Stuttgart: Deutsche Verlagsanst., 1924.

The Art of Influencing the Masses in the United States of America: The author, a prominent professor at the Berlin University and the Propaganda Ministry's own Hochschule fuer Politik, is recognized as the Nazis' foremost expert on the United States. In this book he analyzes the factors and forces influencing public opinion in the United States. In another lecture, he distinctly warned against the prevalent German tendency of underestimating America as a potential world power when he said: "America is much more important for us and it has much greater influence on the development of European politics than most of us realize. It would be wrong either to underrate and slight, or to fail to study the United States just as thoroughly and systematically as other great powers in the world. Such past shortsightedness caused us to make a serious blunder and we simply cannot afford to repeat it."

447. Schultze-Pfaelzer, G. *Propaganda, Agitation, Reklame.* Eine Theorie des Gesamten Werbewesens. Berlin: Stilke, 1923.

Propaganda, Agitation, Advertising: Another one of his books is *Wir suchen Deutschland* (We search for Germany), a free discussion with the author, Otto Strasser, Major Buchrucker of Kuestrin fame, and Herbert Blank. The book is remarkable for the open-mindedness of the debate.

448. Schwertfeger, B. "Die Propaganda," In *Handbuch der Politik.* (Third edition.) 1922.

Propaganda.

449. Six, F. A. *Die politische Propaganda der NSDAP im Kampf um die Macht*. Heidelberg: Winter, 1936.

The Political Propaganda of the Nazi Party During Its Struggle for Power: A young German professor of journalism at Koenigsberg University, who became quite prominent as a Nazi representative at various international student gatherings prior to the war, presents a valuable insight into the aims and techniques of the Nazi propaganda machine and a detailed description of its machinery. The book is fully reviewed in the Survey.

450. Stark, G. *Moderne politische Propaganda*. Muenchen: Eher, 1930.

Modern Political Propaganda: A Nazi party propagandist reveals the methods and techniques of Nazi propaganda.

451. Stark, L. "Der Propagandakrieg," *Militaer-Wochenblatt*, 1935, 20.

Propaganda War: Basing his conclusions on experiences gained during the last war, the author predicts that propaganda will be the chief weapon in the war "to come." He says: "Next to armed action, intellectual offensives will decide the conflicts of the future."

452. Stern-Rubarth, E. *Propaganda als politisches Instrument*. Berlin: 1921.

Propaganda as a Political Instrument: The author, formerly chief editor of the official news agency and now living in London, outlines the political importance of propaganda with this book, thus providing the Nazis with a blueprint which they are widely using now. Stern-Rubarth surveys the history of propaganda, its manipulations of symbols and slogans, its techniques in exploiting martyrdom, faith, and superstition, and its transmission at home and abroad through all the media of mass communication. He suggests Pan-Germanism as the most effective political goal toward mobilizing the sympathies of Germany and the world.

453. Sturminger, A. *Politische Propaganda in der Weltgeschichte.* Salzburg: 1938.

Political Propaganda in World History: An excellent historical review.

454. Thimme, H. *Weltkrieg ohne Waffen. Die Propaganda der West-maechte gegen Deutschland, ihre Wirkung und ihre Abwehr.* Stuttgart: Cotta, 1932.

World War Without Weapons. The Propaganda of the Western Powers, Its Effects and Counterdefense: Generally follows the thesis, originated by Ludendorff, that the western powers owe their victory to clever British propaganda on the one hand, and to complete lack of German counterpropaganda on the other. High praise is given to the American system of propaganda which presented the war to its people as a struggle of "progress and humanity" against "barbarism and the suppression of freedom." The author, who had at his disposal various documents of the General Staff, makes a valuable expose of Allied propaganda and espionage operations in Switzerland and Holland. Like so many other German experts and historians, however, he tends to whitewash the military defeat of the Central Powers by blowing up the effectiveness of Allied propaganda.

455. Wanderscheck, H. "Schoepferische Propaganda," *Muenchner Neueste Nachrichten,* 1933, 228.

Creative Propaganda.

456. —. *Weltkrieg und Propaganda.* Berlin: Mittler, 1936.

World War and Propaganda.

457. Wrochem, A. v. *Die Vernichtungspropaganda gegen das deutsche Volk.* Berlin: Mittler, 1925.

The Destructive Propaganda Directed Against the German People: This tendentious little book is important because its author is a high official of the Propaganda Ministry and the War Ministry's liaison officer for civilian propaganda.

b) Press

458. Binder, H. *Was wir als Kriegsberichterstatter nicht sagen durften*. Muenchen: Privately published by the author, 1919.

What We War Correspondents Were Not Permitted to Say: An extremely important brochure written by an official of the German High Command's press department during the last war, revealing Major Nicolai's technique of news handling. Speculating on the reasons for defeat, Binder comes to the conclusions that Germany, despite intensive preparation down to the last minute detail, lost the war because of unexpected eventualities.

459. Boemer, K. *Die Freiheit der Presse im nationalsozialistischen Staat*. Oldenburg: Stalling, 1933.

The Freedom of the Press in the Nazi State: The author (recently killed in Russia) was the head of the Propaganda Ministry's foreign press department until an indiscretion caused his dishonorable discharge and prosecution before the People's Court. In a lecture before the defunct Anglo-German Academic Association, he purports to explain why journalists of the Third Reich have more freedom than journalists of other nations. The Nazi press is free because it is "independent of financial, economic and political interests," and for the first time, it is able to "serve the interest of the people as a whole." An interesting example of the use of ingenious Nazi sophistry to explain a nonexistent situation.

460. —. *Das internationale Zeitungswesen*. Berlin: Gruyter, 1934.

The International Newspaper World: A somewhat outdated reference book on the world press, by one who certainly knew how to influence it.

461. —. *Das Dritte Reich im Spiegel der Weltpresse*. Leipzig: Armament, 1934.

The Third Reich as Mirrored by the World Press: Commenting on propaganda techniques the world over, Professor Boemer makes the assertion that German propaganda represents nothing but the truth. He is frank, however, in stating that the first requisite of propaganda is to formulate suitable psychological attitudes toward various groups in the population. Complicated issues must be boiled down into slogans to be hammered again and again into the mass consciousness. Propaganda, he concludes, must be directed and supported by absolute authority.

462. —. "Die Methoden auslaendischer Pressepropaganda," *Nationalsozialistische Monatshefte*, 1934, 10, 913.

Methods of Foreign Press Propaganda.

463. Eltzbacher, P. *Die Presse als Werkzeug der auswaertigen Politik*. Jena: Diederichs, 1918.

The Press as an Instrument of Foreign Policy: Stating that the press is the principal means of influencing foreign policy, the author describes the French and British press as willing instruments of their governments. A permanent German press organization, subsidized and given privileges, is advocated to serve the aims of the government's policy.

464. Hoenig, H. O. *Das Aktuelle in der deutschen Presse*. Dresden: Dittert, 1938.

Topical News in the German Press.

465. Kaiser, F. *Die Zeitung als Mittel der Nationalerziehung*. Leipzig: Noske, 1934.

The Newspaper as a Means of National Education.

466. Lueddecke, Th. *Die Tageszeitung als Mittel der Staatsfuehrung*. Hamburg: Hans. Verlagsanst., 1933.

The Newspaper as a Means of State Leadership: The author was the co-ordinator of the German press soon after the Nazis' seizure of power. Believing that press and government have a common purpose, he outlines ways and means of organizing and unifying press, state, and political party. Highly interesting is the discussion of Nazi party propaganda in contrast to the propaganda of the liberal parties and the relationship between the German and Russian systems of directing news.

467. Muenster, H. A. *Publizistik. Menschen—Mittel—Methoden.* Leipzig: Bibl. Inst., 1939.
Publicism; Men, Means, Methods: The author of this popular little reference book is a professor at the Leipzig University.

468. Menz, G. M. H. *Die Zeitschrift als Fuehrungsmittel.* Leipzig: Noske, 1935.
The Periodical as a Means of Leadership: An unoriginal lecture by the director of the Institute of Publications Research at Leipzig University. He presents the magazine as a state instrument rather than commercial enterprise.

469. Nennstiel, K. *Presse und Propaganda.* Weimar: Fink, 1936.
Press and Propaganda.

470. Starcke, G. *Die Presse der Deutschen Arbeitsfront.* Leipzig: Noske, 1936.
The Press of the German Labor Front: A press agent of the Nazi Labor Front describes the organization of the co-ordinated German labor press (twenty million readers).

471. Stiewe, W. "Das Bild als Nachricht," *Zeitung und Zeit,* 1933, 5.
Picture as News: The author is editor-in-chief of one of the biggest German illustrated papers, *Die Neue I. Z.*

472. —. *Das Pressephoto als publizistisches Mittel.* Leipzig: Noske, 1936.

The Press Photo as a Means of Publicism: An excellent guide to the use of press photos in German propaganda. Stiewe describes what pictures to use, how and where to reproduce them. The presentation of a picture depends on what psychological effect is sought. Stiewe's work must be regarded as the last word on the propaganda value of press photography in Germany.

473. Toennies, F. "Die Bedeutung der Presse fuer die oeffentliche Meinung," *Der Weg zur Freiheit,* 1928, 8, 17.

The Significance of the Press for Public Opinion.

474. Traub, H. *Zeitung, Film, Rundfunk.* Berlin: Weidmann, 1933.

Newspaper, Film, Radio.

475. Waldkirch, W. *Weltpresse und Weltkrise.* Ludwigshafen: Waldkirch, 1936.

World Press and World Crisis.

477. —. *Die zeitungspolitische Aufgabe.* (3 volumes,) Ludwigshafen: Waldkirch, 1935.

The Political Task of the Newspaper: Volume one is devoted to a historical review of the newspaper; volume two discusses the political effects, and volume three the political power of the newspaper.

478. Wiss, W. J. "Das Pressewesen der Vereinigten Staaten und die hinter ihm stehenden Kraefte," *Z. f. Politik,* 1938, 11-12, 680-688.

The Press of the United States and the Forces Behind It.

479. Zankl, H. L. *Zeitungsbild und Nationalpropaganda.* Leipzig: Noske, 1938.

Newspaper Make-up and National Propaganda: Practical advice on how to increase the effect of propaganda by clever composition.

480. Zerkaulen, H. *Die kulturpolitische Sendung der deutschen Zeitung.* Leipzig: Noske, 1934.
The Cultural and Political Mission of the German Newspaper.

c) Leaflet

481. Riesch, E. "Das Flugblatt in Luftkrieg," *Archiv fuer Luftrecht,* 1933, 3, 65.
Leaflets in Air War.

482. Schottenloehr, K. *Flugblatt und Zeitung. Wegweiser durch das gedruckte Tagesschrifttum,* Berlin: Schmidt, 1922.
Leaflet and Newspaper.

d) Film

483. Belling, C. *Der Film im Staat und Partei.* Berlin: *"Der Film,"* 1936.
The Role of Films in State and Party: The Nazi party's director of propaganda presents a short history of his organization's film propaganda, its purpose, organization, and success. He describes the film as an "instrument to build up the will of the New Germany," appraising its value as a means of popular enlightenment and education.

484. Guenther, W. *Der Film als politisches Fuehrungsmittel.* Leipzig: Noske, 1934.
The Film as a Means of Political Leadership.

485. Wagner, —. "Film oder nicht?" *Militaer-Wochenblatt,* 1938, 19, 1224.

Movies or No Movies? An army officer analyzes the practicability of motion pictures for military education and propaganda.

486. Wehlau, K. *Das Lichtbild in der Werbung fuer Politik, Kultur und Wirtschaft.* Seine geschichtliche Entwicklung und gegenwaertige Bedeutung. Wuerzburg: Triltsch, 1939.

The Role of Film in Political, Cultural, and Economic Propaganda: An analysis of the history and present importance of motion picture propaganda.

e) Radio

487. Anon. "Welt-Rundfunk," *Z. f. Geopolitik,* 1937, 8, 685-716.

World Radio: Limitation of space prevents us from listing all the articles which Haushofer's *Zeitschrift fuer Geopolitik* has published on radio. The following are samples of the scope and contents of these articles. The present title includes a series of contributions on "German Radio and International Understanding," "Economy and Radio," and "The Mediterranean as a Radio Sphere."

488. Anon. "Welt-Rundfunk," *Z. f. Geopolitik,* 1937, 10, 869-900.

World Radio: A series of articles entitled "Radio and Geopolitics," "The American Radio," and "The Radio in Canada."

489. Anon. "Welt-Rundfunk," *Z. f. Geopolitik,* 1937, 12, 1049-1078.

World Radio: Includes "Radio without Borders," and "England and its Radio."

490. Anon. "Welt-Rundfunk," *Z. f. Geopolitik,* 1937, 2, 145-176.

World Radio: Contributions by H. Dressler-Andress, K. v. Boeckmann, V. Yloestalo, H. Fritzsche, A. A. Guilliland, H. Schaefer, F. Springer.

491. Anon. "Welt-Rundfunk," *Z. f. Geopolitik,* 1937, 4, 321-352.
World Radio: Includes "Television—Possibilities and Accomplishments," "Radio News," "Radio World Exchange," "The Magic of Radio," "South African Radio" and others.

492. Goebbels, J. *Nationalsozialistischer Rundfunk.* Muenchen: Eher, 1935.
National Socialist Radio: An article devoted to platitudes.

493. Hadamovsky, E. *Der Rundfunk im Dienste der Volksfuehrung.* Leipzig: Noske, 1934.
Radio in the Service of the State Leadership: Hadamovsky outlines the definitive functions and programs of radio under Nazism.

494. —. *Dein Rundfunk.* Muenchen: Eher, 1934.
Your Radio: A popular radio book to go with the *Volksempfaenger,* a cheap receiving set designed to make radios available to every German and to exclude the possibility of foreign reception by having the radio tuned for German stations only.

495. Sphinger, F. "Rundfunk und Geopolitik," *Z. f. Geopolitik,* 1937, 7, 468-473; 8, 548-554; 9, 631-641; 11, 777-780.
Radio and Geopolitics.

496. Vowinckel, K. "Zur geistigen Blockade Deutschlands im Weltkrieg," *Z. f. Geopolitik,* 1937, 3.
The Intellectual Blockade of Germany: During the last war, the British succeeded in cutting the German-American cable off Emden, and thus deprived the Germans of getting their news across to the United States. The author, believing that the invention of radio makes such a "news blockade" impossible, outlines the tremendous importance of radio as a medium of German war propaganda.

497. Wagenfuehr, K. "Ein Jahr Aetherkrieg ueber Spanien," *Funkwacht*, 1937, 12, 27.

One Year of Radio War in Spain: A description of radio propaganda methods used during the Spanish Civil War where Germany tested her radio propaganda techniques as a dress rehearsal for the coming war.

f) Geopolitics

498. Anon. "Bauerntum und Geopolitik," *Z. f. Geopolitik*, 1936, 5, 328-336.

Peasantry and Geopolitics.

499. Baumann, M. "Die deutsche Aufgabe der Seeschiffahrt," *Z. f. Geopolitik*, 1935, 6, 366-369.

The German Task of High Sea Merchant Shipping: Members of the German merchant marine are considered "geopolitical agents," and this article points out their place and role in Germany's geopolitical work.

500. Billeb, E. "Geopolitische Auswirkungen der Luftfahrt," *Z. f. Geopolitik*, 1937, 12, 996-1004.

Geopolitical Effects of Aviation.

501. Fittbogen, G. "Sprachinselforschung und Volkstumkunde," *Z. f. Geopolitik*, 1935, 5, 320-325.

Research in "Language Islands" and Ethnology.

502. Haushofer, K. (editor) *Zeitschrift fuer Geopolitik*. Vol. 1, No. 1. Heidelberg: Vowinckel, 1933-1942.

Journal of Geopolitics: This unique periodical is entirely devoted to the findings of General Haushofer's geopolitical agents. Its study provides an insight into the amazing advance work done by Germany to find soft spots in the political, social and economic structure of foreign nations for future exploitation. Also see Mitteilungen der Deutschen Akademie.

503. —. "Pflicht und Anspruch der Geopolitik als Wissenschaft," *Z. f. Geopolitik,* 1935, 7, 443-448.
Duties and Demands of Geopolitics as a Science.

504. —. "Geopolitik als Grundlage jeder Raumordnung," *Z. f. Geopolitik,* 1936, 2, 128-130.
Geopolitics as the Basis of Every Geographical Order.

505. —. "Raumueberwindende Maenner," *Z. f. Geopolitik,* 1937, 3,186-188.
Men Beyond Space: Haushofer outlines "geopolitical work in a certain direction," meaning the co-operation of his collaborators for Germany's grandiose preparations for world domination.

506. Jantzen, W. "Kartenplakate fuer Aufklaerung und Werbung," *Z. f. Geopolitik,* 1936, 10, 696-700.
Geographical Posters as Enlightenment and Propaganda.

507. —. "Aussprache ueber Geopolitik," *Z. f. Geopolitik,* 1935, 6, 393-399.
Speeches on Geopolitics.

508. Kerrl, H. "Satzungen der Reichsarbeitsgemeinschaft fuer Raumforschung," *Z. f. Geopolitik,* 1936, 2, 130-134.
Statutes of the German Society of Geographical Research.

509. Langen, E. "Zur juristischen Geopolitik Europas," *Z. f. Geopolitik,* 1935, 5, 296-301.
Legal Geopolitics of Europe.

510. Offe, G. "Geopolitik und Naturrecht," *Z. f. Geopolitik*, 1937, 3, 188-201.
   Geopolitics and Natural Right.

511. Rauecker, B. "Die geopolitische Bedingtheit der Sozialpolitik," *Z. f. Geopolitik*, 1936, 5, 345-350; 6, 416-421; 7, 474-478.
   The Geopolitical Conditions of Social Politics.

512. Ritterhausen, H. "Politischer Machtfaktor Gold," *Z. f. Geopolitik*, 1937, 9, 781-785.
   Gold—a Factor of Political Power.

513. Schepers, H. "Geopolitische Grundlagen der Raumordnung," *Z. f. Geopolitik*, 1936, 1, 17-32.
   Geopolitical Principles of Germany's Geographical Order.

514. Schumacher, R. v. 'Zur Theorie der geopolitischen Signatur," *Z. f. Geopolitik*, 1935, 4, 247-265.
   Theory of Geopolitical Signs: A list of the markings used in making geopolitical maps, i.e., maps for the political leader indicating the industrial establishments, the natural resources and defense establishments of foreign nations.

515. Siewert, W. "Flugzeug und Erdraum," *Z. f. Geopolitik*, 1935, 8, 508-516.
   The Airplane and the Earth.

516. Vowinckel, K. "Geopolitik und geopolitische Geographie," *Z. f. Geopolitik*, 1935, 10, 688-693.
   Geopolitics and Geopolitical Geography.

517. —. "Tagung der Reichsarbeitsgemeinschaft fuer Raumforschung auf der Marienburg," *Z. f. Geopolitik*, 1937, 8, 665-668.
   A Report on the Congress of the German Society of Geographical Research in Marienburg.

The listings above are samples of the mass of geopolitical material contained in the *Zeitschrift fuer Geopolitik*. A complete listing is obviously impossible. We recommend a careful study of the periodical as essential to obtain a complete understanding of what geopolitics means in present-day Germany and a realization of the menace it represents to the world.

g) Espionage

518. Adler, A. *Die Spionage.* Eine voelkerrechtliche Studie. Marburg: Ehrhardt, 1906.
    Espionage: Investigates espionage from the standpoint of international law.

519. Hahn, B. *Industrie-Spionage.* Erlangen: Krahl, 1935.
    Industrial Espionage: A comprehensive dissertation, chiefly from the legal point of view.

520. Heinz, —. "Spionageabwehr," In *Jahrbuch des deutschen Heeres,* 1938, 120-127. Leipzig: Breitkopf & Haertel, 1939.
    Counterespionage: A captain of the German Army outlines espionage laws and describes agencies engaged in counterespionage.

521. Lettow-Vorbeck, P. E. v. *Die Weltkriegsspionage.* Muenchen: Moser, 1931.
    Espionage During the World War: This monumental collection of special articles by numerous contributors was sponsored by the German War Ministry. It presents a comprehensive picture of espionage operations during the last war, with suggestions for the "war to come."

522. Nicolai, W. *Geheime Maechte. Internationale Spionage und ihre Bekaempfung im Weltkrieg. und heute.* Leipzig: Koehler, 1924.

Secret Powers; International Espionage and Counterespionage during the World War and Today: An exposé of espionage methods written by the former chief of the German intelligence service. Also see No. 356.

523. Ronge, M. *Kriegs- und Industriespionage*. Zuerich: Amalthea, 1930.
War and Industrial Espionage: A scholarly work by a former Austrian general.

524. Schwartz, W. *Industriespionage*. Breslau: Kuntze, 1937.
Industrial Espionage.

525. Urbanski, A. v. "Flugzeug und Spionage," *Militaerwissenschaftliche Mitteilungen*, 1936, 8, 635-647.
Airplane and Espionage: An excellent article by a general, formerly head of the Austrian intelligence service. Discusses the problems of effective "espionage from the air" during peacetime, aerial observation of a deployment, border fortifications, sabotage, and the use of the airplane for propaganda purposes.

h) Fifth Column

526. Bauer, H. "Deutsche Offiziere im Dienste suedosteuropaeischer Staaten," *Mitteilungen der Deutschen Akademie*, Muenchen, 14, 317.
German Officers in the Service of Southeastern European States.

527. Beyer, H. J. "Zur Frage der Umvolkung. Zur Psychologie der Umvolkung," *Auslandsdeutsche Forschungen*, Stuttgart, 1937, 1, 317.
The Question of Changing Nationality. Psychology of changing nationality.

528. Ehrich, E. *Die Auslandsorganisation der NSDAP*. Berlin; Junker & Duennhaupt, 1937.

The Foreign Organization of the Nazi Party: The chief of the organization's press departments presents a candid picture of the agency's structure and functions.

529. Feldkeller, P. "Voraussetzungen der Diplomatie," *Die Tat*, 1936, 2.

Prerequisites of Diplomacy.

530. Fittbogen, G. *Wie lerne ich die Grenz- und Auslandsdeutschen kennen*. Dessau: Duennhaupt, 1923.

How to Become Acquainted With Germans Abroad.

531. —. *Was jeder Deutsche vom Grenz- und Auslandsdeutschtum wissen muss*. Muenchen: Oldenburg, 1924.

What Every German Should Know of the Germandom Abroad and on the Border: Border-Germans are those foreigners of German origin who live in the vicinity of the German frontiers, like Sudeten-Germans, Hungarian-Germans, Italian-Germans, etc. Foreign Germans are foreigners of German origin living in more distant countries, particularly overseas. According to Hitler, all Germans irrespective of their present nationality or allegiance, whether living inside or outside the Reich, whether first, second or tenth generations, belong to the "blood-community of all Germans."

532. Gennrich, P. *Der Krieg und unsere Volksgenossen im Ausland*. Magdeburg: Holtermann, 1915.

The War and Our Fellow Germans Abroad.

533. Grothe, H. *Die Deutschen in Uebersee*. Berlin: Zentralverlag, 1932.

Germans Overseas.

534. —. *Grundfragen und Tatsachen zur Kunde des Grenz- und Auslanddeutschtums.* Dresden: V. D. A., 1926.
Basic Problems of the Science of Germandom on the Border and Abroad.

535. Hauff, W. v. *Die wirtschaftlichen und politischen Aufgaben des Auslanddeutschtums.* Karlsruhe: Braun, 1925.
Economic and Political Tasks of the Germandom Abroad: As may be seen from these books, the problem of "Germandom abroad" was in the center of German nationalistic interests long before Hitler came into power. In fact, the Nazis expropriated existing organizations and developed their activities to an unprecedented extent.

536. —. "Die psychologische und soziologische Einstellung der Auslandsdeutschen zu ihrer Umgebung," *Forschungen zur Voelkerpsychologie und Soziologie,* Leipzig, 1927.
The Psychological and Sociological Attitudes of Foreign-Germans to their Environment.

537. Haushofer, K. *Der nationalsozialistische Gedanke in der Welt.* Muenchen: Callwey, 1932.
The Nazi Philosophy in the World.

538. Mai, R. *Auslandsdeutsche Quellenkunde.* Berlin: 1936.
Foreign-German Sources.

539. Mannhardt, J. W. *Grenz- und Auslandsdeutschtum als Lehrgegenstand.* Jena: Fischer, 1926.
Border- and Foreign-Germans as Subjects for Teaching.

540. Melching, L. "Umvolkung als psychologisches Problem," *Z. angew. Psychol.,* 1938, 54, 2, 138-140.
The Change of Nationality as a Psychological Problem: Report on the first congress of the German Institute of Foreign-Germandom.

541. Schumacher, R. v. *Volk vor den Grenzen. Schicksal und Sinn des Auslanddeutschtums in der gesamtdeutschen Verflechtung.* Stuttgart: Union, 1936.

A Nation Outside Its Borders: The subtitle of this rather important book deserves translation because of its typically Nazi confoundedness. It reads something like "Fate and Meaning of Germandom Abroad within the Total-German Entanglement."

542. Spohr, W. *Deutsche in Uebersee.* Berlin, 1931.
Germans Overseas.

543. Thierfelder, F. *Die wirtschaftliche Bedeutung des Auslanddeutschtums.* Stuttgart: Union, 1934.
The Economic Importance of Germandom Abroad.

5. POSITIVE AND NEGATIVE FACTORS
AFFECTING CIVILIAN MORALE

544. Baumgarten, O. *Der sittliche Zustand des deutschen Volkes unter dem Einfluss des Krieges.* 1927.
The Morality of the German People Under the Influence of War.

545. Bramesfeld, E. "Die Welt des Arbeiters und die soldatische Lebensform," *Soldatentum,* 1936, 120-128, 158-168.
The World of the Workers and the Military Way of Life: The author is a professor at the Darmstadt Institute of Technology.

546. Fischer, —. "Die Bekaempfung des Panikproblems im zivilen Luftschutz," *Soldatentum,* 1939, 18-23.
Solution of the Panic Problem in Civilian Air Raid Precautions.

547. Grunsky, H. A. *Seele und Staat.* Berlin, 1935.
Mind and State.

548. Grunwaldt, H. H. "Ueber die psychischen Bedingungen des Luftschutzes," *Wissen und Wehr,* 1937, 6.
The Psychological Conditions of Air-Raid Precautions.

549. Hampe, E. *Der Mensch und die Luftgefahr.* Berlin: Raeder, 1936.
Human Beings and Danger from the Air: A popular volume on German air-raid precautions.

550. Hanslian, R. "Die grosse Beunruhigung, oder die Nation unter Gas," *Z. f. d. ges. Schuss- und Sprengstoffwesen,* 1937, 1.
The Great Disturbance, or the Nation Under Gas.

551. Hartmann, G. v. "Militaerische Notwendigkeit und Humanitaet," *Deutsche Rundschau,* 1877-78, XIII-XIV.
Humanity and Military Necessity.

552. Himmler, H. *Die Schutzstaffel als antibolschewistische Kampforganisation.* Muenchen: Eher, 1936.
The Black Corps as an Anticommunist Fighting Organization: The author, as it is well known, is the commander-in-chief of the entire German police system, the Fouche of Nazi Germany.

553. Knipfer, —, and Hampe, E. *Der zivile Luftschutz.* Berlin: Stollberg, 1934.
Civilian Air-Raid Precautions.

554. Lueders, M. E. *Das unbekannte Heer.* Berlin: Mittler, 1937.
The Unknown Army: The organization of women for war.

555. Metzsch, H. v. *Der einzige Schutz gegen die Niederlage.* Breslau: Hirt, 1938.
The Only Protection Against Defeat: A call for the mobilization of Germany's morale forces.

556. Peres, W. *Gas und Bomben drohen!* Leipzig, 1932.
Gas and Bombs Threaten!

557. —. *Wirkung von Sprengbomben, Gasschutz und Luftschutz.* Berlin, 1932.
The Effect of Explosive Bombs, Gas, and Air-Raid Precautions.

558. Perignon, L. "Die psychologischen Grundlagen der Selbst-schutzausbildung," *Soldatentum,* 1939, 299-305.
The Psychological Bases of Education for Self-Defense: The author is a high official of the German air-raid-precaution service.

559. Rohden, H. "Betrachtungen ueber den Luftkrieg," *Militaer-wissenschaftliche Rundschau,* 1937, 2, 198; 3, 347; 4, 504; 5, 716.
Air War.

560. Schwarz von Berk. *Die sozialistische Auslese.* Breslau: Hirt, 1934.
Socialistic Selection.

561. Stern, W. "Jugendliches Seelenleben und Krieg," *Beih. Z. angew. Psychol.,* 1915, 12, 1-181.
The Mental World of the Youth and War: With contributions by K. W. Dix, C. Kik, A. Mann.

COMMITTEE FOR NATIONAL MORALE

The Committee for National Morale, a voluntary, private, non-profit organization, was formed in July, 1940, in the conviction that morale represents a decisive force in human affairs which needs to be thoroughly understood and intelligently utilized for the national safety and welfare. High morale is basic and indispensable to every undertaking in the present supreme crisis.

The problems of morale are complex and many-sided, and must be studied from varied points of view which must also be intelligently co-ordinated. The Committee brings to these studies a distinguished personnel of some 100 outstanding specialists in the different relevant fields: psychologists, sociologists, political scientists, educators, historians, physicians, physiologists, psychiatrists, propaganda and public opinion analysts, publicists, radio and motion picture experts, students of foreign affairs, military scientists, social workers, national economists, etc.

The Committee for National Morale undertakes:

1. Fact finding and research on the major problems of morale; publication of the results for both the specialist and the general public.

2. The formulation of controlling principles of morale in every kind of situation.

3. The planning and promotion of practical measures to protect and enhance the country's morale
in all groups and in every typical activity.

Among the Committee's major accomplishments are: preparation, upon invitation, for a Cabinet Sub-Committee of the President of the United States, of a 500-page report on morale with
recommendations many of which have been realized in existing
measures and morale-building agencies; the present "German
Psychological Warfare," a critical survey and bibliography of German methods of military psychology and propaganda warfare;
"The Axis Grand Strategy—Blueprints for the Total War," a comprehensive study of German methods of modern warfare; and numerous independent research projects, such as a study to discover
penetration and intensity of Axis propaganda in the United States;
character studies of the German, French, Italian, Hungarian,
Chinese and Japanese peoples, and a series of confidential projects,
executed upon invitation for government and private agencies.

Members of the Committee for National Morale

AMERICAN TRADITION:
James Truslow Adams
Van Wyck Brooks
Prof. Robert McElroy
Prof. Ralph Barton Perry

ART, MUSIC:
Dr. Phyllis Ackerman
Samuel L. M. Barlow
Dr. Walter J. Damrosch
Edwin Hughes
Miss Irene Lewisohn
Dean Everett V. Meeks

Arthur Upham Pope
S. Stephenson Smith

EDUCATION & HISTORY:

Dr. James Rowland Angell
John Farrar
Dr. Horace M. Kallen
Dr. Frank Kingdon
Dr. Kurt Lewin
Sidney Mandell
Prof. Robert McElroy
Prof. Ralph Barton Perry
Arthur Upham Pope
Dr. George N. Shuster
Dr. Ordway Tead
Prof. Goodwin B. Watson
Prof. Kimball Young

FOREIGN AFFAIRS:

Louis Adamic
E. C. Carter
Mrs. Florence Conrad
Elmer Davis
Clark Eichelberger
Ladislas Farago
Dr. Henry Field
Lewis Frederick Gittler
Francis Hackett
Mrs. J. Borden Harriman
Dr. Ernst Jackh
Dr. Tibor Koeves
Prof. Owen Lattimore
Prof. Max Lerner
Douglas Miller
Prof. Frederick L. Schuman

Lisa Sergio
Count Carlo Sforza
Johannes Steel
Robert Strausz-Hupe
Raymond Gram Swing
Sigrid Undset
Prof. Rustem Vambery
Pierre van Paassen

FOREIGN MINORITIES:
Louis Adamic
Mrs. Rita W. Morgenthau
Dr. M. W. Royse
Count Sforzino Sforza

JOURNALISM, PUBLIC OPINION:
George Backer
Joseph Gollomb
Samuel Grafton
John Gunther
Henry Hoke
Eliot Janeway
Edgar Ansel Mowrer
Chester H. Rowell
Robert Aura Smith
Gabriel Vogliotti

LIAISON:
Mrs. Ruth Cranston
Harry B. Price
Richard C. Rothschild
Mrs. George Rublee
Marshall Shulman
George O. Tamblyn
Mrs. Thomas M. Taylor

MEDICINE, PHYSIOLOGY:

Prof. Walter B. Cannon
Dr. Alfred E. Cohn
Dr. John F. Fulton
Dr. Victor Heiser
Dr. Foster Kennedy

MILITARY SCIENCE & HISTORY:

Major William Moseley Brown
Major George F. Eliot
Ladislas Farago
Captain Walter Hauck
Prof. Hans von Hentig
Stefan T. Possony
Frederick P. Todd
Dr. Alfred Vagts
Kurt H. Weil

NATIONAL ECONOMY:

Frank Altschul
Robert P. Bass
Rev. Dr. John P. Boland
J. Noble Braden
Leonard W. Cronkhite
William K. Doggett
Austin M. Fisher
Rudolph Fluegge
Arthur J. Goldsmith
Mrs. Elinore Herrick
Paul M. Herzog
Prof. Wesley Clair Mitchell
Gifford Pinchot
A. Philip Randolph
George Rublee
Vernon A. Samuels

Herbert Bayard Swope
Dr. Wallace H. Wulfeck

OPINION & ATTITUDE TESTING:

Dr. Matthew N. Chappell
Dr. George Gallup
Dr. Frank N. Stanton

PSYCHIATRY, NEUROLOGY:

Dr. John W. Appel
Dr. Karl M. Bowman
Dr. D. Ewen Cameron
Dr. Foster Kennedy
Dr. David M. Levy
Dr. Karl A. Menninger
Dr. Adolf Meyer
Dr. Henry A. Murray
Dr. Winifred Overholser
Dr. Edward A. Strecker
Dr. S. Bernard Wortis

PSYCHOLOGY:

Prof. Gordon W. Allport
Prof. Edwin G. Boring
Prof. Hadley Cantril
Dr. Leonard Carmichael
Dr. Leonard Doob
Dr. Eric Erikson
Dr. Erich Fromm
Geoffrey Gorer
E. Y. Hartshorne
Dr. Ernst Kris
Dr. Kurt Lewin
Prof. Gardner Murphy

Dr. H. A. Overstreet
Prof. Carroll C. Pratt
Dr. Floyd L. Ruch
Dr. Ruth Sherman Tolman
Prof. Goodwin B. Watson

RADIO, MOTION PICTURES:
Dr. James Rowland Angell
Elmer Davis
Maurice C. Dreicer
Monroe W. Greenthal
Sidney E. Samuelson
Dr. Frank N. Stanton
Walter Wanger

SOCIAL SCIENCES:
Theodore Abel
Dr. Conrad Arensberg
Gregory Bateson
Dr. Ruth Benedict
Dr. Eliot D. Chapple
Watson Davis
Dr. Leonard W. Doob
Geoffrey Gorer
Hans von Hentig
Dr. Kurt Lewin
Ronald Lippitt
Dr. D. W. Lockard
Dr. Alexander H. Martin
Dr. M. W. Royse
Dr. Margaret Mead
Prof. Kimball Young
Prof. Harvey U. Zorbaugh

SOCIAL SERVICE, CIVIC AGENCIES:
Irene Arms
Mrs. Rita W. Morgenthau
Miss Irene Lewisohn
Mrs. Gifford Pinchot
Ronald Lippitt
D. A. Saunders
E. M. M. Warburg

YOUTH & CHILD DEVELOPMENT:
Gregory Bateson
Prof. Charlotte Buehler
Dr. Alfred E. Cohn
Dr. David M. Levy
Ronald Lippitt
Dr. Margaret Mead
Dr. Alexander Meikeljohn
Prof. Goodwin B. Watson

COACHWHIP PUBLICATIONS
CoachwhipBooks.com

HANDBOOK
FOR SPIES

ALEXANDER FOOTE

PSYCHOLOGICAL WARFARE

Your Wife

••• SHE WOULD PREFER YOUR SAFE RETURN

PAUL M. A. LINEBARGER

PROPAGANDA
TECHNIQUE
IN THE
WORLD WAR

HAROLD D. LASSWELL

COACHWHIP PUBLICATIONS

CoachwhipBooks.com

BASTOGNE

The Story of the First Eight Days
In Which the 101st Airborne Division Was
Closed Within the Ring of German Forces

COLONEL S. L. A. MARSHALL

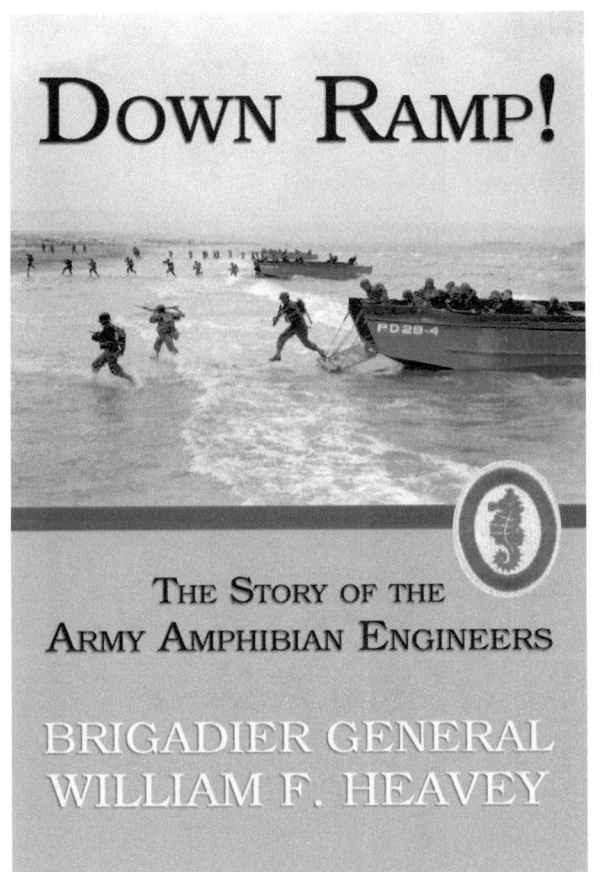

DOWN RAMP!

THE STORY OF THE
ARMY AMPHIBIAN ENGINEERS

BRIGADIER GENERAL
WILLIAM F. HEAVEY

COACHWHIP PUBLICATIONS
CoachwhipBooks.com

THE WAR OF 1812

Henry Adams

COACHWHIP PUBLICATIONS
COACHWHIPBOOKS.COM

YORKTOWN

THE STRATEGY, PEOPLE, AND EVENTS
SURROUNDING THE FINAL BATTLE IN THE
AMERICAN WAR OF INDEPENDENCE